COMMITMENT AND CONNECTION

Service-Learning and Christian Higher Education

Edited by

Gail Gunst Heffner
Claudia DeVries Beversluis

University Press of America,® Inc.
Lanham · New York · Oxford

Copyright © 2002 by
University Press of America,® Inc.
4720 Boston Way
Lanham, Maryland 20706

PO Box 317
Oxford
OX2 9RU, UK

ISBN 0-7618-2455-3 (paperback : alk. ppr.)

CONTENTS

PART III: DEVELOPING FACULTY

PART IV: BUILDING INSTITUTIONAL SUPPORT

PREFACE

THIS BOOK IS THE PRODUCT of the Calvin Center for Christian Scholarship, which was established at Calvin College in 1976 to bring together scholars to think and write about important current issues in the light of the Christian faith. The Center is based on the twin convictions that the resources of the Christian tradition have much to offer scholarly reflection, and that the fruits of scholarship have much to offer to communities of faith. The Center has also aimed to bridge some perennial gaps in the modern academy: between faith and reason, the different disciplines, experts and laity, diagnosis and prescription.

The present volume meets these aims admirably. Gail Gunst Heffner and Claudia DeVries Beversluis have gathered voices from a wide range of disciplines to reflect on the virtues and limitations of academically based service-learning, particularly within the framework of a Christian liberal arts college. Achieving integrity between faith, learning, and practice—or as the editors say, between head, hands, and heart—is an ancient challenge in Christianity as in every religion, and that challenge looms very large for today's academy as well. To build up students as moral agents, faculty as integrated persons, universities as communities within their surrounding locales: all these are needs of the hour that are well addressed by the approaches to teaching and learning set out in this volume. It is our hope that people of many viewpoints will be able to learn and take encouragement from the visions and practices recounted here, just as the contributors have from many sources in their own development.

The Calvin Center is grateful to the editors for their dedication in seeing this volume through, and welcomes responses to the rich body of reflections that they have promoted.

James D. Bratt, Director, Calvin Center for Christian Scholarship

ACKNOWLEDGMENTS

THE THEMES OF THIS BOOK, *Commitment and Connection*, were illustrated again and again in the work of many colleagues. It is a rich blessing to be a part of the academic community at Calvin College where faith, teaching, scholarship, and service are not only emphasized individually but are seen as part of an integrated whole. The enthusiasm and momentum surrounding service-learning at Calvin College has benefited from rich dialogue and interaction among both faculty and students. And, our partnerships with the local community have enriched our work significantly. We would like to thank our colleagues, our students, and our community partners for what we have learned together.

We are grateful to the Calvin Center for Christian Scholarship for the financial support and encouragement that made this collaboration possible. We would especially like to thank the capable staff of the CCCS, Donna Romanowski and Amy Bergsma, for their encouragement and their attention to detail in moving this manuscript to publication. The commitment and support from our administrative assistants, Amy DeVries and Carole Korfker, were also invaluable to this project.

Finally, we would like to thank our families whose commitment and connection to us give depth and purpose to the commitments and connections described in this book. For our husbands, who partner with us day in and day out, we are deeply grateful. This book is written with the hope that our children, David, Maria and Claire Beversluis and Andrew, Daniel and Elisabeth Heffner will develop a passion for service that grows out of lively intellectual work and deep faith.

INTRODUCTION

Connections

THIS BOOK BEGAN as a debate—a playful debate about whether Calvin College should host a conference or write a book about academically based service-learning. A number of us had participated in a faculty development workshop on the "scholarship of engagement" (Boyer 1996) to consider creative ways to connect teaching, scholarship, and service.

We all came from different starting points. Some of us had begun to explore the ways academically based service-learning could transform a class. Some of us were interested in exploring how our research could become more community based and collaborative. Others wanted to connect what they were doing in the classroom in academically based service-learning to larger conversations in their disciplines about the engagement of the academy in pressing contemporary issues.

At Calvin, we had seen rapid growth in academically based service-learning in recent years, and we were receiving many inquiries about our program from other universities and colleges—particularly faith-based colleges. We began to wonder how to meet the need to explain what we do to a larger audience. Thus, the playful debate—should we host a conference? Should we write a book? Do we have something to contribute to the public discourse about how higher education *connects* to contemporary civic, social, economic, and moral problems? More particularly, could our faith-based perspective add to the growing literature about service-learning in a way that has been largely absent to this point?

Our experience has shown us that service-learning can be a bridge that connects faculty and students in concrete ways to issues and problems faced by people who, like us, struggle to make sense of their life experiences. Service-learning connects head and hand and heart in immediate and lasting ways. Service-learning connects theory with action, action with emotion, and emotion with theory. Service-learning connects teaching and scholarship and service, leading faculty to lives of greater integrity and purpose. Service-learning connects college and community as college and community members develop working partnerships to address real human problems. Service-learning connects current school experiences to future lives of purpose and commitment.

All of these connections have been examined and celebrated in an extensive literature on the purposes, logistics, and outcomes of service-learning. This book is about yet another level of connection—the connection between service-learning and lives of faith. It is our thesis that service-learning, as articulated and practiced by the authors of this book, works as the connecting link between the mission of a college to equip students "for lives of Christian service" and the actual skills, virtues, knowledge, and passion needed for those lives. Additionally service-learning can function for faculty as a significant connection between scholarship and service, leading the college into a renewed, wholistic relationship with its various communities.

An Introduction to Service-Learning

Service-learning as a term was first coined in the late 1960s to describe the efforts to link educational goals for students with their active participation in the local community. The term reflects the desire of educators to move students beyond "doing good" toward a richer understanding of themselves, their communities, and academic course content. Robert Sigmon, an early service-learning pioneer, describes the purpose of service-learning as "the linking of service with learning to create a congruent service ethic throughout the campus culture and within the curriculum" (Sigmon 1994, 1).

Service-learning prospered in the 1990s as colleges and universities searched for ways to equip students to meet the expanding social needs in their communities and in the world. The popularity of the service-learning movement in the 1990s also dovetailed with an exploding interest in the ways in which colleges build character. This movement has focused on citizenship development—a model that emphasizes active learning in and with the community. Current examinations of service-learning explore the impact of service-learning on students, faculty, and the communities where service-learning is practiced.

The current volume joins this examination of service-learning but with a distinctly Christian voice. We have asked practitioners of service-learning at Calvin College, a Christian liberal arts college in the Reformed Protestant tradition, to present their experiences with and analyses of service-learning. These authors do not simply describe their attempts to incorporate service-learning, they use the tools of a variety of disciplines to articulate both the reasons for and the impact of service-learning in the college curriculum.

We believe there are challenges in this volume for both Christian and public institutions of higher education. The Christian higher-education community too often thinks of service as charity and needs the focus of justice and active citizenship that is provided in the larger service-learning movement. Within the Christian community, service-learning is about more than educating students for active citizenship; it is about preparing students to live a life of faith and modeling reciprocity between college and community. For public colleges and universities, this book asserts that service-learning, motivated by faith, contributes to the common good and is an important resource within the public square. It demonstrates that the critical thinking, empathic capacity, and passion for justice that arise from service-learning are central to a life of faith—not contrary to it.

Much of the contemporary service-learning movement has religious roots. Stanton, Giles, and Cruz (1999) compiled the stories of the pioneers of the service-learning movement and noted that several of these pioneers described their roots in a faith tradition. The authors note three characteristics that motivated these pioneers. The first was

> a drive to be of service, whether that service meant helping those in need or changing society, which was nurtured by parental and community role models, challenging friends and mentors, and a turbulent society struggling with the demons of war, racism, and poverty.

The second was

> a critical, questioning stance toward life, society, and its institutions, a stance nurtured as well by the social, spiritual, and political movements of the time.

The third was

> an impulse to connect thinking with action or vice versa—to bring about
> "useful" education or more thoughtful service (Stanton, Giles, and Cruz,
> 1999, 50).

Many of the heroes described by these service-learning pioneers, activists such as Dietrich Bonhoeffer, Reinhold Niebuhr, and Martin Luther King Jr., lived lives of sacrificial service grounded in a deep understanding of the demands of a religious vision of the world.

A Context for Faith-Based Service-Learning

Faith-based service-learning exists at the crossroads of several important contemporary conversations: conversations about the role of faith in the public square, about the role of higher education in the development of communities, about the role of education in moral and civic development of students, and about the integrity and spirituality of teaching and learning.

Faith in the Public Square

A lively intellectual conversation surrounds the role of faith in sustaining civil life. Can people of faith contribute to civic discourse on important social, economic, and political issues? Does service offered in the name of faith necessarily mask the hidden agenda of religious conversion? Can strong religious convictions coexist and make space for pluralistic discourse? For many observers of the American political scene, a discussion of the role of religion in public life conjures up images of the political involvement of the religious right, the intolerance of religious agendas, and the mission to save souls at the expense of bodies and civility. The more recent academic conversations about the role of religion in the public square, however, are more hopeful and more nuanced.

The debate over the role of faith in the public square is not just an ivory-tower exercise because political parties and state agencies make platforms and decide funding contracts in relation to faith-based organizations. The 2000 presidential campaign included conversations about Charitable Choice, a provision of welfare-reform legislation that prohibits discrimination against religious service providers in the awarding of government service contracts. The recent initiative by the Bush administration to implement Charitable Choice through the establishment of a White House Office of Faith-Based and Community Initiatives has the potential to contribute to American communities through the generation of *institutional* social capital (in addition to physical and financial capital). Part of the impetus for this legislation is the realization that religious social-service agencies and their holistic service provision have been effective in meeting many social needs. This legislation recognizes that service providers cannot just leave their religious convictions and commitments at the door, and that, in fact, religious commitments may strengthen the service that is provided by the agency. Charitable Choice allows state and local governments to work more closely with faith-based groups that help the poor and provides strong protections for the religious freedom of clients who are receiving services from faith-based organizations. Controversy about Charitable Choice legislation is raging, and the role of faith-based institutions is being scrutinized and argued in the public square as never before. Because of the implementation of Charitable Choice legislation, hundreds of religiously based social service organizations are finding enhanced funding for the work that they do, and government agencies are finding new and valuable allies to provide social services.

Central to the argument that supports the role of faith in sustaining civic life is the conviction that both the values of religious people and the structure of religious institutions are good for community life (e.g., Smidt, forthcoming). Andrew Greeley, for example, calls religion a "powerful and enduring source of social capital in this country, and indeed of social capital that has socially and ethically desirable effects" (Greeley 1997, 592-93). Religion, he argues, is not only a source of social bonds and volunteerism within religious institutions but a significant source and motivator of service *outside* of the religious sector. Religious social capital alone cannot generate a renewal of trust, but it is a source that must not be ignored. Richard Wood (1997) describes the success of church-based organizing in the central city when most other organizing efforts had failed, and he concludes that it is the presence not only of trust and respect but also of broad social networks in religious institutions that contribute to the success of these efforts.

If faith-based agencies and faith-filled citizens are assets to the public square, then it makes sense to look more closely at the faith-based institutions of higher education that are preparing future citizens for an active role in the public square. Is there a particular role for faith-based *institutions* of higher education to play in shaping public discourse about the need for societal transformation?

Role of Higher Education in the Development of Communities

Although much of the service-learning literature focuses on its effects on higher education, a growing emphasis within the movement is a focus the role that universities play in their communities. Bringle, Games, and Malloy (1999), for example, argue that universities and colleges are abdicating their moral obligations unless they bring their teaching, scholarship, and service to bear on pressing community needs. "Public and private colleges and universities have been subjected to a steady stream of criticism throughout the 1990s, both for a lack of research that addresses our major environmental, economic, and social problems and for a failure to prepare graduates fully to meet the challenges of socially responsible citizenship" (Reardon 1998, 57).

The establishment of ongoing partnerships between the university and the community is one way in which educational institutions have attempted to enrich students' educational experiences and encourage faculty to conduct research relevant to the community. Community residents are not enthusiastic about being treated merely as "subjects to be studied" because, in the past, university research into the causes of social problems often failed to address potential solutions. An emerging research paradigm, participatory action research, seeks to enhance the problem-solving capacities of community participants by actively involving residents, business leaders, and elected officials in every phase of the research. Ernest Boyer, former president of the Carnegie Foundation for the Advancement of Teaching, stated that in order for higher education to advance intellectual and civic progress in this country, the academy must become a more vigorous partner in the search for answers to our most pressing social, civic, economic, and moral problems (Boyer 1996, 11). He calls for higher education to broaden the scope of scholarship to include the scholarship of engagement so that the rich resources of the university or college will be connected to addressing societal problems.

In the present volume, Gail Gunst Heffner argues that faith-based colleges often have religious perspectives and convictions that lead them to engage with the local community in ways that can build social capital. Christian colleges have a unique contribution to make because of the religious social capital they can draw upon and simultaneously build. This is accomplished in two ways: first, by strengthening the bonds of mutual trust that exist between the faith-based college and the existing denominational or parachurch social-service agencies, and second, by connecting people, who did not previously know each other, to work together on issues of common concern. Heffner describes the work of Calvin College in developing academically based service-learning as a serious attempt among faculty and students to learn *with* the community, *through* the community, and *from* the community, not merely *in* the community. It is important for the Christian college to build relationships beyond denominational and cultural lines while maintaining its own unique sense of vision.

Faculty and students in psychology often experience a tension between their training in empirical research methods and their personal concerns with forming helping relationships. Glenn D. Weaver describes a collaborative approach to research, which brings students, professor, and family members of Alzheimer's dementia patients together as an investigative team to explore the dimensions of change that Alzheimer's patients experience over the course of the illness. Through in-depth interviews, family members describe their loved one's experience of change over time. These interviews have brought family members into a process of collaboration through critiquing specific interview questions and through raising new questions to be considered. Their comments have enabled the researchers to refine and change the research question(s) as the researchers' understanding grew of the larger contexts of meaning as expressed by family members closest to the Alzheimer's patients. There are several ways this collaborative research effort exemplifies academically based service-learning. As a serious initial attempt to investigate a set of issues not previously addressed in empirical studies, the major objective of the interview project has been to develop new knowledge, not only for the student service-giver but also for professor, family members, care facilities, and, as the program matures, eventually for the larger professional community through publication. The findings are generating considerable helpful local knowledge that allows families to learn from one another's experiences and suggests ways in which both families and institutional staff can be more sensitive to considering patients' spiritual needs. The research project has given the professor (and the students) opportunities to develop a variety of research skills in addressing challenging empirical questions for which no single method of investigation has been widely established and to be of service to a larger community simultaneously.

The Nursing Department was one of the first departments at Calvin College to recognize the value of establishing a community partnership to undergird the academic work it was doing with students while at the same time moving beyond merely using the community as a laboratory. Gail Landheer Zandee describes her experience of using service-learning as an opportunity to teach students how to be community advocates by modeling this in the development of clinical experiences. The goal is to teach students "the value of involving the communities in improving the community's health [but] we don't always model it in how our clinical experiences are arranged" (Bellack 1998, 99). Zandee's chapter describes how service-learning partnerships have the ability to demonstrate to students the essential elements of health promotion. Partnering with Catherine's Care Center, a neighborhood health clinic, Zandee has been able to draw upon community resources to help her teach her students that to be an effective community health nurse, they must learn to truly listen and collaborate with community members. Instead of teaching nursing students that they need to rescue a hurting community, students need to recognize that the community is an expert that needs to be listened to and respected as a partner in the process of moving to a higher level of wellness. Partnerships take time to develop—for trust to deepen, for reciprocity to happen, and for sustainability to be achieved. Then when real partnerships develop, there is mutual benefit for the community and for the college.

Listening to community voices as an initial step in community development is echoed in the chapter by Daniel R. Miller. He argues that the study of history can go beyond the transmission of cognitive knowledge to provide students with an empathetic understanding of the people and groups they study. Miller's motivation is drawn from the Old Testament when God called the Israelites to show hospitality to the aliens who came to reside among them, since they too, were once strangers in the land (Deut. 10:19). In his chapter, Miller describes several examples of how academically based service-learning builds the capacity for empathy among students by their involvement with diverse peoples. Several departmental undertakings have managed to combine methodological training and cross-cultural experience and have afforded students the opportunity to form relationships with people whose ethnicity, religion, and historical experiences differ from that of most Calvin students. In particular, Miller has integrated a service-learning assignment in his Latin American history course as a concrete way to understand U.S. immigration. Miller contends that whatever opinions students form about Mexican immigration or any other issue involving Latin Americans, they should be shaped at least in part by personal contact with the people most directly involved. By listening to and preserving stories of immigration and survival, the students helped give voice to a marginalized community. The gift of these stories to the Grand Rapids Museum allowed community members to value their own stories as an important contribution to the larger community.

Service-learning does not automatically produce improved conditions for those in need. When not carefully monitored and evaluated, service-learning can fail to address real community need, and, instead, it merely creates a charity mentality in the service providers. Kurt Ver Beek issues a strong word of caution in his chapter on international service-learning. Many service-learning experiences that seek to "serve" the poor neither understand nor address their true problems and consequently provide service and learning that is mediocre at best. Students and professors intrude into poor people's lives, often trying to fix problems they do not understand. The service learners end up thinking better of themselves, worse of the poor, and become too busy doing to take full advantage of learning opportunities. Ver Beek argues that this so-called service without understanding does not empower the poor nor build up their capacity. It is often neither equitable nor sustainable. Christian colleges and universities have a particular responsibility to learn more before they seek to intervene in the lives of the poor; and a solid understanding of what development means is essential. Ver Beek suggests that development is about people, not about factories, computers, tractors, or money. True development is about transforming people, empowering them to change their own future, to make a better tomorrow for their children. Thus, true service-learning is about development and must focus on solving core community problems. Ver Beek asserts that until service-learning takes true development seriously, the service they provide will be of little or no benefit to the poor, and the learning they acquire will be mediocre at best.

Role of Higher Education in the Moral and Civic Development of Students

If faith-based colleges and universities have a particular contribution to make to public discourse and civic engagement at the community level, then we must also look more closely at the kinds of faith-based education we provide to future citizens of this public square. How is this education best accomplished? What are the skills, virtues, and knowledge needed by our students? What pedagogy works toward the development of these virtues? These questions are at the heart of the third area of active conversation relevant to a consideration of faith-based service-learning. Writing in *The Journal of College and Character*, Thomas Erlich of the Carnegie Foundation summarizes the convictions of many educators when he says,

> We believe that higher education must aspire to foster both moral and civic maturity and must confront educationally the many links between them. . . . Institutions of higher education have the opportunity and obligation to cultivate in their graduates an appreciation for the responsibilities and rewards of civic engagement, as well as to foster the capacities necessary for thoughtful participation in public discourse and effective participation in social enterprises (Erlich 2001, 2).

What is the best way to build character in college? Erlich describes both the central skills, knowledge, and virtues associated with character development and the need for active pedagogies that "engage students in the practice of grappling with tough moral and civic issues, as well as examining them in theory" (Erlich 2001, 6). He highlights service-learning as a pedagogy that has demonstrated effects on students.

In this present volume, John E. Hare argues that higher education can play a role in the moral development of students and that service-learning in particular can significantly contribute to moral growth in students. He cautions against expecting this contribution to carry too much weight, however. Service-learning can produce *an occasion* for the acquisition of virtue but cannot produce the virtue itself. He argues that students have been sitting in classrooms for fifteen years, and they inevitably go into various modes of engagement and disengagement reserved only for the classroom. This is a kind of habitual screen. What service-learning does is enable students to get past the screen, at least briefly, and it confronts them with an opportunity to engage in a different kind of task. They have to interact socially with a group of people they tend to dismiss, and this enables them to do ethical thinking on the other side of the screen.

Developing a capacity for increased empathy is a significant contribution to the moral development of students (and faculty). As Robert J. Hubbard outlines in this volume, current trends in performance-studies emphasize cross-cultural communication and performance as a tool in the creation of empathy. Hubbard describes the use of academically based service-learning in the performance-studies classroom as a way to engage with the community in an honoring way while building empathy in the lives of students. Students collect oral histories from community members, translate their stories into monologues and perform their stories in a community setting. The concept of performing as a sign of tribute or as a living offering dates back to the very origins of art. Sometimes students become uncomfortable when collecting oral histories that express less than rosy portraits or troubling revelations from their interviewees. Through this experience, however, students gain a richer, more complex understanding that far surpasses simplistic, idealized, and one-dimensional views that students often carry into the project.

Recent Calvin College graduate, Laura Hoeksema Cebulski, articulates the impact that service-learning has had on her education and on her life. In this chapter, Cebulski describes the dilemmas she has faced and the lessons she has learned in her various service-learning experiences. Her words are testimony to the power service-learning can have.

> A college that places emphasis on service takes the training of the mind and synthesizes it with training of the heart. Not emotionalism, devoid of reason, but rather thoughtful, meaningful, useful compassion to the community it resides within. This intersection of mind and heart is what I found in my service-learning experiences. Never did I find service experiences to mock my intellectual pursuits; rather they complemented my study with a good dose of reality, with a good dose of heart. It is a worthy goal of any college to produce graduates who cannot only think well, but also love well.

Michelle R. Loyd-Paige describes the impact that academically based service-learning has had in her sociology courses on diversity and inequality in North America. She has found that the religious and ethnic backgrounds of students are often associated with distancing behaviors and the "color blind syndrome." When students articulate that "I don't see color, I only see people," a statement often made in an attempt to be sensitive and inoffensive, in reality they are dismissing the social significance of race in American society. However, merely creating *awareness* of problems—inequalities, exploitations, the suffering of others—can lead to despair if it is not combined with action that empowers students to bring about social change. In this chapter, Loyd-Paige describes the transformative process of change she undertook with this class over a number of semesters. In the beginning, pedagogically the class was lecture based, had no experiential piece and asked questions, but provided few answers. This strategy was intended to support critical thinking but had the latent effect of leaving the students without a context for viewing themselves as agents of change. To remedy this, a theme of biblical reconciliation was added in conjunction with a service-learning component. The goal was to help students move from an attitude of tolerance of diversity to active engagement in bringing about reconciliation through healed relationships. Service-learning helped students to experience first-hand both the simplicity of reconciliation (it is centered in relationships) and the complexity of reconciliation (it is a process that demands time and is not always rewarding).

Creating some level of disequilibrium within students can be the spark to challenge them to consider alternative perspectives on the world. Susan Schneider Hasseler argues that prospective teachers come to teacher-education programs with many strongly held beliefs about teaching and learning based on their own prior experiences as students in K-12 classrooms, and many of them have limited experience with issues surrounding poverty. These circumstances make it difficult for students to grasp the complexities of most urban school settings and can cause them to form conclusions about students and parents that are misguided and hurtful. Education professors have a particular responsibility for creating learning environments for education majors that will help students understand the complex contexts that impact teaching and learning and to develop the commitment and skills needed to understand and change the societal structures that so powerfully impact schools. In this chapter, Hasseler offers suggestions for constructing powerful service-learning experiences for teacher-education students.

Service-learning can provide opportunities for students to explore potential career paths and practice skills that are critical for success in a chosen field. Randall Brouwer describes how service-learning in a first-year engineering course provides the opportunity for students to plan and implement a design project that can meet the genuine needs of disabled persons in the community. Community members contribute ideas about devices they would find useful, and students go through the entire design process to develop an actual prototype. Students learn something about what an engineer might do on a day-to-day basis and learn how engineers solve problems—from the point of defining the problem to the implemented solution. A student thus gains experience in working as a member of a design team that may prove to be valuable for the future. Equally important is the experience of interacting with and learning from community members. These various experiences contribute to the development of the skills, virtues, and knowledge needed by our students to become effective servants in the world.

The Heart of Faculty Development

A final area of contemporary conversation that provides context for this book is the focus on the spirituality and integrity of higher-education faculty members. Recent literature points not only to the profound impact service-learning is having on the lives of students but also to its transformative power in the lives of many faculty.

> Academic service learning . . . can contribute to the renewal of the love of teaching that draws so many into higher education in the first place. Many faculty wanted, and still want, to have teaching and learning make a difference—for students, for themselves, and ultimately, for the world. Service learning not only makes that desire real again but also offers a way of affecting it. Second, because service learning crosses so many boundaries, it offers new opportunities to think more consciously and more creatively about relationships, including those of faculty and student, disciplinary and interdisciplinary or multidisciplinary knowledge, campus and community. Third, because service learning is an evolving field, those who enter it have the opportunity to contribute to its development. Fourth, because service-learning calls for a link between what goes on in the classroom and what goes on in a community, it offers a vehicle to faculty, students, and community partners for thinking and responding in new, collaborative ways to the critical issues that confront our local and global worlds (Weigart 1998, 9).

In his address to an audience of service-learning practitioners, Parker Palmer highlighted the ability of service-learning to unite the varied interests of college faculty. When a faculty member cares about a community issue, chooses to make that community issue a target of his or her scholarship, and joins with students to form genuine partnerships with community members, then wholeness and integrity are the result (Palmer 1998).

Others have written about the intersection of service, spirituality, and the teaching vocation. *Trying the Ties that Bind*, a recently published book by Michigan Campus Compact, is a collection of memoirs by faculty who have struggled to make connections—at many levels. The struggle cuts "across themes of teaching, faith, vocation, and community-building" (Cooper 2000). Faculty members in Christian higher education long for these connections as well.

One of the connections that is often missing in higher education is a connection to a specific place and people. Janel M. Curry calls for a deepened understanding of our sense of place as an antidote to the rootlessness that professors (and students) often experience.

In higher education, we work at challenging students to see issues in a framework that goes beyond the limitations of their parochial, or locally based, experiences—college is meant to be a broadening experience. In so doing, we often miss the sense of rootedness and commitment that can develop from making connections to a specific place. When we deepen our understanding of the places where we live, we gain a greater understanding of who we are, of the intricacies of our place, and of our responsibilities. Then we may in turn have the skills to learn to appreciate and care for other places. The Calvin Environmental Assessment Program (CEAP) is a service-learning initiative primarily in the natural sciences, which seeks to develop a habit of stewardship based on attentiveness to place. Faculty dedicate regular lab sessions or course projects to collecting data that contribute to an overall assessment of the environment of the campus and surrounding areas. CEAP is increasing our understanding of what it means to be embedded in a natural and social system and how this knowledge can be put to the service of the campus and the larger community. As Curry articulates in her chapter, CEAP is informed by recent debates in care theory and in the philosophy of science over the particularity versus the universality of knowledge—exemplifying the science of local knowledge and the importance of the embeddedness of knowledge in relationships and real-life settings. CEAP has provided a basis for getting faculty involved in community issues, based on their expertise, and it has served as a way to bring diverse people together. CEAP has contributed to the development of faculty through an increase in cross-disciplinary interaction; the creation of a point of engagement with the college planning process; a growing connection between person and place; and a sense of the wholeness of research, teaching, and personal commitments.

Service-learning provides opportunities for faculty members to become re-energized about their teaching. Mary Ann Walters, winner of the Calvin Exemplary Teaching Award, describes how service-learning in her freshmen composition course has influenced not just her students but also her teaching. Pairing her students with residents in a nearby retirement home, the students interview and build relationships with senior partners who share the stories of their lives. All of the writings that the students do in this course revolve around the relationships they build with their senior partners. The final paper is a life review of the senior partner, which is then presented as a gift at the end of the semester. Many of the senior partners are models of faith, patience, endurance, and generosity. Walters argues that it is one thing to lecture about these virtues. It is much more persuasive to be with someone who embodies them.

Steven Vander Veen describes his work in service-learning as pursuing a call to be an agent of renewal in the context of small-business development. Vander Veen directs the Calvin Small Business Institute, which strives to develop individual and communal gifts for leadership and service in business. It seeks to give students the knowledge, skills, and values to make a difference in the world of marketing and business.

Our volume would not be complete without some history of the institutional support we have received all along the way as academically based service-learning has developed. Rhonda Berg describes the accomplishments and the stumbling blocks, the small steps and the turning points, that have led Calvin College to becoming a leader in service-learning among Christian colleges in the United States. This chapter may be of particular interest to those wanting to understand how to institutionalize service-learning so that it becomes a sustainable and lasting contributor in fulfilling their college or university's mission.

The Calling of the Christian College

Nicholas Wolterstorff, in an influential article, "The Mission of the Christian College at the End of the Twentieth Century," argues that

> people have come to see that scholarship itself is conducted out of differing perspectives and that the integration of faith and learning which beckons us does not consist in tying together two things independently acquired but consists of practicing scholarship in Christian perspective . . . rather, competent scholarship is seen to be a pluralistic enterprise . . . the calling of the Christian scholar is to practice scholarship in Christian perspective and to penetrate to the roots of that scholarship with which she finds herself in disagreement—along the way appropriating whatever she finds of use (1983, 15).

Wolterstorff continues,

> the Christian college cannot neglect the suffering of humanity. It cannot neglect the suffering produced by alienation from God, and it cannot neglect the suffering produced by the natural world. But also it cannot neglect the suffering produced by the social world. It cannot burrow into culture while neglecting society. . . . To act responsibly in reforming society, one must know the structure and dynamics of that society (17).

He argues that the Christian college must enter into a new stage, not losing the contributions of earlier stages in Christian higher education (which focused on piety and evangelism, and the contributions of culture) but moving to a new focus on society—on the Christian *in* society. Wolterstorff articulated three particular challenges for Christian colleges at this historical crossroads:

1. A Christian college must become "much more international in its concerns and consciousness . . . American influence spreads throughout the world—sometimes for good, sometimes for ill; and in turn, our society here is profoundly influenced by what happens across the globe" (17).
2. A Christian college must "explore new ways of packaging the learning it presents to students. When our concern is simply to appropriate the stream of culture, then the relevant packages are available and familiar: physics, literary criticism, music theory, economics, etc. But when our

concern is to equip our students to reform society, then we walk in uncharted terrain" (17).

3. A Christian college must "be far more concerned than ever before with building bridges from theory to practice. Throwing some abstract political science at the student along with some abstract economics and sociology will not do the trick. The goal is not just to understand the world but to change it. The goal is not just to impart to the student a Christian world-and-life-view—it is to equip and motivate students for a Christian way of being and acting in the world" (17).

The authors of this volume contend that academically based service-learning is one way to meet this challenge to explore new ways of packaging the learning so that students are equipped to reform society and are motivated for the task of being, and living as Christians in the world.

We cannot dictate to students exactly how to live and be in the world, but we offer them opportunities to explore the world, to probe, to ask hard questions, to interact face to face with people whose life experience has been different from most of our students. We offer them opportunities to see how theories are actualized in practice and of how practice is informed by theory. Steven Garber, in his book *The Fabric of Faithfulness*, raises an important question. "How do students learn to connect presuppositions with practice—belief *about* the world with life *in* the world—in the most personal areas and the most public arenas?" Garber argues, "True education is always about learning to connect knowing with doing, belief with behavior; and yet that connection is incredibly difficult to make in the modern university" (1997, 43). It is precisely this sort of connection that service-learning helps to facilitate.

The Calvin authors of the chapters that follow find inspiration for, and articulation of, their teaching aims in the larger mission statement of Calvin College. Put most simply, Calvin College exists to "train young people, by means of a liberal arts curriculum and according to the Reformed tradition, for a life of Christian service in any vocation." So service *and* learning are at the heart of the college's mission—learning *for* the purpose of service. Calvin is a confessional Christian college, with living commitments to a particular religious tradition. Central to this tradition is the conviction that God created this world, its institutions, and its peoples for joy and delight, for shalom (Plantinga 1997). We do God's work when we delight in the world, study its intricacies, and use our creative gifts. But the world is not what God intended: human rebellion has corrupted both the natural world and the social world. People live with suffering, injustice, pollution, illness, war—a distinct lack of shalom. Our central task as a college is to equip students to do God's reconciling, restorative work with people, societies, and the natural world.

All of our learning, and all of our service, is undergirded by the theology of the Reformed branch of historic Christianity. This Reformed tradition brings at least five historical strengths to Calvin College's enactment of service-learning.

A Holistic Theology

The theology that finds expression in both the mission of Calvin College and the service work of its students and faculty is characterized by a holistic understanding of human personhood and a complex grasp of both individual and structural patterns of injustice. This service is done humbly in the name of Christ but must be based on a sophisticated understanding of persons and institutions. This service must minister to bodies and minds, individuals and structures, and the living and the nonliving worlds. "Saving souls" is not more noble than saving jobs or saving lakes: all are restoring what God intended in creation. Feeding minds and feeding bodies are essential but so is the study of food systems and political inequities. Artistic and creative pursuits, economic and academic work, all can be the work of service if they are done for the glory of God and the restoration of the human community. Our new core curriculum statement says it this way: "In the Reformed tradition, the life of Christian service is not limited just to the church and its missions, it is found in every vocation where God's creative and redemptive purposes are pursued" (Calvin College 1999, 2). This holistic concept of service mandates high-level academic work.

An Emphasis on Learning

How is learning necessary as a grounding for service? If service is so important to the Christian life, why not just stop paying tuition, move out of the dorm and into the central city, and free up professor and staff to bring cups of cold water to the thirsty world? The answers to these questions give power to Calvin College's mission as a liberal arts institution.

Since Tertullian asked his famous question, "What has Athens to do with Jerusalem?" the worlds of higher education and the church have been constructed as being in conflict with one another. But, of course, this has been a simplistic and misguided view. Much of the impetus for scientific discovery, philosophical inquiry, and artistic expression was found through a religious view of the world. Intellectual forebears of Calvin College such as Augustine in the Patristic era, John Calvin in the time of the Reformation, and Abraham Kuyper in late nineteenth century Europe all saw intellectual work as a central task of the Christian community. The bedrock belief that faith, learning, and service are central to each other forms the foundation for most Christian colleges. The Dean of the Chapel at Calvin writes:

> I believe we could summarize our calling in Christian college education as follows: in an academic setting, with the peculiar tools, perspectives, and resources of academe, we have to equip ourselves with the knowledge, the skills, and the attitudes that can be thrown into the struggle for shalom, the battle for universal wholeness and delight. The calling is exceedingly broad. We must never narrow it down to personal piety. But our role in the calling at this place is particularly academic" (Plantinga 1997).

Christian colleges stand as testimonies to the conviction that learning itself is an act of Christian obedience and a preparation for work in the world.

A Tempered Transformational Vision

The college trains in doctrine and faith by engaging the world, by educating Christians beyond simple belief to effective belief, by equipping Christians to transform the world in their individual areas of calling (Van Harn 1996, x).

Transforming the world is not a small task, and yet it is at the heart of the educational mission of many Christian colleges. This "transformational mission" is the direct result of a belief that education is not a morally neutral task but exists for the purpose of witnessing to God's purposes for the creation. But the Reformed tradition is permeated with an awareness of human weakness, weakness that can be found in both the servers and the served. It is this awareness of personal and institutional limitation that tempers our "transformational vision." Calvin's mission statement puts it this way: "We are called to correct the exploitation and oppression of people, to alleviate pain in the world, and expunge evil from ourselves." And our core statement echoes this need to know ourselves and our weaknesses: "Thus Christians learn to shun what is evil and to cling to what is good. In so doing, however, they also learn how often good and evil are twisted around each other, so that each seems to grow out of the other, generating the great ironies and mysteries that fill the history of our world. They learn how often we deceive ourselves about where real good and evil lie, and how such deception dulls and distorts our grasp of reality" (Calvin College 1999, 2).

A Legacy of Service

It is not difficult to make the case for the role of service in a life of faith. The biblical injunction to "let justice roll down like water and mercy like an ever rolling stream" (Amos 5:24) has been a rallying cry for service in the Judeo-Christian tradition since its very beginning. Our heritage of faith shares this mandate and embodies it through both individual lives of service and a rich legacy of service-oriented institutions. In the Grand Rapids metropolitan area, where our college is located, a large proportion of the nonprofit agencies were begun by religious organizations or with religious motivations to help the poor, cure the sick, or integrate the marginalized. The Reformed communities of which we are a part have national and international agencies that not only provide immediate relief, but work on long-term developmental projects throughout the world. Many of these institutions are more than one hundred years old. A large percentage of Calvin alumni find their life's work in nonprofit service agencies, and many more devote extensive vocational time to volunteerism in their communities. Our legacy of service can be found in the long history of the volunteer and service-learning movement at Calvin, a history that is recounted in the chapter by Berg in this volume.

Genuine Partnership

The conviction that all people are created in the image of God demands that we always take others seriously. We can never do service to another, but rather, we participate with the other in a partnership designed to mirror, in a very small way, God's intention for shalom in this world. Both the server and the served have inherent dignity, voice, and power, which must be respected and enhanced. The desire to see others as whole persons, the awareness of personal and institutional weakness, and the eagerness for learning and grace give us the motivation for developing genuine partnership with others. Because the Reformed tradition emphasizes the goodness of creation and created institutions, we can look for movements toward justice and peace wherever they are found and join hands with others in those movements.

Service and Other Christian Colleges

All Christian colleges are not alike, and differences in educational philosophy, faculty, and curriculum can be seen that are related to the theological commitments of each college. Most Christian colleges have a legacy of service and see education for service in the world as central to their educational mission. We have described some of the strengths of the Reformed perspective; other traditions bring different strengths to their understanding of and motivation for service in the world. Some traditions, for example, bring a strong emphasis on the role of service in developing or demonstrating virtue and personal piety. Other groups have had a particularly strong prophetic voice in the world with service as the enactment of that voice. Still other traditions focus on the experiential nature of theological understanding and stress the need for multiple voices for an inclusive theology. Yet other groups emphasize Christ's identification with the poor and our need to imitate that identification in our Christian lives. All of these traditions offer powerful, faith-filled motives for service, and all of them can enliven our understanding of the practice of service-learning. The chapters in this volume represent the reflections of one community of Christian scholar-teacher-servants. We invite faculty in other institutions, especially faculty with the rich resources of a theological tradition, to work out the implications of their faith for their own work as scholars, teachers, and servants.

Calvin College, the home institution of the authors of this book, has recently adopted a new core curriculum. The "Statement of Purpose" begins with these words—words that are also a fitting beginning for this book:

Of the several formulations of educational mission to be found in Calvin's Expanded Statement of Mission, none is more succinct or more precise than the following: "Calvin College seeks to engage in vigorous liberal arts education that promotes live of Christian service" (Van Harn 1996, 33). The distinctive feature of this mission is not vigorous liberal arts education, for hundreds of institutions of higher education across the North American continent are engaged in that very project. Nor is it to be found in the promotion of lives of service; for many schools are likewise engaged. Rather, it is the combination of these two elements under the heading of "Christian" (Calvin College 1999, 1).

Service, learning, and faith—this book is about the intersection of these three central elements of Christian higher education. Literally hundreds of books have been written about the ways that any two of the three concepts interact: i.e., how service and learning come together, how learning and faith are related, and how faith and service intersect and enrich each other. This book, however, combines all three concepts in what the authors believe is a natural alliance among three rich veins of treasure for the committed life.

References

Bellack, Janis, P. 1998. Community-based nursing practice: Necessary but not sufficient. *Journal of Nursing Education* 37 (3): 99-100.

Boyer, Ernest L. 1996. The scholarship of engagement. *Journal of Public Service and Outreach* 1 (1): 11-20.

Bringle, Robert G., Richard Games, and Edward A. Malloy. 1999. *Colleges and universities as citizens.* Needham Heights, Mass: Allyn and Bacon.

Calvin College. 1999. *An engagement with God's world: The core curriculum of Calvin College.* Grand Rapids: Calvin College.

Cooper, David D. 2000. *Trying the ties that bind: Essays on service-learning and the moral life of faculty.* Kalamazoo, Mich.: Fetzer Institute.

Erlich, Thomas. 2001. *The Journal of College and Character.* Online at: *www.collegeandcharacter.org,* April 22, 2001.

Garber, Steven. 1997. *The fabric of faithfulness: Weaving together belief and behavior during the university years.* Downers Grove: InterVarsity Press.

Greeley, Andrew. 1997. Coleman revisited: Religious structures as a source of social capital. *American Behavioral Scientist* 40 (5): 587-94.

Palmer, Parker. 1998. Integrity of teaching. Paper presented at Michigan Campus Compact Faculty Institute on Service-Learning. Olivet, Mich.: Olivet College.

Plantinga, Cornelius, Jr. 1997. Educating for *Shalom.* Admissions brochure. Grand Rapids: Calvin College.

Reardon, Kenneth M. 1998. Participatory action research as service-learning. In *Academic service-learning: A pedagogy of action and reflection,* edited by Robert A. Rhoads and Jeffrey P. F. Howard. San Francisco: Jossey-Bass.

Sigmon, Robert. 1990. Service-learning: Three principles. In *Combining service and learning: A resource book for community and public service.* Raleigh, N.C.: National Society for Internships and Experiential Education. Edited by Jane Kendall and Associates.

Smidt, Corwin. 2002. *Religion, social capital, and democratic life.* Waco: Baylor University Press. Forthcoming.

Stanton, Timothy K., Dwight E. Giles, and Nadinne I. Cruz. 1999. *Service-learning: A movement's pioneers reflect on its origins, practice, and future.* San Francisco: Jossey-Bass.

Van Harn, G. 1996. *An expanded statement of the mission of Calvin College: Vision, purpose, commitment.* Grand Rapids: Calvin College.

Weigart, Kathleen Maas. 1998. Academic service learning: Its meaning and relevance. In *Academic service-learning: A pedagogy of action and reflection,* edited by Robert A. Rhoads and Jeffrey P. F. Howard. San Francisco: Jossey-Bass.

Wolterstorff, Nicholas. 1983. The mission of the Christian college at the end of the twentieth century. *The Reformed Journal* 33 (6): 14-18.

Wood, Richard, 1997. Social capital and political culture: God meets politics in the inner city. *American Behavioral Scientist* 40 (5): 595-605.

PART I

BUILDING COMMUNITY

Chapter 1

CREATING SOCIAL CAPITAL THROUGH SERVICE-LEARNING AND COMMUNITY DEVELOPMENT AT FAITH-BASED LIBERAL ARTS COLLEGES

Gail Gunst Heffner

Introduction

SCHOLARS IN MANY DISCIPLINES have discussed the concept of social capital at great length within the past decade. In this chapter, I will examine the theory underlying social capital as a concept and define several types of social capital that will bear upon the discussion of higher education as an engine for social capital formation. I will next turn to an exploration of the particular role of religious social capital and argue that there is a unique contribution being made by religious institutions in the formation of social capital in society at large. I will explore how higher education can both create social capital and destroy it. Then, I will examine the unique role of liberal arts colleges with a particular eye to faith-based liberal arts colleges in the building of social capital. Christian liberal arts colleges are in a position to (and have a particular responsibility to) increase the stock of social capital in their local communities. I will use Calvin College as an example of a Christian liberal arts college that has been and is investing in the local community in ways that build social capital. Finally, I will consider challenges that institutions of higher education will need to meet if they want to position themselves as social-capital creating enterprises in the future.

Theories of Social Capital

Robert Putnam, a noted scholar of social capital, asserted in his article "Bowling Alone" that American social capital has been in decline over the past two to three decades. His research examined rates of voter turnout, trust in public officials and elected representatives, and participation rates in voluntary associations among other indicators. He has argued that Americans are less engaged in face-to-face contact with neighbors and colleagues and less involved in civic activities and organizations than in decades past (Putnam 1995, 68).

Jane Jacobs first coined the term *social capital* in her classic book, *Death and Life of Great American Cities* published in 1961. More recently, James S. Coleman developed the theoretical underpinnings of the concept. Coleman distinguished social capital as different from natural capital, physical capital, human capital, or economic capital. *Economic capital* (the most commonly understood term) refers to financial resources that can be employed to productive ends; *human capital* refers to skills, knowledge, education, and training that enhance the productivity of individuals. *Natural capital* is based on the value of the services provided by the ecosystem; *physical capital* refers to tools, machines, and other productive equipment developed by humans using natural capital. *Social capital* refers to the networks, exchanges, trust, and reciprocity that exist between and among people. Stated another way, social organization among people affects economic exchange. All these sources of capital serve as resources, which can be applied to solve problems.

Social capital is defined by its function. It is not a single entity, but a variety of different entities having two characteristics in common: They all consist of some aspect of a social structure, and they facilitate certain actions of individuals who are within the structure. Like other forms of capital, social capital is productive, making possible the achievements of certain ends that would not be attainable in its absence. . . . A given form of social capital that is valuable in facilitating certain actions may be useless or even harmful for others. Unlike other forms of capital, social capital inheres in the structure of relations between persons and among persons. It is lodged neither in individuals nor in physical implements of production (Coleman 1990, 302).

What is noteworthy here is that in order to determine if a particular action generates *social* capital in a given setting, it must be analyzed by whether it promotes interactions, exchanges, and trust among people. Social capital is important because it enables people to accomplish that which what would not be possible without it. Social capital is a valuable resource that should not be overlooked (because people use social resources to accomplish their goals) whether it be to obtain a job, pursue higher education, or solve a neighborhood problem.

Putnam's research in Italy found that regions with a high degree of social capital and civic engagement (as exemplified in cooperatives, mutual-aid societies, and neighborhood associations) benefited from higher rates of economic growth, educational achievement, and efficient government.

These communities did not become civic because they were rich. The historical record strongly suggests the opposite: They have become rich because they were civic. The social capital embodied in norms and networks of civic engagement seems to be a precondition for economic development as well as for effective government (Putnam 1993, 37).

Social capital, according to Coleman, Putnam, and others, consists of networks and norms that effectively enable people to act together to pursue shared objectives. Social capital can serve as a bonding function to bring closer together people who already know each other as or a bridging function to bring together people or groups of people who did not previously know each other (Gittell and Vidal 1998, 15). The underlying assumption here is that as people connect with each other, trust will develop and this can lead to social and economic well-being. This sense of trust and cooperation becomes a resource that forms the glue in a given community, and it can be built or lost, developed or squandered.

While it may be obvious that close ties among people in a community are beneficial, research shows that so-called weak ties have an equally important function to play. Granovetter defines the strength of a tie as "a combination of the amount of time, the emotional intensity, the intimacy (mutual confiding) and the reciprocal services" shared among people (Granovetter 1973, 1361). Weak ties have the benefit of expanding a person's knowledge base and sphere of influence beyond his/her close-knit inner circle and can prevent a person from becoming too insulated and narrow in perspective. Weak ties serve as a bridge to other people, ideas, perspectives, information, and so forth.

The fewer indirect contacts one has the more encapsulated he will be in terms of knowledge of the world beyond his own friendship circle; thus, bridging weak ties and the consequent indirect contacts are important . . . those to whom we are weakly tied are more likely to move in circles different from our own and will thus have access to information different from that which we (normally) receive (Granovetter 1973, 1371).

To analyze social capital within the context of how it functions (i.e., to bond or to bridge) leads us to consider the institutions that serve either to build or to destroy it. Social capital is generated in multiple activities through various mediating structures. Research has shown that church congregations play an important role in the formation of social capital in the local community. Neighborhood associations and community development corporations play a vital role by mobilizing residents to act on issues of mutual concern. Larger national organizations such as the Local Initiatives Support Corporation (LISC) (Gittell and Vidal 1998) or the Industrial Areas Foundation (IAF) (Warren 1998) focus on community organizing as a means to build social capital and foster community-building.

Social capital provides the theoretical constructs to help us view communities on the strength (or lack thereof) of their *capacity to act* for mutual gain. Note that this is not automatically positive. Communities can also take negative collective action to exclude those not considered part of the "in" group, which has often been the case with minority discrimination. The social capital in a given community is its capacity to act for good (or ill) to bring about a community's desired goals for improvement. All communities have internal strengths and can make decisions to act in ways that lead to the improvement of the community. This stands in contrast to a dominant perception that low-income communities are only places of need or deficits; their strengths often remain invisible to outsiders.

Religious Social Capital

Many social scientists avoid religion as a basis for social analysis, but in recent years, it has been recognized as influential in shaping corporate and/or communal life. Robert Putnam asserted that while religious affiliation is by far the most common associational membership among Americans, religious sentiment seems to be less tied to institutions and to be more self-defined. Church-related groups are the most common types of organization joined by Americans—so Putnam surmised from the aggregate results of the General

Social Survey. However, Putnam asserts that while individuals may be becoming more religious, he does not equate this with increased social capital because participation in groups has declined since the 1960s (Putnam 1995, 68-69).

A number of scholars argue that Putnam fails to recognize the unique role that religion has played in building social capital. In his study of religious congregations, Ram Cnaan argues that local religious congregations are one of the key foundations of social capital and human capital production at the local level. "They operate as sources of skill acquisition, social interactions, mutual exchanges, mutual obligations, and trust [the lack of] which are roadblocks to the promotion of social activism and civic engagement" (Cnaan 1998, 1).

Donald Miller, in an unpublished paper that considers the nature of civic engagement in a changing religious environment, asserts that religion has more potential to contribute to America's social capital than any other institution in society. His research demonstrates the complex ways in which religion in America is simultaneously becoming more privatized and more engaged in civic life. However, religious institutions are filled with people who have a vision for the possibility of a better society and thus are more willing to get involved. "Religion is one of the few institutions that is trusted in many inner city neighborhoods" (Miller 1998, 24).

Richard Wood argues that church-based organizing in urban areas has become more successful than other efforts because religious institutions are among the few settings that still generate trust. "In many urban areas those settings that previously generated trust and sustained broad social networks have deteriorated badly: unions, blue-collar workplaces, cultural associations, families and so forth" (Wood 1997, 601). But the level of interpersonal trust that can still be engendered because of shared religious convictions should not be underestimated.

Cnaan emphasized three points regarding theological teachings that serve as a foundation for the building of social capital:

> First, teachings of the major religions emphasize mutual responsibility, the need to assist strangers in need, and most importantly, the legitimate claim of the weak and needy upon the community. Second, the major religions have advocated for social care and compassion for the needy regardless of location and economic conditions. Third, religious teachings, even when they are not put into practice, are still part of the socialization process of younger

generations into the faith tradition and serve as instructions for desired behaviors of compassion and social care. If we assume that religion has a powerful and lasting effect on people's attitudes and behaviors, then religious teaching may contribute to a more civil and caring society (Cnaan 1998, 36).

In a comprehensive study on civic participation, Verba, Schlozman, and Brady (1995) concluded that religion is the predominant institution that provides opportunities for women, people of color, and the poor to enhance their human capital and acquire the civic skills needed for political participation. When one builds human capital and enhances skill acquisition, one increases interactions and exchanges, which eventually grows into increased obligations and trust (i.e., increased social capital).

Andrew Greeley, in a study of religious structures as a source of social capital, studied the volunteer phenomenon in the United States and indicated that social and ethical concern is increasing. Americans are significantly more likely to volunteer than are people from any other country according to the World Values Study, and American volunteer rates increased dramatically between 1981 and 1990. Greeley found that religion generated social capital not only for its own projects but for many other kinds of voluntary efforts as well. Greeley concluded that, "religion is (at least potentially) a powerful and enduring source of social capital in this country, and indeed of social capital that has socially and ethically desirable effects" (Greeley 1997, 593). Religious social capital alone cannot generate a renewal of trust, but it is a resource that must not be ignored.

Much has been written about *congregations* as the foundation for social capital formation (see Ammerman, 1997; Coleman, 1990; Cnaan, 1998; Miller, 1998; Wood, 1997), but is it congregations, per se, who are the predominant religious institution in the building of social capital? Or, can this be broadened to include other religious institutions such as Christian colleges, which are also influential because they are driven by a moral imperative and are embedded in a particular locale or place? While there is a unique role that church congregations can play in the local community, other religious institutions, such as Christian colleges, must not be overlooked as a potential source for the generation of social capital within the larger society.

The Role of Higher Education in the Formation of Social Capital

I think it needs to be said from the beginning that the primary role of colleges and universities is not to build social capital. Historically, the role of higher education has been to advance and transmit knowledge, and this has been accomplished mainly through teaching and research. Colleges and universities have played a foundational role in the formation of human capital. However, we ask the question: Is it not possible to go about our primary mission or purpose in such a way that we build social capital as an important and necessary byproduct? We will consider how this might take shape.

Ernest Boyer, former president of the Carnegie Foundation for the Advancement of Teaching, stated that in order for higher education to advance intellectual and civic progress in this country, the academy must become a more vigorous partner in the search for answers to our most pressing, social, civic, economic, and moral problems (Boyer 1996, 11). He calls for higher education to broaden the scope of scholarship to include the scholarship of engagement in addition to that of discovery, integration, the sharing of knowledge, and the application of knowledge. If colleges and universities undertake the scholarship of engagement as Boyer advocates, the rich resources of the university or college would be connected with our addressing societal problems. "Campuses would viewed by both students and professors not as isolated islands, but as staging grounds for action" (Boyer 1996, 20).

The historic mission of several leading urban American universities in the late 1800s (Johns Hopkins, Columbia, the University of Chicago, and the University of Pennsylvania) was to create a better city and society through advancing and transmitting knowledge. The model employed was essentially one that integrated research, teaching and service to make structural change and impact the lives of people and their communities. Harkavy's research identified World War I as the end of an era in history where faith in human progress was the driving force. Disillusionment and despair led many academics "to retreat into a narrow scientistic approach. Scholarly inquiry directed toward creating a better society was increasingly deemed inappropriate" and less important than empirical science in the larger research universities (Harkavy 1996, 6). Today, however, there is an ongoing conversation emerging about the role of research and scholarship as it relates to the civic engagement of the university. In some places, faculty are linking their teaching and their research with their service rather than keeping each a disparate responsibility.

Historically, colleges and universities have played an important role in public life by facilitating events, colloquia, or forums that bring people together for conversation, debate, and careful consideration of issues of importance to the community and the world. Broadly speaking, colleges and universities build social capital by being a bridge to connect groups of people who did not previously know each other. Colleges and universities are gathering places for people to explore ideas, to consider differing viewpoints, to debate, and to learn together. Scholars and teachers from varying academic backgrounds gather with colleagues to dialogue and consider the merits of opposing perspectives. Students from varying ethnic, racial, and economic backgrounds gather in classrooms, residence halls, and coffee shops to talk and debate. Insofar as these dialogues foster respect and openness to new ideas and perspectives, trust levels between and among people are strengthened. Athletic events, concerts of all types of music, and theatre productions encourage people to gather for recreation rather than stay isolated. Such types of interaction and face-to-face contact can increase levels of trust and demonstrate that a college is able to contribute to the formation of social capital. When the university as an institution builds bridges beyond the walls of academia and makes connections to the larger culture a certain measure of social trust is engendered.

Colleges and universities build social capital by bringing people, who have some previous knowledge of one another, together to work on issues of common concern. They educate and train the next generation to become leaders. In this role, universities contribute to the formation of human capital, but also, insofar as it helps people (students, alumni, and so forth) discover their vocational callings by connecting them to others in their respective fields, the university helps to form social capital.

A college or university needs to be consciously aware that it can contribute to the destruction of social capital also. If it portrays an image of exclusivity or superiority, the public will be less likely to view it as an institution concerned with the common good. A simple example of how social capital can be destroyed is related to off-campus student housing. If the university's students are viewed as a liability within a given neighborhood because of violations of zoning, overcrowding, too many cars on residential streets, noise, or overuse of alcohol, social capital in that locale has a negative effect.

Colleges and universities can use their resources to both bond (bring people together who already know each other) and to bridge (leverage their resources to connect people who have not known each other; i.e., foster weak ties). If a college is serious about making a difference in its community, it must attempt to link those in need with outside resources and opportunities. Social capital is not really valuable unless it connects someone to something new. A local college student could tutor an at-risk child. This cultivating of so-called weak ties (or bridges to social capital because the child and the college student were not part of the same social network originally) connects the child to outside resources that may help her learn to read so she can advance in school.

Unique Role of Faith-based Liberal Arts Colleges

While it is commonly accepted that public institutions of higher education have a responsibility to engage in community service in addition to research and teaching, less attention has been paid to the role that private liberal arts colleges play in service to the community. Teaching has been viewed as the primary mission of liberal arts colleges. In a recent journal article, Fear, Lelle, and Sandman identified four reasons why private liberal arts colleges have been absent from the debate about higher education's public service mission:

1. Private liberal arts colleges often lack the financial and human resources with which to conduct community service or other innovative activities.
2. Unlike state universities and community colleges that are chartered to serve defined, distinct, and known geographic areas, the geographic service area of private liberal arts colleges is self-determined.
3. Growing secularization of private higher education and the quest for financial stability and prestige has been a limiting factor.
4. Private liberal arts colleges lack institution-appropriate definitions of service (Fear, Lelle, and Sandman 1998, 52).

Other researchers claim that private liberal arts colleges, particularly church-related colleges, have always had a service mission. Church-related private colleges could more appropriately be labeled as "public Christian colleges," because they were often founded for the public interest to serve the common good. Some Christian colleges participated in social reform activities, such as Oberlin's Anti-Slavery Society (Ringenberg 1984, 77).

Liberal arts colleges often have religious perspectives and convictions that lead them to engage with the local community in ways that build social capital. The size of many liberal arts colleges is an asset that can facilitate more interaction and connectedness between college personnel and community members and can lead to a greater sense of reciprocity between the two. There are mutual benefits to be gained for community organizations and for colleges when they share a sense of common purpose in addressing local problems. The potential is there, but institutions need to be intentional about making connections that fit clearly with their own sense of purpose or mission.

A Christian college has a unique challenge and responsibility to flesh out its religious convictions in the way it educates and equips its students. As Nicholas Wolterstorff states it, "the Christian College must become far more concerned with building bridges from theory to practice. The goal is to equip and motivate students not just to understand the world but to change it." Wolterstorff argues that Christian colleges need to move beyond merely introducing students to the breadth of high culture and actually help students and faculty engage with society. Wolterstorff has made careful distinctions between culture and society.

Culture is something different from society. Culture . . . consists of *works* of culture. Society, by contrast, consists of *persons* who interact in various ways. From that interaction arises social roles, social practices, and social institutions. And here in college you may learn how to appropriate for yourself various offerings of the stream of culture, when you leave here you cannot simply appropriate culture. You will have to fill certain social roles, engage with your fellows in certain social practices, participate with them in certain social institutions (Wolterstorff 1983, 16).

One role of a Christian college is to help people make connections between how they think/believe and how they live so that healing and shalom may come in all dimensions of human existence.

Christian colleges have a unique contribution to make because of the religious social capital they can draw upon and simultaneously build. For many faith-based colleges, strong denominational ties, which can be employed for mutual gain, already exist. When faith-based colleges collaborate with denominational or parachurch social-service organizations, they are strengthening their bonds of mutual trust and thereby increasing the stock of social capital. This is a unique resource available to religious colleges that does not exist for public universities.

Some faith-based colleges are intentional about building bridges to other denominations or racial-ethnic groups in their particular locale. Sharing a common faith perspective, despite different denominational affiliations, is a resource to draw upon when larger issues need to be addressed collaboratively. Additionally, by interacting and working with those who do not share the same religious convictions, new opportunities and new ideas emerge, which expand the possibilities for all involved.

Calvin College: A Contributor to the Formation of Social Capital

Calvin College is a comprehensive liberal arts college that stands in the Reformed tradition of historic Christianity. The college has always had a clear sense of mission, which begins with faith and the call to serve God. The *Expanded Statement of the Mission of Calvin College* states that our "confessional identity informs all that we seek to do. It shapes our vision of education, scholarship, and community" (Van Harn 1996, 13). Calvin College's present mission is further articulated: "Remembering that we are called to obey God as whole persons in every area of life, we believe that education should explicitly connect the way we think with the way we live" (Van Harn 1996, 18). Three convictions have special status at Calvin.

> First, the aim of Christian education is to let faith find expression throughout culture and society. Second, the life of faith, and education as part of that life, find their fulfillment only in a genuine community. Third, the Christian community, including its schools, is called to engage, transform and redeem contemporary society and culture (Van Harn 1996, 32).

Unlike some institutions of higher education, Calvin does not lack an institution-appropriate definition of service.

> In particular, the college must make sure to maintain its historic strength in serving the denominational community while broadening the scope of that service to include more civic, professional, and other religious organizations. Applied scholarship is the readiest avenue for such service. To qualify as

scholarship, it must reflect persistent intellectual engagement with the substance of the arts and sciences; to qualify as service, it must challenge, instruct, and learn from its audience (Van Harn 1996, 50).

One of the specific ways that Calvin College has fleshed out this understanding of service and contributed to the formation of social capital has been through Academically Based Service-Learning (ABSL). Calvin College has invested significant resources to connect faculty and students to the Grand Rapids community in reciprocal relationships. Numerous faculty-development workshops have been held to help Calvin faculty understand how service-learning can be used as a pedagogical tool. Ongoing assistance is available to help faculty construct discipline-specific assignments for students who are involved in academically based service-learning so that they can begin to see the connections between theory and practice in the courses they are taking.

At Calvin College, ABSL has been defined as service activities that are related to and integrated with the conceptual content of a college course and that serve as a pedagogical resource to meet the academic goals of the course as well as to meet community or individual needs. Academically based service-learning at Calvin is a serious attempt among faculty and students to learn *with* the community, *through* the community, and *from* the community, not merely *in* the community.

Much of the current literature about service-learning focuses on the moral and civic development of students. Service-learning contributes to the development of human capital in the form of increased skills and advanced education for particular students. Additionally, it has been documented that service-learning is a valuable teaching tool that contributes to a faculty person's professional development. While these are not insignificant, something is missing if an equal emphasis is not also placed on community development. Ira Harkavy asserts that

> the service-learning movement has not "rightly placed" the goal. It has largely been concerned with advancing the civic consciousness and moral character of college students, arguing that service-learning pedagogy also results in improved teaching and learning. Although service to the community is obviously an important component of service-learning, it [often] does not focus on solving core community problems. . . . Urban colleges and universities are in a unique position . . . [to move to] strategic

academically-based community service, which has as its primary goal contributing to the well-being of people in the community both in the here and now and in the future. It is service rooted in and intrinsically tied to teaching and research, and it aims to bring about structural community improvement (Harkavy 1996, 2-3).

Unless service-learning is cast in a community development context that fosters the building of social capital, it remains largely an academic exercise.

The specific examples of academically based service-learning given in the chapters of this book demonstrate some of the possibilities available to a Christian college that desires to invest in its local community so as to build social capital. Serious and sustained engagement and partnerships with local organizations has been undertaken to increase connectedness among diverse peoples, to increase capacity building, and to give voice to those who have felt ignored and powerless. Calvin is committed to building community partnerships at many levels and has established significant relationships with both geographical and professional communities.

An example of bridging social capital is Calvin College's commitment to the Pathways to Possibilities program, a precollege program for ethnic-minority students. The broad goal of Pathways to Possibilities is to help inner-city children and youth value learning, seek academic success, become aware of career and higher-education opportunities, and strive to live responsible lives. Various program initiatives provide opportunities for urban minority youth (and their parents) to develop the knowledge and skills necessary for successful entry into higher education.

The Pathways to Possibilities program is a collaborative effort involving Calvin College and churches from four different denominations. Some of the churches are members of the denomination in which the college is also a member but not all of them. This program demonstrates how a Christian college can use its resources to build both bonding (as seen in the social networks of existent denominational ties) and bridging social capital (as seen in the new weaker ties across racial, ethnic, and denominational boundaries). Once established, these networks need to be maintained and nurtured for them to remain viable.

Conclusion and Future Challenges

Private liberal arts colleges are in a unique position to contribute to their local communities. The activities described above, though beneficial, may not necessarily build social capital and lead to community development unless there is a clear sense of reciprocity, mutual trust, and cooperation. This is accomplished both through our close ties (in the case of a Christian college through collaboration with other Christian institutions where religious social capital is found) and through our weak ties (with people and institutions who do not share our perspective). As Granovetter states, "Weak ties are more likely to link members of *different* small groups than are strong ones, which tend to be concentrated within particular groups" (Granovetter 1973, 1376). Granovetter's research asserts that strong ties (like kinship and intimate friendship) are less important than weak ties (like acquaintances and associations) in sustaining community cohesion and collective action.

This points to the importance of Christian colleges' building relationships beyond denominational and cultural lines while maintaining their own unique sense of vision. Reciprocity and mutuality are key ingredients in the building of social capital. They can be fostered best when the institutions (or individual people for that matter) can not only articulate their own distinct identity but also recognize their need for others. One's unique identity does not have to be lost in order for collaboration and mutuality to occur. Christian colleges need to remain true to their mission as they work in the local community but must realize they have as much to gain from their so-called weak ties as they do from their strong ties. I want to close by outlining three broad challenges that higher education needs to recognize in if it wants to be in a position to create social capital.

First, colleges and universities need to connect their research to identified needs in the community. Given the particular needs and demands of the twenty-first century, colleges and universities need to focus some portion of their research capabilities and resources on local community issues. We need to connect to local constituencies in ways that will enable our research findings to be used by those who most need the information our research uncovers. In other words, we need to find ways to construct our research in collaboration with those who will benefit from the results of our research. Too often good research is conducted, but the findings are hidden in the pages of a journal rather than being employed to bring about needed change. Simply put, our research and scholarship (in many disciplines) needs to be connected to real people.

A Christian liberal arts college can make significant contributions if it uses its research capabilities to serve the local community. Liberal arts colleges have often been overlooked as potential resources for community-based research. The assumption is that only larger universities have the capacity and the mandate to be involved in research. Liberal arts colleges can make a unique research contribution (without having to leverage huge amounts of research dollars) if faculty creatively connect both their teaching and their research by involving students.

A growing body of literature affirms the value of community–based research, which is seen as contributing simultaneously to scholarship and to the direct needs of the local community. Collaborative research makes a distinction between research in a community (as a place) and research with a community (as a social and cultural entity). Community members are valued as collaborative partners in all phases of the research process, and there must be a clear return for the community on the investment it has made in the research. Participatory-action research, a type of collaborative research, demands that those most affected by the research be involved in setting research parameters, posing the research questions, and determining how the research findings will be used at the conclusion. Research so defined can make a significant contribution to community development and can increase trust levels, which build social capital. If this does not happen, opportunities to build social capital are missed.

Second, many colleges and universities need to develop a stronger sense of place. This is clearly connected to their understanding of their role in the local community. Social capital cannot easily be built when people do not have a sense of commitment to and/or embeddedness in a particular place. Eric Zencey challenges those in academia to cultivate a sense of connectedness to the place where they live and work.

> Academics in all disciplines ought to work to acquire a kind of dual citizenship—in the world of ideas and scholarship, yes, but also in the very real world of watersheds and growing seasons and migratory pathways and food chains and dependency webs. What is needed is a class of cosmopolitan educators willing to live where they work and to work where they live, a class of educators willing to take root, willing to cultivate a sense of place. These educators could exemplify in their teaching and in their lives their own

manner of accommodation to the fruitful tension between local and universal, particular and general, concrete and abstract (Zencey 1996, 19).

Colleges and universities face difficulties in creating social capital when many of their personnel do not view themselves as rooted to a particular locale.

Third, colleges and universities need to recognize the huge issue of power and the "uneven playing field" that exists between academia and the community in terms of leveraging resources. This is complicated and beyond the scope of this chapter but it needs to be said that uneven power relationships can negatively affect the formation of social capital and must not be overlooked. It is difficult to foster reciprocity when there are glaring economic and social inequities.

These are challenges that all institutions of higher education both public and private and secular and religious need to consider if they are serious about wanting to be engines of social-capital formation. A college or university *can* make unique contributions to both the formation of human capital and the formation of social capital. Because of its unique religious perspective, a Christian college has a responsibility to generate and invest social capital in the place where it is embedded.

References

Ammerman, Nancy Tatom. 1997. *Congregations and community*. New Brunswick, N.J.: Rutgers University Press.

Boyer, E. L. 1996. The scholarship of engagement. *Journal of Public Service and Outreach* 1 (1): 11-20.

Cnaan, R. A. 1998. *Bowling alone but serving together: The congregational norm of community involvement*. Paper presented at conference, Religion, Social Capital, and Democratic Life Conference. Grand Rapids: Calvin College, 1998.

Coleman, J. S. 1990. *Foundations of social theory*. Cambridge: Harvard University Press.

Fear, F. A., Mark A. Lelle, Lorilee R. Sandman, 1998. A legacy rediscovered: Public service at private colleges. *Journal of Public Service and Outreach* 3 (2): 48-53.

Gittell, R. and A. Vidal. 1998. *Community organizing: Building social capital as a development strategy.* Thousand Oaks, Calif: Sage Publications.

Granovetter, M. S. 1973. The strength of weak ties. *American Journal of Sociology* 78 (6): 1360-80.

Greeley, A. 1997. Coleman revisited: Religious structures as a source of social capital. *American Behavioral Scientist* 40 (5): 587-94.

Harkavy, I. 1996. *Service Learning as a vehicle for revitalization of education institutions and urban communities.* Paper delivered at the American Psychological Association Annual Meeting, Toronto, Canada.

Miller, D. E. 1998. *Religion, privatization, and civic life: The nature of civic engagement in a changing religious environment.* Paper presented at conference, Religion, Social Capital, and Democratic Life Conference. Calvin College: Grand Rapids, 1998.

Putnam, R. D. 1993. *Making democracy work: Civic traditions in modern Italy.* Princeton, N.J.: Princeton University Press.

_____. 1995. Bowling alone: America's declining social capital. *Journal of Democracy* 6 (January): 65-78.

Ringenberg, W. C. 1984. *The Christian college: A history of Protestant higher education in America.* Grand Rapids: Eerdmans.

Van Harn, G. 1996. *An expanded statement of the mission of Calvin College: Vision, purpose, commitment.* Grand Rapids: Calvin College.

Verba, Sidney, Scholzman, Kay Lehman and Brady, Henry E. 1995. *Voice and equality: Civic voluntarism in American politics.* Cambridge: Harvard University Press.

Warren, M. R. 1998. Community building and political power: A community organizing approach to democratic renewal. *American Behavioral Scientist* 42 (1): 78-92.

Wolterstorff, N. 1983. The mission of the Christian college at the end of the twentieth century. *The Reformed Journal* 33 (6): 14-18.

Wood, R. L. 1997. Social capital and political culture: God meets politics in the inner city. *American Behavioral Scientist* 40 (5): 595-605.

Zencey, E. 1996. The rootless professors. In *Rooted in the land: Essays on community and place,* edited by Willem Vitek and Wes Jackson. New Haven, Conn.: Yale University Press: 15-19.

Chapter 2

LISTENING TO THOSE WHO REMEMBER: SERVICE-LEARNING AND COLLABORATIVE RESEARCH

Glenn D. Weaver

B Y THE TIME THAT they complete the senior research seminar, undergraduate psychology majors often feel that their commitments to the discipline are leading them into two opposed cultures. Through courses in statistics, experimental psychology, and the research seminar itself they have gone through rites of passage into the culture of experimental behavioral science. Here the practice of "good" psychology lies in mastering a set of technically defined procedures for collecting data to test theory-driven hypotheses. These procedures both assume and help to confirm a hierarchy of authority based on theoretical knowledge. Principle investigators who have expertise in connecting theoretical predictions and appropriate research methods stand at the top (professors usually assume this role), research assistants who administer procedures to experimental participants stand one step below (students usually assume this role, deriving authority only to the degree that they adhere carefully to the preestablished methods), and research participants whose psychological experience the experiment is designed to explain stand at the bottom. Ideally, behavioral measures in research are kept simple to prevent participants from importing unique interpretations that might differ from those specified by investigators as tests of the hypotheses.

There is another culture of psychology that students engage in at points throughout the major. It can be seen in developmental psychologists' discussions about how to interact effectively with preverbal children in order to understand what they are thinking or in clinical psychologists' considerations of how to match therapies effectively to clients' expressions of their own goals and needs. Students frequently model different standards for good psychology in this culture when they work in an undergraduate internship with practitioners in one of the applied specializations: school, counseling, or industrial-organizational psychology.[1]

In these settings of professional practice, the structure of knowledge-based authority is somewhat less clear than in the culture of behavioral science. To be effective, a school psychologist has to work within political systems that have no clear connection to theories of diagnosing learning disorders, a counseling psychologist must adjust therapies to the limits of a health-care system that covers treatment for only certain kinds of disorders, and an industrial psychologist must fit workers, skills to the economic concerns of the corporation. In the context of these demands, the well-being of individual clients must still be served. This is psychology's other culture of helping services and local meanings. It is coincidentally the culture that most psychology majors have significant familiarity with from their ordinary life experiences and the culture that will for most of them guide their work after they graduate.

These different discipline-based ways of approaching and understanding persons each represents a different set of values important to the mission of liberal arts education. Planning and conducting scientific behavioral research builds appreciation for honesty and critical rigor in examining biases of data interpretation, coherence in arguing from evidence to tentative conclusions, and parsimony in the type of explanations one pursues. Practicing psychology in a helping profession confronts one with needs to empathize with clients, to be courageous in improvising techniques where no clear guidelines may exist, and to work for justice when clients are unfairly discriminated against in the evaluations they receive. Unfortunately, when students separate these sets of values into these different cultures of the discipline early on, they may never generalize across cultures to realize the importance that all of these values have for effective service in their later professional and nonprofessional lives.

Although my students have made me aware of this tension in psychology's cultures for many years, I experienced it as a personal challenge to action when our family needed psychological services fifteen years ago. Following progressive difficulties with memory and several episodes of disorientation and confusion, my mother was hospitalized for a battery of diagnostic tests. The

---

[1] This distinction between psychology's two professional cultures has been discussed in a number of previous articles. (See, for example, Kimble 1984; Van Leeuwen 1988.)

psychologist who administered tests of her cognitive functioning carried out the procedures in a careful, standardized manner. The test questions and exercises focused on simple behavioral measures of memory and reasoning. The following day, her medical doctor reported the results of the examination and suggested the diagnosis of Alzheimer's dementia. My mother and father returned home to manage as best they could, but it occurred to me that other than a diagnostic label and a rather grim prognosis, our family had little further insight into the psychological meanings that her condition might hold for her life than we did before.

The meanings that the disease would hold took shape in our family journey together over the next five years. Because both of my parents' lives centered in their Christian faith, many of the psychological changes that the disease caused were experienced through their relationship to this faith. Thus, as my mother's ability to remember episodes from her present life diminished, her identity seemed to focus more and more on events important to the shaping of her faith in her distant past. When even these memories began to drop away, her experience of self grew much more constricted and the common assurances of faith less accessible. For my mother, this was a time of serious spiritual trial. My father and I became increasingly sensitive to these upsets in her identity and continually searched for ways to help uphold her identity.

Some years into the disease, after my mother had moved to a nursing facility, I participated in a nationally funded research project on Alzheimer's dementia that was being conducted at the facility. The study was designed to determine relationships among the measures of the severity of residents' dementia, the type of care that they received, and other dimensions of their mental health and overall quality of life. Family members were asked to fill out questionnaires that covered each of these areas. As was true with the tests used in my mother's diagnosis, the questions were simple and behaviorally based, e.g., how frequently does a family member visit this resident in the nursing facility? How many interpersonal contacts does the resident have with other residents during a typical day? There were also several short behavioral inventories of symptoms of anxiety and depression. The questionnaire was sent by a research group that family members knew little about and was to be mailed back to a researcher whom they had never met.

Although my father and I completed the measures, we shared an annoyance and resentment about the way in which this study was done. We had no reason to believe that the intentions of the researchers, or the purpose of the study had anything directly to do with my mother's well-being, or the well-being of our family. The scale items we marked appeared simple and direct, but many were quite difficult to judge accurately because they took no account of the larger contexts of meaning in which we observed my mother's day-to-day experience. Evaluations of her interpersonal contacts had to take into consideration the social skills of her roommates and the nurses and aides working with her at the time. Judgments of her emotions had to consider the role of her social context that had been changing dramatically since the beginning of the disease. We were most put off by the fact that the questionnaire allowed no mention of spiritual experience in rating her overall quality of life. If it had, however, I'm certain that my father would have hesitated to explain this most sacred quality of my mother's life in writing to a stranger whose real interests in my mother remained unknown.

I combed the research literature for empirical studies that examined the relationship between the psychological changes that occur throughout the course of Alzheimer's dementia and the meanings that these changes hold for one's faith and spiritual life. Several studies documented the relationship between decreased church attendance and increased symptoms of depression in elderly persons suffering dementia, but none of these studies sought to determine the direction of this relationship (did decreased church attendance contribute to the depression or vice versa?) or sought to describe the meaning that this decline held for the person who had the disease. Altogether there were very few investigations of any dimensions of demented persons' own perspectives and interpretations of their condition.

It appeared to me that one could do potentially interesting and helpful research on these issues by asking family members who had lived through stages of dementia with an Alzheimer's patient systematically to describe changes in their loved one's experiences over time. It also appeared clear that this research would have to be collaborative in nature. Nyden and Wiewel define collaborative research "as research in which all parties, researcher and client are equal partners. There is equal participation in defining the research problem and the research strategies" (Nyden and Wiewel 1992, 45). The nursing residences in which the study would be conducted, as well as staff in these residences would have to support the study as an expression of their institutional mission and potential contribution to the well-being of the residents for whom they cared. Family members would have to understand and share a sense of the importance of the study and have full opportunity to influence the types of questions asked and evidence pursued. The research assistants who administered the interviews would have to be able to establish a climate of interest in and mutual trust to explore past episodes with the family members who would be sharing stories about their loved ones.

So, I came back to those senior psychology majors mentioned earlier with an opportunity to explore research that might bridge the divide between the cultures of behavioral science and the helping services. The students' relative youth and lack of professional identity made potentially important contributions to this research project. I remembered that while my father was always guarded in what he told medical doctors and psychologists about my mother's experiences (perhaps simply trying to fine-tune his answers to what he took to be their specific professional concern), he was usually comfortable with openly telling our family's story to young aides or volunteers who offered the time to listen and showed interest in asking questions from their own experiences in life.

The first student to volunteer assistance in this research did so both because she was thinking about a professional career in counseling and because her grandmother had suffered considerable anxiety and confusion about her faith over the course of her Alzheimer's dementia. After volunteering as a helper in a nursing-care facility the previous summer, Jill wanted to do an independent study that would allow her to continue this type of service and to understand her grandmother's experience better. We decided that she would spend approximately eight hours each week during the semester interacting with residents at the Verblauw Unit, the Alzheimer's care unit of Fulton Manor, a senior care residence near campus. She also did extensive research and reading of the literature on psychological changes in dementia. Our principle learning goals were for her to get to know several residents and their families well; to understand how to help support them during her time on-site each week; to sensitively share with the families the results of the existing research that might be helpful to them; and, with the families' guidance, come to an understanding of how subsequent studies might ask useful questions about the relationship of dementia to a person's spiritual identity.

Jill developed genuine friendships with two residents and their families. The questions that the families asked her about the nature of memory processes and how memory is related to one's sense of self-identity helped to guide her searches of the literature. Jill's personal interest in the spiritual dimensions of their loved ones' suffering helped families to reflect more intentionally on their lives together and the resources of their faith. She accepted the invitation of one family to accompany them with their loved one on a forty-five minute drive each Sunday to worship with a congregation that included members diagnosed with a range of severe mental disorders and social problems. At the end of the semester, we collaborated on the first draft of a standard interview that could be used in further research. The interview focused on the dimensions of change that both families had described in their loved ones' experiences: changes in memory, in close interpersonal relationships, in expressions of self-identity, and in spiritual practices as well as expressions of spiritual well-being and changes in the actions of family members toward the Alzheimer's patient.

The next step involved pretesting this interview with a larger sample of families to make certain that it communicated questions clearly and focused on issues that they had found important in their experiences. At this stage, a group of five upper-level psychology majors volunteered to meet for a research discussion group every other week throughout the semester and to spend time visiting and interacting with Alzheimer's patients and close family members each week either in a nearby residential facility or at the families' homes. These visits provided stimulation for the patients and collaboratively brought family members into the process of critiquing and refining the interview as it was administered to them.

Our research discussions offered opportunities to consider how the results of our planned study might provide a service to the families and the care facilities that would volunteer to participate in it. We considered the importance of effectively, personally communicating the mission of service that helped to motivate the research and the hope that better empirical understanding of relationships among the dimensions we were trying to measure could contribute to the ways in which families and residence staff provided care. The helping services cultural values of empathy and justice were clearly invoked here. In our meetings, it also became clear that the methodological concerns and epistemic values of the behavior-science culture were important to our efforts to detect real, reliable relationships among the descriptions of change on these dimensions that would generalize across residents' experiences and so be of genuine use in improving care.

The fruits of this further collaboration gave the structured interview a new look. Several students discovered that elderly family members were having difficulty keeping the different dimensions that the interview measured in mind when they were asked about them in sequence over the span of the interview (which ran approximately one hour). They suggested that it would be easier to keep descriptions of changes on all of these dimensions in better order if participants could visually map them out on parallel strata of a time-line covering the years of the Alzheimer's patient's illness. When we modified the interview to include this written mapping exercise, our collection of reported events representing psychological changes increased.

Before using the interview in a larger-scale investigation, we felt it was important to secure not only the endorsement but the real collaboration of the several residential-care facilities in the community that would provide our family contacts. The director of our college's service-learning center established contacts with administrators at two area facilities and set up meetings to discuss the nature of the research. In follow-up conversations, we considered how the project fit with the mission of each of these facilities, one aspect of which was to provide knowledge in care giving that results in the provision of excellent care to residents (Fulton Manor, 1995). The student-researchers and I coauthored a letter that explained the research-as-service intentions behind the project and extended an invitation to families and staff to be active collaborators with us. We also held small-group strategy sessions with interested care staff (aids, nurses, chaplains) to plan their involvement in the study.

The institutional ethics-review boards at both facilities approved our proposal and included in their monthly newsletter mailing our letter inviting families to participate, along with a response postcard. In response to the initial invitation forty-six families indicated that they were willing to participate in our one-hour structured interview. To accommodate this number, I brought on another four students who were enrolled in my abnormal psychology course. Students in this course can receive extra-participation credit for completing a two-hour weekly service-learning assignment as volunteers in agencies that provide services to persons diagnosed with various forms of mental disorder (as defined by the DSM IV nosology).[2] Those students who choose this option can then write one of their short case-study assignment about the subjective

---

[2] The official diagnostic system of the American Psychiatric Association, 1994.

experience of symptoms as shared in an interview given by one of the clients with whom they worked.[3] Five upper-level majors in the course who were interested in empirical research were invited to conduct our structured interview in the research project as a way of fulfilling this service-learning opportunity.

So far about half of the interviews that we hope to do have been completed. It is too early to report meaningful results. Our research group (students, me and several staff at the facilities) has continued to meet to discuss techniques for interpreting interview material that will satisfy a level of analytic rigor defined by the culture of behavior science, be adequate to understanding the meanings communicated by families, and realize helping culture concerns for the well-being of residents. In this regard, we have actually had some animated discussions about whether and how data-analysis techniques such as content analysis or time-series analysis would help in realizing all of these objectives.

If the interview material does suggest patterns of reported changes in memory, relationships, self-identity, spiritual experience, and family members' actions, it will still be premature to conclude that it is an accurate picture of the psychological experiences of Alzheimer's patients throughout the course of the illness. Given the flexible, reconstructive nature of memory, it may tell us more about how families create after-the-fact narratives to make greater sense of their loved ones' journeys. In any event, there should be a springboard for further collaborative research to try to address these possible explanations in ways that may be of help to families. Already, several residence staff and family members have agreed to work with us on considering sensitive ways to conduct interviews with Alzheimer's residents themselves.

Calvin College's policy statement on academically based service-learning defines it as: "activities which are designed both to contribute to the meeting of community or individual needs and to aid in the development of the knowledge and understanding of the service giver" (Calvin College, 1993). There are several ways in which this collaborative research effort may exemplify this statement of purpose.

---

[3] This service-learning option has proven to be not only an effective exercise in understanding the phenomenology of mental illness but also a good way to teach the ethics and interpersonal skills of maintaining confidentiality and respecting clients' control over their own case narratives.

As a serious initial attempt to investigate a set of issues not previously addressed in empirical studies, the major objective of the interview project was to develop knowledge not only for the student service-giver but also for professor; family members; care facilities; and, as the program matures eventually, perhaps, for the larger professional community through publication.

In the interim, the interview material is generating considerable helpful local knowledge that may allow families to learn from one another's experiences and suggest ways in which both families and institutional staff can be more sensitive to considering residents' spiritual needs. The project has given students opportunity to develop a variety of research skills in addressing challenging empirical questions for which no single method of investigation has been widely established.

There were additional, immediate ways in which the process of the study helped to meet community and individual needs. Every student assistant met and spent time with the Alzheimer's resident whose family they interviewed. Students' efforts to listen to residents and come to know their histories were typically welcomed by residents and family members as an enrichment of their lives together. Families especially appreciated the respect that this research method gave to their experiences of suffering. Several have mentioned that the collaborative search for greater understanding of the psychological effects of the disease gave them a greater sense of empowerment in response to life experiences that made them feel powerless. They have asked that we share the outcome of the research with them as results become available and indicated interest to meet again to discuss and critique the conclusions. Administrators at the facilities value the project as an appropriate way to expand the implementation of their institutional missions and seem willing to consider whatever resulting local knowledge may aid their delivery of care.

As the research has progressed, we have faced some challenges and detours in our path. In order to offer this learning experience to all qualified students who wish to participate, it has been necessary to spend considerable time training new students who join the research team each semester. The same has been true for establishing relationships with care-facility staff and administrators when there are changes in professional positions. Although we have so far been able to maintain the objectives of the research that we originally agreed upon collaboratively, this turnover makes us realize that we may have to renegotiate some of these objectives before the study is complete.

Perhaps our greatest challenge has come from having to work around several nationally funded (noncollaborative) studies that are ongoing at these care facilities and prohibit additional research with the families involved until the studies are complete.

At a higher level of disciplinary understanding, the experience of collaborating with professor, residents' families, and institutional staff as research partners has helped some psychology majors to build bridges between the previously mentioned two cultures of psychology. Students experienced firsthand that being able to empathize with families and express genuine compassion encouraged family members to share richer accounts of their loved ones' experiences than might have been obtained by administering prematurely conceived behavioral scales. Engaging family members in this investigative alliance helped these students ask better questions in their research. It also fostered convictions that when research is carefully, honestly, and critically conducted in this fashion it can make an important behavioral-science contribution to effective compassionate care.

Jill, the student who helped to initiate this research, reflected on her semester's experience this way:

> Clearly remembering and upholding the lives of the persons with whom I worked does not mean they are lifted out of their experiences of chaos and despair. I do not believe that human community, regardless of its degree of love and commitment, can free the Alzheimer's sufferer. Instead I want to share the bittersweet hope I experienced this semester. I believe there is a genuine hope that comes to all those affected by Alzheimer's dementia when a community is willing to meet them, to partially join them (for we can never fully know), to remain with them amid the despair and chaos. For it is in this state of shared human weakness that hope in the God who promises to remember and uphold is possible. I have come closer to understanding the number of ways in which remembering and upholding is a matter of bringing oneself into the life of another.

Undergraduate education may aspire not only to communicate theoretical knowledge and develop skills of critical inquiry in students, but also to nurture such qualities of wisdom.

References

American Psychiatric Association. 1994. *Diagnostic and statistical manual of mental disorders,* 4th ed. Washington, DC: Author.

Calvin College. 1993. *Report of the ad hoc committee on service-learning.* (Available from Calvin College, Service-Learning Center, 3201 Burton SE, Grand Rapids, MI 49546).

Fulton Manor. 1995. *Verblauw Alzheimer's Care Unit: Mission, philosophy, goals.* (Available from Fulton Manor Verblauw Alzheimer's Care Unit, 1450 E. Fulton SE, Grand Rapids, MI 49503).

Kimble, G. A. 1984. Psychology's two cultures. *American Psychologist* 39(8): 833-839.

Nyden, P., and W. Wiewel. 1992. Collaborative research: Harnessing the tensions between researcher and practitioner. *The American Sociologist* 23 (4): 42-54.

Van Leeuwen, M. S. 1988. Psychology's two cultures: A Christian analysis. *Christian Scholar's Review* 17(4): 406-424.

Chapter 3

RECIPROCITY AND PARTNERSHIP: THE MULTIDIMENSIONAL IMPACT OF COMMUNITY-DRIVEN NURSING PRACTICE

Gail Landheer Zandee

Introduction

E VER SINCE LEAVING the full-time clinical practice world of nursing in 1993 to enter the academic world of educating nurses in the Hope-Calvin Department of Nursing, I have felt dual loyalties. As a community health nurse educator, I was not only wanting to advocate for the health of the community as I had done for years in the practice setting, but I was also wanting to advocate for the education of my nursing students. The problem was that these loyalties started to compete against each other when I began using the traditional clinical placements for students. Most baccalaureate nursing students gain community health clinical experience by providing nursing services in public health departments and/or community agencies. In these settings, nursing students end up caring for clients who are already being serviced by nurses. Students do use some of their time to provide additional services for clients, but in many instances care is duplicated so that students can learn. In these traditional clinical placements, there were times that the community (both agency staff and community residents) felt as if they were being "used" for students to gain experience. During those same times, I felt as if I was asking the community to be our student laboratory. To my dismay, I was creating a learning environment for my students that was conflicting with my values as a community-health nurse.

33

Defining the Problem and Seeking a Solution

It was not until June of 1997 that I realized the validity of my dilemma and a potential solution to eliminate it. That summer, I participated in a faculty development workshop provided by the Service-Learning Center at Calvin College. In the workshop, we reviewed the definition of service-learning. The concept of service-learning has been around for many years. However, depending on the recipients and areas emphasized, the meaning of service-learning can be quite different. Sigmon provides a typology of service and learning in which he describes four types:

1. Service-LEARNING is where the "learning agenda is central while the service setting is secondary."
2. SERVICE-learning, on the other hand, emphasizes the service being provided while the learning is secondary.
3. Service learning (without a hyphen) is when the services and learning goals are separate. "No expectation is stated that the service experience will enhance the learning nor that the learning will enhance the service."
4. Lastly, SERVICE-LEARNING (with a hyphen) gives equal weight to the service being provided and the learning occurring. The hyphen symbolizes that the needs of the community are linked with the learning objectives of students. "All parties to the arrangement are seen as learners and teachers as well as servers and served" (Sigmon 1996, 10).

It suddenly became clear to me that traditional clinical placements for nursing students were service-LEARNING in nature. Students were placed in community agencies more for the impact it would have on their learning than the impact it had on the community. The learning goals were primary while the service outcomes were secondary. That is why there were times when the community felt as if they were being used and I felt as if the community was our laboratory for learning. The answer to my dilemma seemed to be found in the fourth definition of service-learning. If I initiated a SERVICE-LEARNING experience for clinicals, I could give equal weight both to the service being provided and to the learning. Although this would ease the professional tension I felt, I began to wonder if using this process would in some way lessen the learning. If I did not make learning the central focus, would that mean learning would be compromised?

Literature Support

With the new idea that was churning and the questions it was raising, it was obvious that it was time to go to the literature. First, I turned to *The Essentials of Baccalaureate Education for Professional Nursing Practices*. This document states that "patient advocacy is, and will continue to be, a hallmark of the professional nursing role" (*American Association of Colleges of Nursing* 1998, 4). In traditional service-LEARNING placements where the learning is central and the service is secondary, there was a risk that this process may model to students that their needs are more important than the community's. As a community-health nurse who wanted to hallmark community advocacy, this concept was directly contrary to what I wanted to teach. The reality is that listening, collaborating, and partnering with the community are essential to being effective as a community-health nurse. Using SERVICE-LEARNING might allow me the opportunity to teach students how to be a community advocate by modeling how clinical experiences are arranged.

As a Christian nurse teaching at a Christian college, I also found biblical support for using SERVICE-LEARNING. All people are created in God's image and deserve dignity and respect. Giving equal weight to service and learning would allow us opportunity to give the community dignity and respect and lessen the risk of using them. In addition, the mission statements of both Hope and Calvin colleges support engaging with students in an education that promotes service to Christ and humanity.

As I dug into the literature further, I learned that SERVICE-LEARNING was gaining momentum in the professional realm of nursing. However, to my surprise, I found that just using service-learning was not enough. The literature was encouraging the creation of service-learning community-campus partnerships. A partnership is formed when the community and college (employee(s), department(s)/division(s), or college as a whole) engage in a significant area of endeavor. An organization called Community Campus Partnerships for Health (CCPH) taught me the most about what it means to have a partnership. This organization advocates using service-learning partnerships for health-profession education, and they have written many documents on how to integrate them. In one document published by CCPH, the authors (Maurana, Beck, and Newton 1998) list seven principles of an effective community-campus partnership (*see list below*). One of the highlights of this list is the requirement that both the community and the campus need to be committed to the relationship. Goals for enhancing the relationship and the outcomes need to be set regularly and mutually. A partnership signals longevity and mutual commitment.

Draft Principles of Good Partnership

- Partners have agreed upon mission, goals, and outcomes.
- The relationship between partners is characterized by mutual trust, respect, genuineness, and commitment.
- The partnership builds upon identified strengths and assets.
- There is clear and accessible communication between partners, making it an ongoing priority to listen to each need, develop a common language, and validate/clarify the meaning of terms.
- Roles, norms, and processes for the partnership are established with the input and agreement of all partners.
- Partnerships evolve.
- There is feedback to, among, and from all partners, with the goal of continuously improving the partnership and its outcomes (Maurana, Beck, and Newton 1998, 47).

Bellack supports the value of having nursing students experience clinicals that are service-learning partnerships. She makes the distinction that "learning in the community is not the same as learning with the community" (Bellack 1998, 99). She goes on to say that although we teach students "the value of involving the communities in improving the community's health" (99), we do not always model it in how our clinical experiences are arranged. *The Essentials of Baccalaureate Education* also supports the partnership approach by encouraging educators to prepare baccalaureate students with the skills to "initiate community partnerships" and form "partnerships with patients and the interdisciplinary health care team" (*American Association of Colleges of Nursing* 1998, 13, 16). Community-health nurses will rarely be effective if they see their role as a top-down one with the goal of rescuing the community. In contrast, the community needs to be seen as an expert. They need to be listened to and respected as a partner in the process of moving to a higher level of wellness.

In addition, service-learning partnerships have the ability to demonstrate to students the essential elements of health promotion. Lindsey and Hartrick (1996) highlight some of the essential elements of health promotion: empowerment, autonomy, egalitarianism, partnership, collaboration, community participation, self-determination, accessibility, mutual aid, and shared responsibility. If a clinical experience is based on a service-learning partnership, community participation will be essential. All partners will need to collaborate, all will have shared responsibility, and the equality of the partners will be stressed. A good partnership should emphasize the empowerment of the community and the student. What a better way for community-health educators to teach students about the essential elements of health promotion than by modeling these elements.

In summarizing the literature, it was evident that there was much support for using service-learning partnerships in place of traditional community-health clinical placements. In fact, after researching the issue, I was beginning to believe that this method was not only going to translate into better service for the community, but it was also going to result in enhanced learning for the student.

Initiating a Service-Learning Community Campus Partnership

In initiating a partnership, I needed to seek out potential partners and begin to dialogue with them on this topic. During the summer workshop offered by the Service-Learning Center, I had met an individual from the community who looked to be potential partner. Our initial meeting involved two members from the community and two members from campus. The partners who were present were a director of a center-city neighborhood association, a community organizer from a clinic affiliated with the neighborhood association, a Calvin College service-learning director, and me. The staff from the service-learning center had worked with the neighborhood-association director previously in

SERVICE-LEARNING contexts. She facilitated conversations and the building of our relationship. We began by sharing our mission, our goals, and our desired outcome of a partnership. The community representatives shared how the neighborhood association had recently collaborated with others from the community to create a clinic that emphasized primary care for the uninsured and underinsured in the neighborhood. Their goals were to do a more detailed neighborhood assessment and increase awareness of the availability of the clinic in the community. I shared the objectives of the course and my commitment to having a service-learning partnership.

Throughout the semester, we held additional meetings and brainstorming sessions on possible collaborative initiatives. By the end of the semester, we had mutually decided on objectives for the partnership. The student's objectives were achieving course outcomes and developing an appreciation for the strengths and needs of an uninsured and/or underinsured population. The community's objective was having two hundred neighborhood residents participate in health-promotion activities offered through home visits and a health fair leading to ongoing wellness practice. These objectives were included in a proposal, and the project received support through a Michigan Campus Compact grant. Students would focus on two vulnerable population groups—children and the elderly. Clinical time would be spent strategizing, organizing and designing care for the target population; conducting home visits to residents of the neighborhood; evaluating care given by themselves and others; and proposing ideas on how care could be improved. In May, the students would collaborate to provide a health fair in the neighborhood.

Because partnerships evolve over time and trust had to develop, a mutual decision was made to have the partnership site encompass half of the clinical experience. Thus, students would spend half of their clinical time in the partnership placement and the other half in the traditional placement. This would allow time for the partners to learn more about each other and build a relationship. We wanted to make sure our mission and goals overlapped before we started programs we could not continue. It would also allow me the opportunity to fall back on the traditional clinical placement if student learning proved not to be optimal in the partnership site.

Implementing a Service-Learning Partnership

Over the course of the semester, sixteen students each spent approximately thirty-five hours at the partnership site. The first day, students received an orientation from the neighborhood-association director and the clinic representative. Topics that were covered included the role of the neighborhood association, the history of the clinic, a description of the community and its residents, various community development issues, community organizing techniques, and a walking tour of the neighborhood. Students then spent time reviewing a rough draft of a survey. The survey was meant to gather health-indicator data as well as inform those without insurance about the availability of the clinic. By allowing students the freedom to make additions and corrections to the survey, the students began to develop ownership of the survey and the project they were starting.

One of the highlights of the orientation was the training that the neighborhood association representatives provided in community development and community organizing. Because a neighborhood association's effectiveness is based on these skills, they truly were experts in this area. They were also the experts regarding their community, so the training could be specifically applied to the neighborhood the students would be working in. Chalmers, Bramadat, and Andrusyszyn (1998) studied the changes occurring in community-health nursing practice for the baccalaureate-prepared nurse. They found that community-health nurses felt weak in their training on community development. "In general, they were accepting of community development as part of their role but were unsure that their understanding and preparation were adequate" (113). The community-health nurses who participated in the study go on to predict that community-development and community-mobilization skills will become a larger part of the public health nurse's role for the future.

During the semester, students went door to door in the neighborhood and completed fifty-eight surveys. At each resident's home, students offered screening and health education to those who were interested. Approximately half of those surveyed were open to receiving health-educational material or to being screened. The most frequently requested activities were blood pressure screening, blood sugar screening, information on childhood growth and development, and education on lead poisoning and prevention. One individual under the age of thirty was found to have hypertension and was not aware of it.

The person was referred appropriately and committed to following up on it. Another individual with diabetes had an elevated blood sugar but did not have access to a glucometer. A referral was made, and the local diabetes outreach network provided follow-up care. Both of these individuals were grateful for the student's work and the experience made the students feel as if they were really making a difference in someone's life.

The health fair at the end of the semester was attended by one hundred forty two neighborhood residents. Nursing students provided blood pressure and blood sugar screening and a doctor-nurse team from the neighborhood clinic provided cholesterol screening. Other booths created by nursing students covered the topics of nutrition, stress management, lead poisoning, growth and development, and burn prevention. In addition, nursing students ran a bike rodeo in the parking lot to teach bike safety while representatives from the police department registered bikes. An ambulance was also on site for education and tours. Many businesses from the surrounding community supported the health fair by donating items to be given away as door prizes, including sixteen bicycle helmets.

Evaluating the Service-Learning Partnership

The partnership was created to provide an unavailable service to the community, so we knew there was no duplication of care that was occurring. However, we did not know how the community perceived us and whether we were being effective. To gather data, we asked community residents to evaluate us, and we tried to determine whether we had a positive impact on their health. Of the community residents who participated in door-to-door surveys and screenings, only five (9 percent) mailed back a completed evaluation. All five residents said the visit was helpful and they felt more aware of the services provided by their community clinic. Of the three who received health education, two said they would use the information and one said maybe. One said he would make lifestyle changes based on the information, one said he would not make lifestyle changes, and the other did not answer. In evaluating children at the health fair who completed every booth and the bike rodeo, all of them said the health fair was fun. Nursing students also selected one or two learning objectives for the bike rodeo and each booth to ensure the effectiveness of their individual teaching methods. Of the adults who participated in the health fair, thirteen (29 percent) completed evaluations. All of them said the health fair was helpful and that they would use the educational material received. Eleven (88 percent) said they would make lifestyle changes based on the information received. Although we did receive a positive evaluation of the project from the community, we did not receive the 40 percent response rate that we had hoped. One of our future goals was to collaborate as partners on this issue and strategize on how we could increase our response rate in the future.

All nursing students were able to achieve course outcomes through the partnership experience. According to their journals it was also evident that students were developing an appreciation for the strengths and needs of this underserved population. Many students described the lack of access to health care and how amazed they were at the number of people without insurance. They also described how several people in the community who had insurance were dissatisfied with the services they were being provided through their insurance. Students described the impact it had on them to see that we live in a society of many health-care resources, but the resources are not equally distributed. Others talked about the need for health-care professionals to be willing to give up authority and listen to the community so that we could work *with* them rather than *for* them. One described community cohesion as a strength that was important to build on for increasing wellness, while another described the importance of meeting people where they are in promoting health. In comparing the overall journal write-ups between the two clinical placements, it was obvious that student learning was not compromised at all in the partnership placement. In fact, in my judgment the learning was enhanced because of it.

Not only did students describe their understanding of the strengths and needs of an underserved population, but they also grew in their understanding of how to care for the community as the client. Traditional community-health clinicals in our department have focused on caring for the client and/or family in the context of the community rather than caring for the community as client. Because of this, nearly all of the journal entries were written with emphasis on the individual and/or family as the client. In the literature, however, public-health nurses of today are saying that their practice has shifted from emphasizing individuals and families to emphasizing the community. "Public health nurses now act as facilitators, rather than experts, helping communities identify health concerns. They work with the community, rather than with individuals, to implement solutions to a broad range of health related problems"

(Chalmers, Bramadat, and Andrusyszyn 1998, 113). The community-campus partnership component of this clinical emphasized the community as a whole. Because of this, the majority of the journal entries for the partnership site emphasized the community as client. This translated into a stronger learning environment for the student.

Student evaluations of the clinical experience were collected at the end of the semester. Strengths listed by students were the ability to see the big picture of how public health operates with community as client, the independence and creative thinking that it encouraged, the health fair, having their own project to design and implement, being involved with a project with wide-reaching and long-term effects, emphasis on health promotion, and how the site was an effective application of the theory class. All students recommended using this clinical placement as a site for the next year.

The primary challenge of the experience was dividing clinical time between the traditional and partnership placements. It was difficult for students and the instructor to adjust back and forth between the two placements, which led to a lack of continuity in the experience. Although the division of time allowed trust to slowly develop with the community, I would recommend looking for alternative ways to do this in the future.

One unanticipated and enjoyable outcome of the experience was the learning that I received from the partnership site. I learned much about community development and community organizing and have grown in my professional skills because of this. Also, because we were creating a new service extension of the clinic, I was able to both teach and practice at the same time. This allowed me to collaborate with the students in creating a public-health program and have the dual role of being their teacher and preceptor. (Traditionally a registered nurse from the community agency assists in overseeing the student).

At the end of the semester, I sat down with the two partners who had worked with me in creating this experience (the director of the center-city neighborhood association and community organizer from the neighborhood clinic) and asked them to evaluate the experience. They thought the semester was a tremendous success and shared that they wanted to continue our community-campus partnership. In June, the community organizer and I attended a workshop sponsored by the Service-Learning Center at Calvin College. At that workshop, we discussed our partnership, the future direction it would take, and formulated shared goals. With our partnership goals in mind and the results of the survey we conducted, the community leaders met in the fall and developed a list of neighborhood objectives for health and wellness. The list is set up very similar to that of *Health People 2000* (U.S. Department of Health and Human Services, 1990) except it is specific to the strengths and needs of their neighborhood. It was a three-year plan that included goals, benchmarks to measure the goals, and yearly objectives that would help us meet those goals. The following spring, nursing students spent their whole public-health rotation at the partnership site. They built upon what the students had started the previous year and worked to fulfill the yearly objectives for health that had been set in the fall. This document was an essential piece of our partnership. It signaled longevity and mutual commitment to the relationship. It gave us the direction we needed to continue our partnership and defined how we would expand it.

Evaluation seemed incomplete, however, if I only looked at the impact the partnership had over the course of one semester. If a partnership truly has value, it will have evidence of this by the support it receives from both the community and campus over time. The partnership was created in the spring of 1998 and will be entering its third year of existence this coming year. Both the community and the campus are demonstrating its value by the fact that the partnership still continues today. In addition, this partnership has been used as a model to create two other partnership sites for students in the Hope-Calvin Department of Nursing. One is with a rural community in West Michigan, while the other is with a center-city homeless population. This is the second way the service-learning partnership concept has demonstrated validity over time.

Conclusion

It is always a risk to step outside the comfort zone of tradition, to try a new endeavor. Because of the multidimensional impact of service-learning partnerships, this was one risk I am glad I took. I encourage you to evaluate your traditional teaching methods and consider whether service-learning partnerships have a place in your area of expertise. It may be a risk you, too, will be very glad you took.

References

American Association of Colleges of Nursing. 1998. *The essentials of baccalaureate education for professional nursing practices.* Washington, D.C.: American Association of Colleges of Nursing.

Bellack, Janis P. 1998. Community-based nursing practice necessary but not sufficient. *Journal of Nursing Education* 37 (3): 99-100.

Chalmers, Karen I., Ina J. Branadat, and Mary Anne Andrusyszyn. 1998. The changing environment of community health practice and education: Perceptions of staff nurses, administrators, and educators. *Journal of Nursing Education* 37 (3): 109-17.

Linsey, Elizabeth, and Gweneth Hartrick. 1996. Health-promoting nursing practice: The demise of the nursing process? *Journal of Advanced Nursing* 23: 106-12.

Maurana, Cheryl A., Barbara Beck, and Gail L. Newton. 1998. How principles of partnership are applied to the development of a community-campus partnership. In *Partnership perspectives*, edited by K. Conners and S. D. Seifer. San Francisco: Community-Campus Partnerships for Health.

Sigmon, Robert L. 1996. *Journey to service-learning: Experiences from independent liberal arts colleges and universities.* Washington, D.C.: Council of Independent Colleges.

U.S. Department of Health and Human Services. 1990. *Healthy people 2000: National health promotion and disease prevention objectives.* DHHS Publication No. PHS 91-50213. Washington, D.C.: GPO

Chapter 4

HISTORICALLY SPEAKING: ACADEMICALLY BASED SERVICE-LEARNING IN THE HISTORY CURRICULUM

Daniel R. Miller

The Experience of the History Department

THE FORMAL IMPLEMENTATION of an Academically Based Service-Learning (ABSL) course in the History Department at Calvin is a fairly recent phenomenon, but it draws on several prior developments. For many years, the History Department has felt a special responsibility to promote the cross-cultural aspect of the college's mission. The discipline of history almost inevitably puts students in contact with "diverse cultures." All members of the department have attempted to make their classes places where such contacts go beyond the transmission of cognitive knowledge to provide students with an empathetic understanding of the people and groups they study. The participatory aspect of the college's mission has also been important to the department, but efforts along these lines have more commonly related to vocational preparation in library and museum internships and in the senior research seminar that concludes the major course of study. In a department where much of the content is long ago and far away and where the skills employed seem more appropriate to the library and the seminar room than to the urban neighborhood, the introduction of ABSL has proven to be a bit of a challenge.

A few departmental undertakings have managed to combine methodological training and cross-cultural experience. The most ambitious is the Archeology Fieldwork program. Each summer, students in the program spend six weeks engaged in fieldwork at the archeological site of Umm el-Jimal in

Jordan. The Calvin students work alongside Jordanian and Palestinian excavators as well as Arab and other archeologists. The collegial aspect of the work is an essential component of the program for the professor who leads the program because it allows students an opportunity to form friendships with people whose ethnicity, religion, and historical experience differ from that of most of the Calvin students he takes on the program. The students generally come away from the experience with very different attitudes about people in the Middle East than those they began with. Of course, their primary mission is to catalogue items found on-site and to write research reports that become part of the archeological record. In that sense, they are engaged in service to a community of scholars around the world.

Service-Learning in the Latin American History Course

The first course in the department to invoke the notion of academically based service-learning explicitly is one that I teach on the history of Latin America. The course appeals to business majors who are interested in international marketing, students in the Third World Development minor who are thinking of becoming aid workers, sociology majors who want background on the Hispanic population of the United States, as well as others whose reasons for enrolling are more idiosyncratic. My general objective in the course is to acquaint these students with Latin America and Latin Americans in ways that combine factual knowledge and empathetic understanding. One issue that I stress is the influence of the United States on the region and its people and another is the influence of Latin Americans, especially immigrants, on the United States. For the last five years, I have included a service-learning assignment in the course to facilitate the achievement of these two course goals.

My decision to utilize an assignment that placed Calvin students in close contact with people from Latin America was motivated in large part by the recollection of an experience that I had as a young man fresh out of college. I worked for a year at a factory in Santa Ana, California, assembling parts for recreational vehicles. My coworkers included a large number of Mexicans who had entered the United States illegally. Having grown up in an all-white suburb of Los Angeles, I had experienced little prior contact with Mexicans and probably shared to some degree the invidious stereotypes that white Californians often expressed about Mexican immigrants. What I actually observed were hard working, cheerful people who sent much of their pay back to Mexico to support parents, children, spouses, and siblings. They faced significant hurdles such as the Immigration and Naturalization Service, which raided our factory three times during that year and deported several Mexican workers. Most returned to work within a few days after spending several hundred hard-earned dollars to get back across the border. Years later, my experiences in the factory influenced my thinking as I considered the possibility of a service-learning assignment. I knew that the immigration issue is complex; certainly the United States cannot absorb all of the world's poor. However, I also remembered what God told the Old Testament Israelites about the need to show hospitality to aliens who came to reside among them, "since they too, were once strangers in the land" (Deut. 10:19). In the end, I concluded that whatever opinions my students formed about Mexican immigration or any other issue involving Latin Americans should be shaped at least in part by personal contact with the people most directly involved.

Initially, the service-learning assignment required students to tutor Hispanic children at Homework House, an after-school enrichment program for elementary students. In the third and fourth years, the Calvin students were assigned to tutor adults in an English as a Second Language (ESL) program that serves Hispanic immigrants. In both places, the Calvin students were required to participate in a minimum of eight 60- to 90-minute tutoring sessions during the semester. In preparation for the assignment, students attended an orientation meeting where a member of the Spanish Department acquainted them with some of the distinctive features of the Hispanic community in Grand Rapids. They also received instruction in the logistics of the assignment—transportation, attendance records, and so forth. The students also watched one or two videos— *El Norte* and *My Family*—and read several articles dealing with Hispanic immigrants to the United States. These materials provided them with a background of knowledge against which to evaluate their experiences in the service-learning activity. I also supplied the students with a list of questions to ask the individuals they were tutoring. Some of the questions were:

> Where are you from? What prompted you to leave and to come here? What was the journey like?

> What do you like best about living in Michigan? What do you miss most about the place where you grew up?

What are your favorite types of music, movies, food, sports, etc.? Is/are the music, food, sports different here than where you grew up?

What are your favorite holidays? How were they celebrated when you were growing up? Are the holidays different here?

Do you have a favorite relative? Tell me about her/him.

Did you learn stories or songs when you were growing up? Can you tell/sing me any?

Do you go to church? Do/did your parents? What kind is it? What is it like?

After each visit, students submitted a 100-150 word informal report in writing or via e-mail detailing what happened and what they thought about the experience. At the end of the semester they wrote a 4-to-6 page essay defining what is meant by the term "Latin American" (or "Mexican" if the more restrictive term fit). I graded their essays on how well they had integrated personal observations with the course material (articles, lecture notes, and films).

Evaluating the Effectiveness of the Service-Learning Assignment

The response of the students to this assignment has been very positive with only a few exceptions, and it displays evidence of significant learning in the form of changed attitudes and insights that would have been difficult to acquire through ordinary classroom instruction. Tutors at the Homework House site quickly noticed that the children were generally adept in mathematics but slow in reading. It was an unsurprising observation, but it helped several of the Calvin students comprehend how easily bright children can be stigmatized as "slow" or "lazy" by virtue of their unfamiliarity with the English language. The students were astonished at how mobile many of the children were, learning that they commuted frequently between Mexico and Michigan or followed a harvest cycle that took them to Florida, Texas, and California on an annual rotation. The deleterious educational effects of these constant uprootings were also apparent to many of them.

The Calvin students noted that even for those students whose parents had secured work that enabled them to remain in Grand Rapids throughout the year, living conditions were less than ideal. The neighborhood of the school was fairly rundown—several students commented that they had always avoided this part of Grand Rapids before—and the children talked much about local gangs and their violent doings. The more thoughtful students made shrewd observations about the relative ease with which the children abandoned their cultural distinctiveness versus the more intractable character of their economic-and social-class status. Despite differences in age and background, the Calvin students had little difficulty establishing friendly relations with the children. The children loved the personal attention they received, and the Calvin students enjoyed the opportunity to use their reading and math skills or in many cases their recently and imperfectly acquired Spanish language ability.

Tutors in the adult ESL program were also impressed by evidence that Hispanic immigration is not a once-in-a-lifetime event but an extended period during which there is much coming and going across the border. They also remarked on how determined the immigrants were to learn English; many of them displayed great eagerness for instruction despite the fact that the class came at the end of a long workday. They correctly noted the importance of good English skills to the immigrants' chances for upward job mobility. Some of the students admitted that the "work ethic" of the ESL learners was far stronger than they had imagined. Several students volunteered to tutor again in the following semester even though it was no longer a course requirement, and many students in both program expressed a new-found respect for the Hispanic people. Following are some of the comments made by students in the fall of 1999:

> "I have known many immigrants [works on a farm] but I had never sat down and talked to them about their experiences before, it was very enlightening."

> "I learned lots about Cuban immigrants from the family I worked with for PARA."

> "The ABSL assignment made the class information real, I met a woman who talked about getting across the border with the help of a coyote and she was kept in virtual slavery for a while after she got here."

Students who responded to a survey taken more than a year after the end of the course were unanimous in their conviction that the service-learning assignment ought to be remain a part of the class. In support of that judgment, they cited the peculiar efficacy of personal contact with Latin Americans as a means to learn about the region. These responses indicate that students are realizing in some measure the cognitive and affective goals of the course that were noted above.

The response of the program directors indicated that they felt that the Hispanic children and adults were being well served by the Calvin tutors. They commented favorably on the punctuality and reliability of the students and on the earnestness they displayed in carrying out their assignments. One of the children at Homework House referred fondly to a Calvin tutor who had worked with him two years previously, suggesting that the personal attention that the children received was indeed appreciated.

As a professor, I have profited personally from service-learning in a couple of ways. During the first year, I joined my students in tutoring children at Homework House on a weekly basis. By participating in the exercise, I was able to assess the effectiveness of the program and respond to students' questions about the assignment more effectively. The fact that I experienced many of the same problems that the students were facing improved class morale. Very heavy time demands prohibited me from participating in the assignment during the subsequent years, but I hope to get involved during the coming semester because the benefits are clearly worth the effort. In addition, preparing course materials to accompany the assignment has obliged me to delve into the literature on the Hispanic community in the United States, and that has represented a permanent gain in my understanding of the larger topic of Latin American history.

Challenges

It would be seriously misleading to imply that the implementation of ABSL in the Latin American history course has been problem free. After two years, I discontinued participation at Homework House for a variety of reasons. Frequent and sometimes unannounced schedule changes in the program, especially in the second year, caused frustration to the Calvin students and made it difficult for some to meet the minimum number of tutoring sessions. The children sometimes refused to pay attention or misbehaved, leaving many of the Calvin students, who had not been trained as teachers, unsure about how to respond. A number of students also complained that they had difficulty acquiring information for their final essay from young children whose ability to communicate was poor and whose memories did not go back very far.

For all of these reasons, in the third year I switched the venue of the assignment to a pair of ESL programs that catered to adult learners. The change proved beneficial as reflected in the quality of the students' observations and in their expressed satisfaction with the value of the assignment, but some problems remain. Two students complained that they were placed with non-English speakers and, since they spoke no Spanish, little communication took place. The placements were designed to avoid such incompatibilities but evidently more careful monitoring is needed to guarantee that result. Another tutor complained that the transience of the ESL students made it difficult for him to get beyond an introductory stage in his investigations. These are serious issues, and they indicate that further refinements are needed in the assignment and in strengthening the partnership between the college and the community organizations.

Another adjustment that I made after the second year was to make the assignment optional. Students who wish to do so may now write a term paper based on academic sources instead of participating in the service-learning project. This change was prompted by my acknowledgment that a course dedicated to exploring the broad chronological and geographical sweep of Latin American history should allow students the option of studying topics that are inaccessible via the service-learning assignment. Even so, three-fourths of the students elected to do the service-learning assignment. Unfortunately, the fact that one-fourth of the class was not engaged in the service-learning assignment made it awkward to use class time for group reflection on the experience, and out-of-class meetings were unappealing to the students due to the busyness of their schedules. An on-line discussion offers the best possibility of getting around this problem.

One other adjustment was to permit students who had a special interest in a particular organization or profession to chose an alternative site for their service. That change allowed students with an interest in elementary education to serve at Homework House during the third year when most students were tutoring in an ESL program. It also permitted one nursing student to serve as a translator at a free medical clinic that served Hispanic women. Her acute observations about the relatively poor attention paid to non-English speaking patients by English-only speaking medical personnel was a more than sufficient reward for a bit of administrative flexibility on my part.

It should be noted that my initial decision to try service-learning and my subsequent experiments with it were aided enormously by the college. One of the directors of the Service-Learning Center suggested the idea and located appropriate sites for the service assignments. The student staff she recruited and trained attended to logistical details such as distributing and collecting sign-up sheets and recording attendance. They also provided some of the orientation for the tutors. The Calvin Job Transportation Service also played a key role because it made possible the participation of students who lacked their own transportation. As these examples illustrate, the commitment of the college to ABSL goes beyond rhetoric to providing institutional supports for faculty who want to give service-learning a try. Without these supports, the effort required to begin such a project might well have proven prohibitive, but with them it was eminently feasible.

Future Directions

The role that ABSL might increasingly play in the History Department is indicated by the Calvin College Garbage Project that took place this past spring. Inspired by the Arizona Garbage Project, "a pioneering archeological program for studying modern American cultural habits," Calvin's professor of archeology assigned students in his archeological fieldwork course to catalogue rubbish left at seven campus collection sites on a typical weekday. Their work was part of the interdisciplinary Calvin Environmental Assessment Project (CEAP). To complete the garbage project, students had to learn and follow proper fieldwork procedures, record data, write up a report on their findings and publish it on the Web. While it served as a test-run for the sorts of procedures that the students would soon be using at Umm el-Jimal, the project had the additional service-oriented purpose of providing the college with data that would be useful for improving food service, waste disposal, recycling, and composting efforts. The Garbage Project represents a useful model of how historical research methodology can be incorporated into a service assignment.

Another expression of ABSL in the History Department is an oral-history assignment that has been incorporated into the African-American history class. Students in the class are instructed in methods of oral history and then sent out to interview elderly African-Americans who moved to Grand Rapids from the South during the Great Migration. Transcript tapes of the interviews are collected by the Grand Rapids city historian in archives devoted to the experience of African-Americans in Grand Rapids. The students also prepare a written account of their interviewees' experience, a copy of which they give to the interviewees to serve as a record of their family history.

This last example inspired me to offer an oral-history project in my Latin American history course during the semester just concluded. Students who elected to do this project attended a seminar on interview methods offered by the Grand Rapids city historian. The seminar taught them how to prepare for, conduct, and record interviews, how to transcribe recorded material in proper format, and how to transform transcripts into a narrative life history. The students also read secondary material and watch videos about Hispanic immigrants to provide them with background knowledge about the subject. In the fifth week of the semester, each student was paired with a "community partner," an immigrant from Latin America who had been selected by the city historian as an appropriate interview subject. Students met with their community partners on four occasions. The first meeting was an occasion to get acquainted, explain the project, gather factual information using a standardized questionnaire, and complete a release form. The second and third visits included audio-taped interviews. The last visit was an opportunity to thank the community partner and receive final corrections to the draft of their life history. Prior to each interview, students submitted interview guides (questions). Students were also required to transcribe their taped interviews and to submit copies of the transcripts along with the narrative life history of their community partner. Community partners received a copy of these life histories. Another copy, along with the tapes and transcripts of the interviews, was placed in the public museum as part of a permanent archive of material on the Hispanic community in Grand Rapids.

This assignment satisfied the criteria for effective academically based service-learning. Students not only learned facts about the immigrant experience, they learned them in the context of a relationship that encouraged them to see the significance of those facts. Community partners received and provided a service. People generally love to tell their stories, and this project gave the community partners an opportunity to do so and to have their stories recorded in an accurate and permanent way. By allowing themselves to be interviewed, they also provide the students with an opportunity to acquire valuable research skills. The public museum served the students by providing training in research methods and locating suitable community partners. In turn, it will benefit from the addition to its archival collection. There were a couple of drawbacks to the project, however. From an administrative point of view, finding enough community partners for future oral histories may not be easy. From the students' point of view, transcribing and sometimes translating three hours worth of audio tape, even with the aid of transcription devices, turned out to be an extremely tedious and time-consuming challenge. Still, all of the participants expressed gratitude that they had been permitted to do the project.

Academically based service-learning resonates well with the mission of Calvin College. With a bit of creative planning and some adjustments born of experience, it can become a vital component of the history curriculum as well. ABSL may not prove appropriate for inclusion in every course in the History Department, but its full potential is only beginning to be realized.

Chapter 5

INTERNATIONAL SERVICE-LEARNING: A CALL TO CAUTION

Kurt Ver Beek

Introduction

B OTH STUDENTS AND UNIVERSITIES in North America are increasingly interested in the global issue of poverty, and many want to *do* something. This desire combined with cheaper international airfares and growing disposable incomes in North America have contributed to an ever-increasing number of university sponsored service-learning trips to the "Third World."[1] Spring break, May term, and full semester programs attempt to combine both learning about and helping these poor countries. Students and professors travel the world, including countries as distant and distinct as Ecuador, Kenya, and Viet Nam to learn while building orphanages, painting health centers, and running after-school programs. What should we think of this growing trend? Are these experiences beneficial to both the students and the poor? Should such programs be expanded or cut back?

Unfortunately, the vast majority of the service-learning experiences, which I have witnessed in my fifteen years in Central America, neither understand nor address the true dilemmas of poverty and consequently provide little or no long-term benefit to the poor. They therefore result in learning that is mediocre at best. Students and professors are intruding into poor people's lives, often trying

---

[1] I have put "Third World" in quotations in this first usage to make clear that I am aware and sympathetic with many of the arguments against using First/Third, Developed/Underdeveloped terminology. However, for ease of use and because it is the most common terminology, I will use Third World for the remainder of this paper.

to fix things they do not understand. This service often causes them to think better of themselves, worse of the poor, and makes them too busy to take full advantage of their learning opportunities. More importantly, this service based on superficial understanding seldom empowers the poor or builds up their capacity. It is often neither equitable nor sustainable. As a result, I will argue using development and service-learning literature and case studies that students must learn more before they seek to intervene in the lives of the poor, that this learning can be experiential even if it is not service-oriented, and that any learning experiences that seek to serve the poor must go through a process of review and evaluation to determine if it is truly contributing to the development of the poor.

Development and Service-Learning

Development is about people. It is not about factories, computers, money, or tractors. These are but useful tools. They are means to an end but only means. True development is about transforming people, empowering them to change their own future—to make a better tomorrow for their children. The United Nations maintains that

> Development is not only a fundamental right but also a basic human need,
> which fulfills the aspiration of all people to achieve the greatest possible
> freedom and dignity both as individuals and as members of the societies in
> which they live (United Nations 1991).

Bryant and White in their classic text on development define it as "increasing the capacity of people to influence their own future," (Bryant and White 1982) and go on to outline four characteristics of a true development process. First, it must be empowering, increasing people's sense of control and power over decisions and events that affect them. Second, it must increase people's capacity—both their ability and their energy to determine their future. Third, it must be equitable—the benefits must not be concentrated on only a small sector of the population and especially not on its wealthier members. Finally, development must be sustainable. Development processes must be carried out in such a way that is sustainable by local economic, human, and environmental resources.

A Christian perspective on development, brings this focus on people and the importance of empowering the poor into sharper focus. Christ gave his disciples two commandments, "Love the Lord your God with all your heart and with all your soul and with all your mind and with all your strength. The second is this: Love your neighbor as yourself. There is no commandment greater than these" (Mark 12:30-31, NIV). In this passage, by putting love of neighbor as one of the two summary commandments, Christ is demonstrating how important people are in his kingdom. In addition, he is challenging his followers to a radical type of love, especially for those in need,[2] which few if any have been able to attain. If Christians both value and put into practice this love of others, rich or poor, then our every interaction with others should be characterized by respect for their God-given and God-reflecting dignity. Second, loving others as ourselves means our seeing that they attain their God-given potential just as we attempt to. Finally, a Christian perspective on development should take seriously people's spirituality. While many nonreligious development organizations avoid or even minimize the faith of those they serve, Christian organizations should recognize the power of faith and spirituality to motivate and transform lives (Ver Beek 2000).

In summary, a Christian perspective on development reinforces the centrality of people and their God-given dignity. It is our responsibility to see that all people fully develop the talents and gifts they were given as well as the centrality of spirituality to many people's lives.

Service-learning is a term used to describe efforts that allow students to meet formal educational goals while at the same time improving themselves and their society. The Southern Regional Education Board program first used the term in the late 1960s. They defined it as "the integration of the accomplishment of a needed task with educational growth" (Kendall 1990). Robert Sigmon asserts that its purpose is "the linking of service with learning to create a congruent service ethic throughout the campus culture and within the curriculum (Sigmon 2000). Clearly, service-learning seeks to have students learn while they do something good, and, as a result, improve learning, pedagogy, and create better and more moral citizens.

---

[2] See the parable of the Good Samaritan in Luke 10:30-36.

Robert Sigmon argues that the best of these service-learning opportunities have three characteristics in common: (1) "Beneficiaries"[3] define their needs, which are then linked to learning expectations for students. The individuals, communities, or agencies seeking assistance should define their needs and requests and then enter into dialogue with the professors and students to match their needs to student's interventions. (2) All involved are learners and teachers as well as servers and served. The students, professors, and beneficiaries should all be both contributing and benefiting from the relationships. (3) Students are challenged to both learn and contribute. They must respect the local knowledge and culture, listen and explore as well as share from their emerging capacity, and gain increased capacity for self-directed learning (Sigmon 2000).

A Christian perspective on service-learning largely complements the characteristics outlined above. I have already mentioned Christ's concern for our serving our neighbor and the poor. Such service, for a Christian, should not be a convenient addition to the curriculum but an integral part of each Christian's life—students, professors, and all others. The goal of service-learning in a Christian context goes beyond creating better citizens. Rather it is for us to become what God originally intended—to fulfill our calling by being loving neighbors. Christians should all be busy learning and acting to better transform this society into what God desires—"let justice roll on like a river and righteousness like a never-failing stream" (Amos 5:24, NIV). Finally, as disciples of Christ, we need only reflect on his example as teacher to see service-learning in practice. Christ's original twelve disciples learned through Christ's teachings and modeling as well as by serving and reflecting on that service. In summary, a Christian perspective on service-learning is consistent with Christ's example, calls us to serve the poor and society in general, and sets the goal not at becoming better citizens but rather at fulfilling who we were created to become—loving servants who by giving, receive.

We can certainly imagine a setting where true development and true service-learning are taking place and complementing each other. Students would be serving and learning in ways that are empowering, capacity building, equitable, and sustainable. In practice, this would mean that the student

---

[3] I use this term recognizing that it is problematic. In the best service-learning situation both the students and the "served" are learners and teachers. However, I know of no better term that captures the idea that the student is "serving" on various levels (individuals, communities, agencies).

intervention would encourage and allow the poor to define their needs, make decisions, and control the processes affecting their lives. The poor would learn new skills and feel increasingly motivated and empowered. New resources would complement but not overwhelm local ones, the poor in the community would benefit and the processes set in motion would be economically, humanly, and environmentally sustainable. The service-learner would contribute limited amounts of resources, ideas, and effort without diminishing local processes. The focus would be on learning from the poor, and recognizing the value of local knowledge, skills, and ideas. Finally, they would be culturally sensitive and knowledgeable about development in order to truly contribute to a development process in a manner that makes their hosts feel comfortable, intelligent, and motivated. After the students left, the community would say—"we did it ourselves."

After reviewing the above scenario, we can also imagine one where attempts to do development and service-learning are clearly in conflict. Students would be serving in ways that disempower, do not build local capacity, and are neither equitable nor sustainable, and, as a result, both their service and learning would be deficient. In practice this would mean that the students and their leaders would be the ones defining the agenda, making the decisions, controlling the processes, and learning new skills. The students would be predominantly the teachers, using and building their knowledge, skills, and ideas. Their resources would overwhelm local ones; benefits would not be distributed equitably; and the processes they set in motion would not be economically, humanly, or environmentally sustainable with local resources. The students would focus on serving the poor with their own knowledge, skills, and ideas rather than learning from them. In this scenario, the poor are primarily the learners and the served. After this type of service, the poor would feel less powerful and not in control of their future. Their knowledge, skills, resources, and ideas would have been marginalized by the students and leaders who were neither culturally nor developmentally aware of the impact of their actions and decisions. After they left, the community would state—"they did it for us."

Regrettably, in my experience, many service-learning experiences that seek to help the poor fall closer to the second description than to the first. I agree with Harkavy who asserts that

> the service learning movement has not "rightly placed" the goal. It has largely been concerned with advancing the civic consciousness and moral

character of college students, arguing that service learning pedagogy results in improved teaching and learning. Although service to the community is obviously an important component of service learning, *it does not focus on solving core community problems* (italics mine). (Harkavy, 1996)

I join Harkavy in calling for service-learning that, while not ignoring the needs of students and professors, instead focuses on creating an empowering and healthy development process for those it is seeking to serve. The following are two contrasting case studies that will exemplify two different types of international service-learning.

Case Studies

In October of 1998, Hurricane Mitch spent six days destroying much of Honduras. The hurricane was followed by a flood, not of water, but of very well-intentioned groups who came to Honduras to help. Many of these groups were college students and their professors coming down during their breaks or after classes were finished for service-learning.[4] Honduras has long been a top destination for international service-learning, the hurricane just increased the flow. Honduras is attractive to groups both because of its poverty and its accessibility. Over the last fifteen years in Central America, I have seen hundreds of service-learning groups come and go. I will present below two case studies to examine some of the issues involved.

"We Came to Serve"

After the hurricane, an engineering professor from a Christian university asked one of his classes to design a house for hurricane victims in Honduras. At the end of the semester, those who were able would fly down to Honduras and build their house for a family.[5] A simple $4,000 house was designed, and a group of

---

[4] While many of these trips are not called service-learning experiences, they fit most common definitions of service-learning, in that participants attempt to provide some service to the community in which they work and at the same time attempt to learn something about the country, culture, and society in which they are serving.
[5] These two case-studies are compilations of the experiences of various groups, however, all of the experiences cited did actually happen. I have attempted to be as even-handed in

twenty students had some orientation meetings to discuss what to bring, what the country was like, learn a little Spanish, and so forth. The group also raised the $30,000 from family and friends to cover their expenses and the cost of the house they would build. The professor contacted a friend who was a missionary in Honduras and who agreed to select an appropriate area and family to receive the house. In their two-week stay in the south of Honduras, the group almost finished the house, working with the assistance of three Hondurans who had lost their jobs because of the hurricane. A local church was paying them $3 a day to rebuild and repair houses. When the group returned home, they told us that they were overwhelmed by the immensity of the destruction, impressed by the hard-working Hondurans, and a little frustrated by how little they had accomplished. They all agreed with the woman who said, "I have so many questions. I wished we would have seen and learned a little more about the rest of Honduras."

When I later visited the family who had received the house, they were extremely grateful to the group for such a wonderful gift. The house was well-built and larger than that of most of their neighbors. Their only complaint was that they would have rather had fewer but bigger bedrooms since the children usually all slept together. However, while I was talking to their pastor, he said that two of the family's neighbors were not speaking with them because they felt they had been more deserving of the house. Some in the community were also upset because the group had mostly stuck to themselves, had brought down all their own food, and usually would not take the food or drinks they offered them. In addition, the students seeming amusement at the Hondurans' more simple building techniques had offended two of their Honduran coworkers. I tried to smooth the waters by explaining that the group had only had enough money to build one house and that they had probably stuck to themselves because they did not speak much Spanish. I also explained that they probably did not accept the food because they were afraid of getting sick and assured them that the group was not mocking their techniques but probably laughing in amazement at how much they could do without power tools.

---

these compilations as possible. I know of many groups who served in ways that were even more destructive to a true development process than the one I relate here.

"We Came to Learn"

A second group of twenty college students from a Christian college planned to go to Honduras for a three-week class to try to better understand why Honduras was poor and what responsibility they held as Christians and global citizens in the face of that poverty. After they arrived, several of them shared that they felt embarrassed when people in the United States, who assumed they were coming to help, looked at them disapprovingly when they found out they were coming "*just* to learn." While in Honduras, the group did spend a day alongside a group of Hondurans, digging out a house in the south of Honduras—and their aching muscles convinced them of the enormity of the task. They also lived with Honduran families—learning firsthand about daily life, the culture, and the struggle to seek true development. These students were also able to learn about Honduran history and culture and about development theories that seek to explain Honduran poverty and possible solutions. They met Honduran leaders, including the president of the Honduran Congress and leading activists for the poor, and could ask for their perspectives on the hurricane and how to best help Honduras. Finally, they were able to visit almost a dozen communities that were devastated by the hurricane, and they were able to see and hear what the *community members* were doing, sometimes with the help of development organizations. At the end of their time, they were encouraged to continue learning and sharing with others what they had learned about Honduras, poverty, and development and to begin to act and support the development work of at least one of the organizations they visited.

After one of the one-day visits to a rural development project, the coordinator said he felt very blessed by their visit. He said it was the first time that a group had come to humbly listen to the people, visit their farms and houses, and see how their lives were changing, without some other agenda. He said he felt very encouraged by the fact that they cared enough to be willing to come "just to learn" from the people.

While these students also lamented that they had only been able to stay for three weeks, they seemed less frustrated with how they had used their time and what they had accomplished. One of the students wrote in her final evaluation, "I learned that in order to really help the poor we need to learn more—to understand the causes of the problems before we try to solve them. I also saw that there is hope—that God works through us and we can support and help organizations that are changing the lives of the poor. I'm excited to go home and learn and do more."

Issues to Consider

The definitions and characteristics of true development and true service-learning as well as the case studies demonstrate that it is possible although perhaps not uncomplicated to combine development and service-learning goals. I believe there are three issues that need to be addressed in all future attempts to do so: evaluating the impact on the poor, evaluating what students are learning, and finally concentrating on learning before serving.

Evaluating the Impact on the Poor

The first, and perhaps the most important issue is whether a specific service-learning opportunity is truly developing and empowering those it is serving. This is the most important question because the service-learning experience is intruding into poor people's lives. Before considering the quality of the learning for students, we need to be relatively certain that our intervention will leave people better off, in developmental terms, than before. Universities have very clear standards for approving psychological experiments or for allowing social-work or psychology students to be involved in counseling settings. They need to be certain that the students are properly prepared, supervised, and evaluated to determine if the intervention will benefit or at least not harm the subjects. Universities can be held liable if they do not follow these standards. However, students and professors travel all over the world, with little or no preparation or supervision and intrude into poor people's lives with neither the knowledge nor the time to evaluate whether or not their intervention was beneficial or harmful.

Professors often evade responsibility by arguing that they are relying on development organizations, missionaries, or other knowledgeable locals to design an appropriate and effective experience. First, such an argument would not protect a university from liability in another setting. The university and its professors are ultimately responsible for the programs that they approve for their students. Second, it is clearly unwise to assume that local leaders, many of whom are equally ignorant about development principles and often depend on the donations of groups such as these to continue working, have the knowledge and ability to design appropriate and effective experiences. In Honduras we know of many organizations and individuals who host service-learning groups but will readily admit that it is not good development though it is a good way to raise money.

I argue that service-learning experiences that are going to affect the lives of the poor need much stronger reviews and evaluations than are currently present. The best situation would be that each service-learning experience that is going to directly affect the poor should be reviewed, supervised, and evaluated by a panel of professionals in much the same way that psychology experiments or standards for students doing counseling are prepared and reviewed. Short of that, we need to begin to set up voluntary reviews by groups of knowledgeable peers, as well as guidelines and standards that professors can use in developing service-learning experiences. In such an effort, questions rising from Bryant and White's four characteristics would be useful:

1. Empowerment: Are we relatively certain that those we serve will be empowered by this intervention? Are they the ones making the decisions, controlling the process? Are the economic and human resources from the outside being given in a manner that contributes to rather than overwhelms a local process? Are we building on the strengths of the local community?

2. Capacity building: Are we relatively certain that those we serve will improve their capacity as a result of this intervention? Will they be learning new skills and gaining new energy and motivations? Finally, will their existing skills, ideas, and motivation be respected and encouraged?

3. Equity: Will the benefits of this intervention be distributed equitably or at least be focused on the most needy in the population? Can we design the intervention in a way so that the community benefits rather than individuals, and if not, can we make sure that the beneficiaries are chosen in a way that prioritizes the most needy?

4. Sustainability: Will this project be sustainable given the human, environmental and economic resources available locally?

Finally, these questions should not only be considered while planning a service-learning component, but they should be monitored and evaluated during and after the intervention. This is normal operating procedure for most university programs, accreditation processes, and professional programs that deal with needy populations. However, service-learning opportunities tend to be evaluated by students and professors and possibly by the host organization regarding the extent to which these two or three groups were "content" and "pleased" with the experience and the resulting learning but not by its end results on those being "served." Harkavy, who levels similar criticisms on service-learning that does not resolve community problems, when citing two model classes at Penn University, mentions only the positive effects of the service-learning program on student, professors, and the school principals but has no figures on the effects on teenage pregnancy, which the program is supposed to be addressing (Harkavy 1996). I argue that service-learning programs, which seek to help the poor, should be planned and approved based on development principles. Then they need to be monitored and evaluated based on their effects on the needy. If they are not accomplishing their goals *for the needy*, they should be changed or eliminated.

Evaluating the Impact on Student Learning

The second issue to consider is whether or not the service-learner is truly learning how to better understand the world, its problems, and how to best address them. The most common message that seems to be transmitted in service-learning efforts is that a poor person has a need, and the student can and should fix it. A poor person in Honduras needs a house; the Illinois students can build one. A Chicago family's house needs paint; Michigan students can paint it. The service-learner in this scenario is learning that they are the ones with the resources, abilities, motivation, and ideas to solve "the problem of the poor." Asking students who are participating in these experiences why they are involved gives good insight into their perspective. Often, the first statement they make is usually about what they *did*. "We all went to Honduras to build a house, to help out after the hurricane," or, "We painted a house for an inner-city family." If you ask specifically what they learned, they might tell you, but it is not how they primarily explain and construct their experience. It is first of all about *doing* something for the poor—learning is often a distant second.

An overemphasis on doing also means that service-learners may often consciously or unconsciously pass up opportunities to learn more about their context and those they are serving. In Honduras, we regularly hear of groups who were too busy to take a break when Hondurans arrived offering coffee and cookies at work sites. As a result, they do not listen to Hondurans—to their joys, needs, accomplishments, and daily struggles. Other groups have turned down opportunities to visit historical sites such as Copan or complain of wasting their time in orientation or talks about Honduras' history. The groups' focus on finishing their project is especially disconcerting when we analyze the costs. The $4,000 house could have been built by much-in-need-of-work Hondurans for an extra $500. The $25,000 the group raised to come down and do the work could have built five more houses. The economics demonstrate that this is not a very cost-effective way to build a house, yet these groups clearly justify their reason for coming as doing not learning.

This does not mean that they do not learn. Unfortunately they often explain their observations in ways that develop or reinforce ideas about their own abilities and motivation and the perceived lack of such in the poor. A student member of a medical brigade recently commented that it was obvious to him why Hondurans were poor—the fact that even those who were not sick "just all stood around all day watching the doctors work" showed him that they either had nothing to do or did not like doing it. It did not seem to occur to this student why a visit by five North American doctors with all their equipment and medicines would be the equivalent of the circus coming to town for very remote villagers. Other groups have explained Honduran poverty by pointing to the number of apparently able-bodied but unoccupied poor males on the streets during work hours or the number of children poor families are raising or the government's lack of social services. Similar stories are common in the United States. A student recently told of repairing a poor family's porch in the United States while the two teenage sons sat inside and watched TV. Despite the fact that the service-learners are usually focused on doing, they do not stop processing their experiences in ways that often only reinforce negative stereotypes about the poor.

Learning that breaks out of stereotypes and opens students' eyes will usually take preparation, guidance, and reflection, which can be missing from certain service experiences. Having students trying to do or fix things without understanding what are the true problems, its symptoms, and real solutions is irresponsible at best. One of my students had spent six weeks in Haiti refurbishing an orphanage but learned nothing during her stay about Haitian history or even what type of government was in power in Haiti. She came away with superficial and stereotypical explanations for Haiti's poverty. This sort of service would clearly be unacceptable in other fields. Calvin College is rightfully proud of a service-learning project in which biology students sample pond water to discover any pollutants. However, if high levels of nitrates are found, the professor is unlikely to propose adding large amounts of phosphates to neutralize the nitrates. She knows that such a solution would be short-lived at best and likely cause other complications. Rather, the students and professor need to find the sources of the pollution and together plan interventions that will help the pond in the short term while resolving the underlying problem. The poor being served deserve the same kind of consideration. Students and professors need to spend much more time with the poor to understand their problems and then together look for solutions that seek to resolve the short-term needs as well as the longer-term problems. Obviously this will require a much larger focus on learning than doing—on understanding development, culture, language, history and local resources, needs, accomplishments, and ideas. This is not something that students or professors should take lightly—we should only intervene with a great deal of respect, fear, and desire to tread carefully and properly.

Learning before Serving

I also argue that service-learners who want to help the poor need to *learn* much more before they *serve*. In addition, even once they are serving the focus should always be very clearly on learning from those they are helping. A predominant focus on learning will undercut any attempt by students to justify their efforts as helping and as a result will not create a savior-complex. Being clear from the beginning that the focus is on learning will also change students' attitudes toward non-doing activities such as having coffee with a poor neighbor woman, visiting historical sites, or having a lecture on the United States role in Honduran poverty. Finally, a learning focus led by knowledgeable and experienced staff will allow students to prepare for, experience and reflect on their encounters in a way that will question their stereotypes, allow them to form new understandings of the problems facing the poor, and begin to develop new alternatives for addressing them.

Focusing on learning does not mean sitting at a desk in front of a blackboard. According to Dewey (1938), *genuine* learning only occurs when human beings focus their attention, energies, and abilities on solving *genuine* dilemmas and perplexities. Before trying to fix poverty in Honduras, students need to meet the poor; listen and talk with them; observe how they plant their corn, build their houses, taste their food, play with their children; and maybe dry the tears of a mother whose child died of malnutrition. Students need to experience poverty, spend time in the Third World, and in the inner city. It is only after such learning that students will understand the *genuine* (rather than their imagined) dilemmas of poverty and be able to begin addressing them.

Conclusions

In conclusion, I want to clarify what I am not saying. First, I am not arguing that students should not try to help the poor. I think that most North Americans (who are nearly all extremely wealthy in global terms) do far too little to address one of the greatest problems that face us in this new century—poverty and inequality. Second, I am not arguing that students (and professors) should not visit Third World countries or other poverty-stricken areas. People need to be exposed to how half of the earth's population, three billion people, lives on less than $2 a day. Third, I do not believe that the problems with the typical service-learning experiences in Honduras are unique. Very similar problems occur in projects in other countries, including North America. Finally, I am certainly not arguing that students should stay in a classroom setting until they have all the knowledge to fix the world's problems.

I am arguing that we need to learn from and about the poor before trying to fix things. Listening to the poor, observing, respecting, and dialoguing about their lives before trying to do something sends the right message. It affirms their value, their God-given dignity and their knowledge. I am also arguing that we can learn a great deal without serving—at least in the traditional sense. Simply listening, observing, and encouraging may often be the best way to both learn and serve others. We, both academics and professional development workers, are responsible to provide students the best learning opportunities possible. It is condescending both to the poor and to students to assume that we fix things without understanding the problems first. By failing to do so, we do a disservice to the poor, the students, and ourselves. By focusing on learning and experiencing life in the Third World, we honor the dignity and complexity of the learning process.

Finally, I am also arguing that once students and their professors are properly prepared and are convinced that serving is appropriate, we need to do so cautiously, asking hard questions and holding ourselves to the highest standards possible. We need to plan interventions, which build on the experience and knowledge of generations of people who have gone before and even then monitor and evaluate our interventions to make sure they are benefiting the poor. Voluntary or even mandatory peer reviews as well as standards and guidelines for such experiences may be helpful or even necessary. Service-learning projects that are planned, implemented, and evaluated by well-prepared groups are much more likely to be empowering-building capacities, both sustainable and equitable. As a result they will be truly good service and learning.

References

Bryant, Coralie, and Louise G.White. 1982. *Managing development in the third world*. Boulder, Col.: Westview Press.

Dewey, John. 1938. *Experience and education*. New York: Macmillan.

Harkavy, Ira. 1996. Service Learning as a vehicle for revitalization of education institutions and urban communities. Paper delivered at the American Psychological Association Annual Meeting. Toronto, Ontario.

Kendall, Jane. 1990. *Combining service and learning*. Raleigh, N.C.: National Society for Experiential Learning.

Sigmon, Robert. 2000. Linking service with learning in liberal arts education. Washington, D.C.: Council of Independent Colleges.

United Nations. 1991. The realization of the right to development. New York: United Nations.

Ver Beek, Kurt. 2000. Spirituality: The development taboo. *Development in Practice* 10:31-43.

PART II

DEVELOPING STUDENTS

Chapter 6

KANTIAN MORAL EDUCATION AND SERVICE-LEARNING

John E. Hare

Introduction

THIS CHAPTER ARISES out of some reflections about an intermediate-level ethics course that I have taught for ten years at Calvin and before that for fifteen years at a secular university. Next, I describe my experience of teaching two sections of the course in one semester with a service-learning component in one section but not in the other. Finally, I analyze what I learned about moral education from this experiment. The discussion is philosophical rather than social-scientific. Although I will mention some numbers from course evaluations, I do not have the competence to produce a quantitative comparison of the two sections, for example, through a multiple-regression analysis. I am planning to attempt this with some expert assistance next time I teach the course. In the present chapter, I am interested in the theoretical understanding of moral education that would justify the inclusion of a service-learning component. My observation is that the literature in service-learning has usually drawn this understanding from Dewey. For example, Thomas Ehrlich (1996) says, "The basic theory of service-learning is Dewey's: the interaction of knowledge and skills with experience is key to learning." Dwight Giles (1991) says, "At least since Dewey, the literature on experiential learning has claimed the superiority of action-reflection and the connected pedagogical approaches that characterize service, over more traditional modes of classroom instruction." McPherson and Negben (1991) describe the effect of community service on teaching in self-consciously Deweyan terms,

[Such an approach] involves and immerses students in relational learning environments and engages multiple senses and intelligences. Learning becomes more accessible by expanding the definition of competence and redefining the relationship of teacher to student and student to learning. The teacher, rather than simply being the provider of information and the evaluator of competence, is the creator of environments where the students learn by doing, working with others, and reflecting on their experiences (See also Harkavy and Benson 1998; Saltmarsh 1996; and Hatcher 1997).

I do not want to deny that service-learning can be justified in such ways, and, in fact, I often talk about my own course in these terms. There is, however, an older theme in the Western tradition of reflection about moral education that Dewey did not recapitulate (see Frankena 1965, especially 192-200). It can be found in Kant, and it came to Kant through Luther, Scotus, Anselm, and Augustine. This is not the place to recount this history in detail, but the theme is explicit in the most vivid discussion of moral education that we have from the ancient world, namely Plato's *Meno*. This dialogue starts with the question of whether virtue is acquired by teaching or by practice. At the end, Socrates is left with the answer that virtue comes by neither of these but by divine gift (*Meno* 99d to the end). Twentieth-century interpreters have been altogether unsympathetic to this answer and have supposed that Socrates is being ironic or hiding what he really thinks. This is an interpretive maneuver that twentieth-century interpreters have also used in order to lessen the significance of Kant's references to God's role in human morality, and I have elsewhere argued that the maneuver should be used only as a last resort where there is not a more straightforward reading available (Hare 1996, chapter 2). I will call the theme of divine gift "the vertical theme," in order to distinguish it from Dewey's emphasis, for example, in the humanist manifesto of which he was an original signatory (1933), that "man is at last becoming aware that he alone is responsible for the realization of the world of his dreams, that he has within himself the power for its achievement." Although Dewey is close to Kant in many ways, his views on religion are consistently horizontal; human moral problems have exclusively human solutions. What I want to do in this chapter is to discuss some differences that it makes to a service-learning component in an ethics course whether the vertical theme is admitted or not.

Especially at a Christian liberal arts institution we need an understanding of the merits of service-learning that is receptive to God's role in human morality. Dewey's view is inappropriate not only because he denies (amongst all the other dualisms) the dualism between Creator and creature but also because the modern scientific worldview has not in fact produced the fruits in this century that Dewey projected. He, himself, came to see by the end of his long life that his earlier optimism about education could not be sustained. We need to be as critical about Dewey as Dewey was about Kant. We should retrieve from our own tradition and outside it whatever we can use, and aim at an understanding that is distinctively Christian and that fits our present circumstances.

What concerns me is that the school's role in moral education and, derivatively, the contribution of service-learning is being oversold because the vertical theme has been forgotten. I am not denying the significant contribution of school in general and service-learning in particular to moral growth in students. My main point in this chapter is to affirm this contribution. But it is dangerous to make this contribution carry too much weight. Too much expectation leads, as Plato says in the *Phaedo* (88-91) to disillusion. I was part of a moral education team at a teaching hospital in Philadelphia for several years, which oversold its potential to produce morally good doctors. I noticed a medical ethics backlash, which was partly caused by the observation on the part of the medical faculty that students were learning fancy argument techniques to rationalize their preferences but were not learning to be good. There is wisdom in the Kantian picture that the ethics teacher can produce an occasion for the acquisition of virtue but cannot produce virtue itself.

Kant's Theory of Moral Education

I will focus in this section of the chapter on Kant's account of moral education, though it would be interesting in a longer treatment to trace the vertical theme backward in its connection with traditional thought about the acquisition of virtue. There are two features of Kant's account that I want to emphasize. First, Kant denies that we can, and therefore denies that we should, make other people morally better. Second, he denies that we can, in any fundamental way, make even ourselves morally better.

The first point is expressed most clearly in Kant's *The Doctrine of Virtue*. He says that we have two fundamental kinds of duties. The first is the duty toward our own perfection (especially our moral betterment), and the second is our duty towards the happiness of others (*Metaphysics of Morals*, 6:386. In referring to Kant, I will use the volume and page numbers of the Academy edition). He is denying here that we have duties toward our own happiness and toward the perfection of others. The reason for this first denial is that he thinks we already have a sufficient inclination toward our own happiness, and duty only comes in to control inclination. Why, however, does Kant deny that we have duties toward the perfection of others? The reason is that the responsibility for being a good person belongs to that person and not to anyone else. (I discuss the difficulty about whether God has such responsibility toward the perfection of others in Hare 1999, 251-62.) What constitutes a good person, for Kant, is the good will in that person. No human being can produce a good will in another human being, and therefore no human being has a duty to do so; but what implication does this have for moral education? Does it mean that a person's moral education is her own business and nobody else should interfere in it?

This is clearly *not* Kant's view. He writes a whole book on education, of which the crowning section is a treatment of how parents and teachers can and should morally educate the children in their charge. The techniques and methods he prescribes are all ways of producing an *occasion* for the fundamental choice that an individual has to make for herself. Moral goodness is not something he thinks we can graft into a person. Kant also thinks that there are precursors for the choice either for or against the moral law. For example, there is the presence or absence of what he calls "discipline," and the provision of discipline is something that *is* within the control of a child's parents and teachers. More importantly for present purposes, even after a person has reached the age of reason, there are encouragements and discouragements we can provide to each other. In particular, Kant emphasizes the *example* we provide to each other. Even though he sees the danger of examples if they substitute for reflection, he thinks that the most effective way to influence others toward morality is by living a moral life oneself. I will return to the question of what this means for teaching an ethics course to undergraduates.

A person is responsible for her own moral perfection, and other people can only provide an occasion for such a choice. This brings us slap against the second feature of Kant's view, which I mentioned. He says that we cannot produce a good will in ourselves either. This is most clearly seen in his *Religion within the Limits of Reason Alone*. The problem, as he sees it, is that we are born with an innate but imputable propensity to evil (*Religion,* 6:31-2). Here he follows Luther, and before him Augustine, in a strong doctrine of the Fall. My complaint is that contemporary Kantians who write about moral education, like Kohlberg, do not repeat this part of Kant's picture, and Kant's picture is not coherent without it. Kant translates this doctrine into strictly moral terms, but he does not cease to believe it in its untranslated form (see Hare 1996, chapter 2). There is a problem here that I will not discuss, namely what is the relationship between moral goodness and salvation. For the purposes of this chapter, I will assume that Kant is right that at the deepest levels of the will we cannot be good without God. He construes the Fall as preventing the development of moral goodness, and this means that we are born with the tendency to put our own happiness above our duty. There is nothing wrong, in Kant's view, with desiring our own happiness; we will do so, he thinks, even in heaven. What is wrong, however, is the ranking, which makes doing our duty merely a means to our happiness. There is a fundamental choice of rankings. What Kant calls "the good maxim" puts duty first and happiness second. What he calls "the evil maxim" reverses this priority. Kant thinks we are born under the evil maxim, and this means that we cannot in our own power restore the predisposition to good with which humans were created. The root orientation of our wills is against this. The only answer to this difficulty, he thinks, is to suppose that there is divine assistance available that can accomplish in us a revolution of the will.

Whether we are Kantians or not, there is something deeply mysterious about the process by which people become morally good. Theologically, the mystery is expressed in terms of how we become pleasing to God and the relationship of this to divine sovereignty and human freedom. God's assistance to us is certainly mysterious, and so is the free human choice of the fundamental orientation of the will. It is mysterious, moreover, what the relationship is between these two. For example, we would like an explanation of how the revolution of the will is related to our experience within time of moral struggle. Even if the revolution of the will has taken place, there are still the traces of the dominion of the evil maxim that are ours by habit, and these traces we still have to fight. In Kant's terms, the "dear self" can be found lurking behind even the most apparently virtuous actions. It is not my purpose in this chapter to make any of this easier to understand. My project is to explore the connection between this complex doctrine and the benefits of service-learning.

Before we go further, however, I need to say something about the distinction Kant makes between physical and practical education. Neither of these terms means just what we now mean by them. The best way to understand them is to connect them with another of Kant's distinctions, that between nature and freedom. He says (*Education*, 9:469), "We may, therefore, call the cultivation of the mind physical, in a certain sense, just as well as the cultivation of the body. This physical cultivation of the mind, however, must be distinguished from moral training, in that it aims only at nature, while moral training aims at freedom." The dichotomy between nature and freedom is one of the many dualisms that Dewey wants to get beyond. He accomplishes this by recapitulating many of the points Kant makes on the "nature" side of the distinction but remains silent about some of the key points (especially the vertical theme) that Kant stresses on the "freedom" side.

Kant puts nurture, discipline, cultivation of skill, and education in prudence under physical education. Many of the details of Kant's discussion here will strike the contemporary reader as harsh and male-centered. *Nurture* he associates with infancy. It involves mother's milk but also cold baths, cool and hard beds, and the ignoring of our babies' cries if they want what is not good for them. *Discipline* is also part of physical education. Kant associates it with childhood, and says that it consists in the restraint of inclinations and unruliness (*Education*, 9:442). "If a man is allowed to follow his own will in his youth, without opposition, a certain lawlessness will cling to him throughout his life." On the other hand, Kant says, the goal is not to break but to bend the will. A broken will produces "slavishness," whereas the destination is a manly autonomy. To this end, Kant says that a child's wishes should be granted whenever they are good for him. Opposition to a child's wishes for its own sake is always wrong. *The cultivation of skill* is produced by exercise and instruction. Mostly, for the preschool child, this will involve play and games (and Kant tells us which games are good, e.g., spinning a top and blind man's bluff). School, however, involves work. He says (*Education*, 9:482), "One often hears it said that we should put everything before children in such a way that they do it from inclination. In some cases . . . this is all very well, but there is much besides which we must place before them as duty." Here it is not moral duty that he has in mind but a precursor (where the authority is external). There will be much that is mechanical in this part of schooling, as Kant conceives of it, involving drill and memorization. Again, however, memorization for its own sake is never the point, just as the restraint of inclination for its own sake is not the point. What is memorized must be itself useful, just as the inclination that is restrained must be itself harmful. And Kant (*Education,* 9:477) is a forerunner of Dewey when it comes to learning by doing—"The best way to understand is to do." Finally, *education in prudence* is designed to guide the child into a knowledge of what is in her own long-term interest and how to secure it for herself. This involves learning, for example, that if she wants to be happy, she must make friends. Kant thinks the child will learn at school how to live happily and acceptably in society.

All this is physical education. Practical education is, as I said, on the side of freedom, and Kant divides it into "ethical didactic" and "ethical ascetic." Here there is much that reminds one of Dewey on the first side of this distinction, which is closest to what Kant calls "nature" as opposed to "freedom." Ethical didactic is itself divided into lecturing and questioning, and questioning is divided into catechism and dialogue (*Metaphysics of Morals,* 6:478). In a *catechism* it is only the teacher who asks questions and the student has to remember the answer, whereas in a *dialogue* both teacher and student ask questions of each other and the students have to use their reason. The best of these ways of teaching is dialogue, which Kant associates with Socrates, but he thinks it can only come after catechism, and he gives an example of what a moral catechism is like. Kant introduces it as follows, "The teacher elicits from his pupil's reason, by questioning, what he wants to teach him; and should the pupil not know how to answer the question, the teacher, guiding his reason, suggests the answer to him."[1]

I want to draw a Deweyan lesson from what Kant says about ethical didactic before going on to ethical ascetic. I have found it confirmed in my teaching of the service-learning component in the ethics course. Kant recognizes that both straight lecturing and catechism become less and less appropriate as

---

[1] The catechism begins this way, "1. Teacher: What is your greatest, in fact your whole, desire in life? Pupil: (is silent) Teacher: That everything should always go the way you would like it to. 2. Teacher: What is such a condition called? Pupil: (is silent) Teacher: It is called happiness (continuous well-being, enjoyment of life, complete satisfaction with one's condition). 3. Teacher: Now if it were up to you to dispose of all happiness (possible in the world), would you keep it all for yourself or would you share it with your fellow-men? Pupil: I would share it with others and make them happy and satisfied too. 4. Teacher: Now that proves that you have a good enough heart; but let us see whether you have a good head to go along with it. Would you really give a lazy fellow soft cushions so that he could pass his life away in sweet idleness? . . . . "

the child matures. The preference for dialogue over catechism shows that he thinks the teacher should be open to questioning as the student gets older. Kant makes explicit appeal to the model of Socrates. This connects with the theme that we learn best by doing. A person who entered into discussion with Socrates was likely to have his *life* up for scrutiny. Thus Nicias says, in Plato's *Laches* (187e), "Anyone who is close to Socrates and enters into conversation with him is liable to be drawn into an argument, and whatever subject he may start, he will be continually carried round and round by him, until at last he finds that he has to give an account both of his present and past life, and when he is once entangled, Socrates will not let him go until he has completely and thoroughly sifted him." The undergraduates should be questioning and answering together with the teacher their own ethical lives. This is much more natural if the students and the teacher are both engaged in a context outside the classroom where ethical issues arise. The students will learn to think ethically by doing reflection together with their teacher about their current and past ethical experience.

Finally, we come to what Kant calls "ethical ascetic." He does not have in mind here the "monkish disciplines" of "pilgrimages, mortifications, and fastings" (*Education,* 9:488). He recognizes that a large part of moral education is learning to "combat natural impulses sufficiently to be able to master them when a situation comes up in which they threaten morality" (*Metaphysics of Morals,* 6:485). This takes us back to the "dear self," and the problem of sin. I think Kant makes two important contributions to the theory of moral education here, neither of which Dewey recapitulates. Both are significant in how we see the contribution of service-learning to the teaching of ethics. The first is a positive point about what belongs in a service-learning component, and the second is a negative point about what should not be claimed for it.

First, moral education belongs together with the vertical theme of divine gift. Kant's view here is balanced. He is concerned to avoid the danger of making morality merely instrumental—a way to please God so as to get into heaven or avoid hell. The theology should not, therefore, precede the moral training. Kant thinks we all have a "seed of goodness" in us at birth, as well as the propensity to evil, and the seed can develop into virtue *given the right assistance.* It is not as though the theology has, so to speak, to come first so as to plant the seed, for the seed will be there already. The problem is that the required assistance is not merely from parents or teachers but from God. "The child must learn to feel reverence toward God, as the Lord of life and of the whole world; further, as one who cares for men, and lastly as their Judge. . . . [The child should be given] an explanation which unites the ideas of *God* and *duty*" (*Education*, 9:495-6, emphasis original). It is not that we should just wait around and pray that God will provide the required help. On the other hand, however, the Christian tradition is, Kant says, the vehicle by which the moral demand has been articulated to him and his contemporaries in Europe, and those of us in this situation need to make use of this vehicle to understand what the demand is and what assistance is available to meet it. This is why Kant thinks the state has a moral interest in maintaining biblical preaching. "The Christian religion makes people humble, not by preaching humility, but by teaching them to compare themselves with the highest pattern of perfection," which is Christ (*Education*, 9:491. See *Religion*, 9:106, and *Conflict of the Faculties*, 7:43). The example of humility and pride is a significant one. Kant is right that the central thrust of the teaching of the New Testament about humility is that we should compare ourselves with Christ, but its key idea is that we should take on Christ's position of servant. Paul tells us, "Let this mind be in you, which was also in Christ Jesus, who . . . took upon him the form of a servant" (Phil. 2:5-8, *KJV*). The point I want to make is that this is a significant difference both from pagan teaching about virtue and from Dewey. Virtue is not an idea whose content is neutral among worldviews. This is an important point that needs to be emphasized to those promoting a virtue-based curriculum for moral education. Aristotle thinks that high station is something of which a person should be proud, and he uses the word *humble* (*tapeinos*, the same term used in the New Testament for the virtue) as a term for the vice of pretending you do not have merit when in fact you do have it. Dewey denies that there is something like original sin in all human beings (in Kant's terms, an innate but imputable propensity to evil) that should occasion our humility, and he does not mention humility among the key dispositions he wants to produce. Here is an example of the sense in which the religious tradition is a "vehicle" of the moral demand (see Hauerwas and Pinches 1997; Meilaender 1984).

The second point is that the obstacle to virtue, as Kant sees it, is so deep that it infects all our efforts to remove it. "Extirpation could occur only through good maxims, and cannot take place when the ultimate subjective ground of all maxims is postulated as corrupt" (*Religion*, 6:37). This means that we should not be looking for some technique of moral education to do the job for us. Dewey is strikingly optimistic about the power of the school, if properly reformed, to accomplish a better society. He talks of education as a "guarantee of a larger society which is worthy, lovely, and harmonious" (Dewey 1959, 41, 49). He says that the new education "has within itself the power of creating a free experimental intelligence that will do the necessary work of this complex and distracted world in which we and every other modern people have to live" (Dewey 1981, 111). We shall see that some proponents of service-learning have taken a Dewey-eyed view of its prospects. But Kant is less sanguine, recognizing that social institutions (without divine assistance) tend not to remove original sin but merely to express it on a larger scale (*Religion*, 6:97, *see also* 6:93-94). This is not to say that we should sit by and leave moral education up to God. As I said earlier, Kant gives us a whole book of suggestions on physical and practical education. He does not put his proposals forward as techniques sufficient (together with "custom") for the production of virtue. Because the obstacle lies so deep, moreover, we cannot tell by observation of other peoples' lives or even of our own whether it has been removed. We are never so easily deceived, Kant says, as in the good opinion we have of ourselves. This is true also of the bad opinion of ourselves we would have if we focused on our status as worms. Kant wants us to be realistic but also *cheerful* (*Metaphysics of Morals*, 6:491). The truth is, as he sees it, we simply do not know the fundamental motivations of our own lives or those of others. We can tell whether actions are in accordance with the moral law but not whether they are done *from* the moral law. We should be doubtful, therefore, about whether we can measure progress empirically, either in ourselves or in others, toward a good will. There are some proponents of service-learning who are less modest, and I will return to them at the end.

A Service-Learning Segment

In this section of the chapter, I will describe briefly the class that I taught. I had two sections of my ethics class in one semester, one with a required service-learning component and one that did not, but otherwise with identical material and format. This gave me the chance to evaluate what contribution the service-learning component made to the students' education. I will start with what the students said, then describe what we did. In the third section of the chapter I will discuss the connection of this service-learning component with what I have just been saying about Kant. I am not describing this segment of the course as a model for how such a thing should go. On the contrary, I think it was in some ways naïve, and I can think of various improvements, but the discussion of what I learned about service-learning requires this description first.

The class had four segments, of which the first two were historical (Aristotle and Kant), the third was applied (abortion and homosexuality), and the fourth was a segment on Christian ethics. In the third segment, we read a number of individual articles that I had collected from various sources. For one of the two classes, I required them to meet for ten hours over the semester, either tutoring at Park School (a school set up especially for teenagers who were pregnant or young mothers), or with the Christian homosexual support group called AWARE. It is the second of these two options that I want to describe in more detail in this chapter. It was more successful than the first, though that was also worth doing. The difficulty with the first assignment was that my students went once a week, and the turnover of Park School students was so rapid that my students rarely got to know any of them well enough.

The students' evaluation of the service-learning component was overwhelmingly positive. There were nine statements on the evaluation form, and the students had to say to what degree they affirmed each statement.[2] Most of them strongly affirmed that the service-learning component connected to the

---

[2] The statements were (1) that the service-learning connected to the course as a whole, (2) that the professor required reflection on it, (3) that the assignments were clear, (4) that the student was prepared by the class for the service-learning, (5) that there was good supervision, (6) that the service-learning was valuable to the organization being served, (7) that there was course-related learning, (8) that there were general skills promoted, and (9) that the transportation provided was sufficient. In the group who worked with AWARE, the results were:

	strongly affirmed	affirmed	neutral	denied	strongly denied
question 1	12	2	0	0	0
question 2	11	2	0	0	0
question 3	5	7	2	1	0
question 4	4	7	2	1	0
question 5	6	4	2	0	0
question 6	4	5	4	0	0
question 7	11	3	0	0	0
question 8	12	2	0	0	0
question 9	6	5	1	0	0

On the four questions that concern this chapter, in other words, (questions one, two, seven, and eight), over 90 percent of the students strongly affirmed the value of the service-learning component, and the remainder affirmed it. The Park School group had a significantly less favorable verdict on these questions.

course as a whole. They had no doubt that this part of the course required reflection and involved course-related learning, and they valued the general skills that it promoted.

There were a number of informal comments on the evaluations. Students said, "We had to directly deal with issues of ethics in a personal setting," "The interaction with issues in both theoretical and personal terms helped me learn more than if theoretical had been the only means of learning," "Learned ability to discuss difficult topics with people who are affected by the topics," "Made me think more about actuality, not all theoretical," "Do again, perhaps with similar readings by both sides," "I had a really wonderful experience. Whoever does the AWARE group must be open minded," "Gives a practical application to the theoretical," "Putting people before the issues puts everything in a new light."

We met once in two large groups (each group was half students and half members of AWARE) for two hours. At each of these meetings, each person was invited to talk briefly about his or her own experience with the issue of homosexuality. I was aware of the possibility that some of the students might be gay, but none of them (if they were) raised this in the large-group sessions. We then arranged ourselves into seven smaller groups, each with two students and two members of AWARE, and these groups met at their own convenience for three 2-hour sessions. I had handed out a sheet with questions, around which they could organize their discussions.[3] Finally, we met in the same two large groups toward the end of the semester and talked about what we had learned.

The whole class did a number of readings together on the topic. We read the 1973 synodical report from the Christian Reformed Church. We read a paper by James Olthuis (1995, 188-205), "When Is Sex Against Nature?" We also read a piece of mine that is not published but that discusses the argument that males and females are complementary to each other such that there is something

---

[3] The questions were: (1) Has the church been faithful in carrying out its ministry toward you? (2) How has your sexual orientation related to your personal faith? (3) Do you think that the Bible has any witness on the issues surrounding same-sex relations? (4) Are there any stereotypes about homosexuals that you want to challenge? (5) Have you encountered discrimination or persecution against homosexuals? (6) What is your opinion of the current state of the debate both inside and outside the church? What do you see as the likely state of this debate in ten years' time? (7) Are there any difficulties that same-sex couples are likely to experience more than opposite-sex couples, other than the difficulties produced by social attitudes? (8) What are your views about same-sex marriage? (9) How might the atmosphere at the college be improved for students who are homosexual?

missing in same-sex relationships other than the inability to procreate (Hare, 1995). My intention was to have a range of different views presented in the readings, and it would have been better to have had more class time and more readings in order to accomplish this.

I required two five-page papers from the section of the class that was not doing the service-learning component. For those doing the service-learning, I required an ungraded journal and a report at the end. The report was either a narrative history about a person's life, as it was affected by the issue of abortion or homosexuality, or a reflective paper on the issue, informed by experience with the service-learning component. On the final exam (which was the same for everybody in both sections) there were three kinds of questions. There were questions directly about the readings, questions that asked for a connection between the readings on homosexuality (and abortion) and the readings on ethical theory, and then questions that called for longer reflective answers. One of this last kind was, "If your younger sibling told you he/she was gay or lesbian, what advice would you give?"

Service-Learning and Kant

In this final section of the chapter, I want to relate the service-learning component of the course to the vertical theme in Kant's account of moral education. I will focus this discussion around the positive and negative points about "ethical ascetic," which I mentioned at the end of the introduction to distinguish Kant's account from Dewey's. The first of these points is that moral training belongs together with the vertical theme about divine gift. I want to describe the difference it made to the service-learning that both students and AWARE members were Christians, held themselves accountable to the same God, and tried to understand their experience in terms of the same sacred texts.

This commonality was, I think, basic to the success of the experiment. In the first meeting that we had, for example, I started with prayer and the leader of the AWARE group closed in prayer. This set the context for the respect that he and I and the whole group were able to maintain even though we had significant differences of view. The students did not on the whole change their conclusions about the issue. They had, by and large, conservative views before the experience, though there was a range and some were more liberal. After the experience there was the same range. I did not quantify this, but my impression is that one person had become slightly more hard-line and one person slightly more liberal. I do not want to place any reliance on this impression, however. Even though the students did not change their conclusions, they did change the considerations that they thought about and introduced into their writing. This is why one student said, as I quoted earlier, "Putting people before the issues puts everything in a new light." For example, only the students who had done the service-learning mentioned in the final exam that they would be worried about a sibling's committing suicide. I am convinced that this difference resulted from the topic of suicide having come up in the small-group discussions. I was part of one such small group, and it came up several times in ours. Here is another example. The students who had not had the service-learning tended to say that they would tell their sibling to go to the pastor of their church. Those who had met with AWARE tended to say that they would advise their sibling to find out if the pastor would be pastorally sensitive on this issue. Again, I am sure this was because of experiences that AWARE members had described. There was more information that the students acquired through the service-learning, for example, about AIDS and local politics. The key change, however, was in sensitivity. Having faces and stories to put to the issue changed the issue for them. It is not that the students changed their minds in the sense of coming down on a different side of the issue; I am tempted to say that they changed their hearts, though that would be misleading in various ways. They saw the struggle that the AWARE members had gone through and were still going through.

They also saw how they, themselves, had been guilty of a kind of contempt. We talked, for example, about the use of the term *gay* as an equivalent for *despicable*. There is a point here that Kant would put in terms of the fundamental principle of morals, which he calls "the categorical imperative." This requires sharing, as far as the moral law allows, the ends or purposes of the people affected by one's actions. Most of the students were not accustomed to the attempt to share ends with people they knew to be gay. What I wanted them to learn is that these were people like themselves—with Christian faith and with sin. Both groups had the desire to be faithful to God and struggled with sexual desires and with desires for acceptance. I wanted the students to see that the members of AWARE had the whole range of ends outside their sexual preference that the students themselves had. They had jobs and homes and political affiliations and churches. The students came to see both how deeply the sexual preference affected everything else *and* that this was only one part of life and should not be mistaken for the whole. One of the AWARE members, for example, was an African American, and he described how much more discrimination he had experienced because of his race than because of his sexual orientation. I think the students started to learn to see these gay people as people, rather than as one-dimensionally gay.

Kant makes the great contribution of seeing that moral education consists partly in coming to see and to control one's own tendencies to pride. The students who were heterosexual tended, I think, to regard themselves as superior to gays for just this reason. This is why gay has been such a convenient term of contempt. In the dominant culture, it has provided a safe way to express superiority. In the theological setting that the students and the AWARE members shared, it was possible to see this pride as a manifestation of the original preference for the self, which Kant calls "the evil maxim." The formal setting of the service-learning component was one of equality. Each small group had two students and two AWARE members, and they had an agenda that they had to agree on together. In fact, the AWARE members tended to be older than the students, and they knew the issue better. They were therefore more ready to talk, and there was a danger of their dominating the conversation. I want to stress here the painful side of what Kant calls "ethical ascetic." The superiority that the students probably felt initially was hard to sustain. Many of them were forced to see that their attitudes had been wrong, even if their views were right. For example, one student vowed to change his language patterns. One student said he would challenge his church to be more caring to gays. Kant gives an example of teaching a child his duties toward others (*Education,* 9:489. See Dewey, 1908, 349). "For instance, were a child to meet another poorer child and to push him rudely away, or to hit him, and so on, we must not say to the aggressor, 'Don't do that, you will hurt him; you should have pity, he is a poor child,' and so on. But we must treat him in the same haughty manner, because his conduct is against the rights of man." Here is moral education in the process of life. The child has to learn about the dignity of all human beings. If he acts in such a way as to demean that dignity, he needs to be shown what this means by our "treating him in the same haughty manner." Promoting pity is, Kant thinks, the opposite; it expresses not equal dignity but a form of contempt. Transferring this idea to the undergraduate context, there is the same kind of moral education in the process of life that should take place. The students come to an ethics course with certain unconsidered feelings of superiority. They may know in a theoretical way that they should not have such feelings, but they need to experience the feelings without disguise and see how intolerable they are through the responses of those they have despised. This kind of reflection is best done in the context of action where there are serious and engaging moral questions at issue.

One question raised in all the groups was whether sexual orientation is chosen. The students were told by the AWARE members that it is not; in Kant's terms, it is "from fortune." If this is right, then even if heterosexuality is granted to be a superior state (and this was controversial in the conversations), "we must seek to avoid every form of pride which is founded upon superiority of fortune" (*Education*, 9:491). It is, I know, disputed to what extent orientation is chosen, and there may be a difference here also between male and female homosexuality. My point here is not to engage in this discussion but to point out that the students came to see another problem about pride in the context of the issue we were discussing.

Kant recognizes that we have a natural tendency toward the vice of pride. It is like bindweed in a garden, which keeps cropping up however much we try to eradicate it. This tells us something about moral education. Undergraduates, just as much as younger students, need to be put in situations in which they first feel the wrong kind of pride and then see that it is wrong. As I quoted earlier, "Man is nowhere more easily deceived than in the good opinion he has of himself." One function of an ethics class, then, is to put students in a situation where their natural inclination is to do or say or think something that morality would prohibit. Then, in reflection and discussion, they can identify what is wrong with this. This is ethical ascetic.

A significant part of the discussion and reflection was focused on texts that both the students and the members of AWARE accepted as authoritative. This was illuminating, because the students had not often had to interpret the Bible in the face of disagreement that was so directly connected to life choices. It was a lesson in both how hard and how important it is to interpret well.

The vertical theme provided the context for the Deweyan justification I mentioned in the introduction of this chapter. The students saw me and the AWARE leader treat each other with respect and trust but not agreement. They saw how this was helped by our common faith. They saw me uncertain about some things and certain about others, and they saw me work hard to make ethical sense of the experience. They and I were in the experience together, and we had a shared sense of risk and excitement about it. I am not trying to make my role glamorous. I was in many ways awkward. I think Kant is right, however, that the most effective way to teach is to show. Most ethics courses, because they stay in the classroom, have limited scope for this kind of example. Kant also says that the most effective way to learn is to do. What the students had to do in the service-learning component of this course was to get to know and understand (within the constraints of ten hours in a relatively formal setting) the lives of two particular gay people. One thing that had concerned me is that we were not really doing any *service* in this service-learning. It seemed all for the benefit of the students and nothing for AWARE. I came to see that this was quite wrong. The members of AWARE were strongly desiring and needing to tell their stories to people in the wider Christian community. This is why they volunteered, and they were pleased with the result. They gladly did it again the following semester with one of my colleagues, and it was again a strongly favorable experience both for them and for the students. We will continue it. The members of AWARE appreciated that the students were taking them seriously as people. This meant that the students were learning to think ethically about life in a life context that was problematic for them. This was why one of the students said, in a comment I quoted earlier, "made me think about actuality, not all theoretical." Sometimes it is suggested that an ethics course leaves mere theory when it gets into application. This is partly right, but it is incomplete. Even before I included a service-learning component, my ethics course had always had components of applied ethics. We discussed abortion, or international relations, or capital punishment, though this is still theoretical in the sense that matters most. It is still books and words and classroom. I am not trying to make a dichotomy between the ivory tower and real life. This dichotomy is false. The classroom (when it is functioning well) brings in wide experience from outside, and life outside the classroom (when it is being lived well) brings in reflection of the kind done in class. So, though there is not a dichotomy, there is a tension. The students have been sitting in classrooms for fifteen years or so, and they almost inevitably go into the various modes of engagement or disengagement that they reserve for the classroom. For some this is boredom, for others the pursuit of academic success. In both cases, however, this is a kind of habitual screen. What the service-learning did was to get past this screen, at least briefly, because the students had to engage in a different kind of task; they had to interact socially with a group they had tended to dismiss. They found themselves doing ethical thinking on the other side of the screen.

I have been discussing the first (positive) point about ethical ascetic—that moral training belongs together with the vertical theme. I now want to go on to the second (negative) one. The obstacle to virtue, as Kant sees it, is so deep that it infects all our efforts to remove it, and we should not therefore be looking for some technique of moral education to do the job. Nor should we think that we can observe the fundamental moral orientation of the will, or measure progress toward it. The literature in moral education has many examples of a contrary view, which is more optimistic both about the moral changes we can produce and about our techniques for measuring them. William J. Penn (1990) gives a succinct statement of some typical assumptions:

> (1) There is a capability present within human consciousness which, when it is developed and exercised, significantly increases the probability of rational consensus on the just resolution of value conflicts. This is the capability Kohlberg and other cognitive developmentalists have identified as principled or post-conventional moral reasoning. (2) the capacity for principled moral reasoning, like the capacity for mathematical and scientific reasoning, can and must be developed by means of focussed, systematic and long-term educational effort. (3) It is necessary to develop this human capacity for moral reasoning to its highest level in order to have rational individual and social direction in modern democratic and pluralistic societies.

Penn then goes on to claim (contrary to Kohlberg) that this capacity for principled reasoning can be directly taught at the undergraduate level, and he claims that he has done so in the courses he has designed. I am not interested here in the details of the specific proposal but in the optimism of such an approach. The comparison with mathematical and scientific skills, together with the optimism that educational technique can produce these outcomes in the student, are both characteristic of Dewey's thought. T. K Stanton (1990) makes the application to service-learning: "The evolving pedagogy of service-learning is a key to *ensuring* the development of graduates who will participate in society actively, ethically, and with an informed critical habit of the mind" (emphasis added). Ronald Lee Zigler (1998) makes the comparison with physiological functions, "All virtues and vices are habits which incorporate objective forces. . .

They can be studied as objectively as physiological functions, and *they can be modified* by changes of either personal or social elements" (emphasis added).

Some writers on moral education write as though students were like plants to be cultivated into virtue or even chemicals to be combined with virtue. Thus Ernest Boyer (1987, 68) says, "it is appropriate for educational institutions that are preparing students to be citizens in a participatory democracy to understand the dilemmas and paradoxes of an individualistic culture and *cultivate* students who are personally empowered and committed to the common good" (emphasis added). Derek Bok (1986, 167) says, "What is more important is to discover ways to *combine* undergraduates with a sense of commitment and civic concern that will cause them to devote their talents in later life to addressing important social problems" (emphasis added). But undergraduates are neither plants nor chemicals. They are free agents, and the basic orientation of their wills is beyond their teachers' control. It is, for Christians, a matter between them and God.

Suppose, like Dewey, we identify the goal of education as training students in some kind of process of reflective inquiry. Dewey (1981, 8:177) gives us a three-stage process. First, "the various parts of information acquired are grasped in their relation to one another." Then, the relation is discerned between what we do and its consequences. Finally, "we put ourselves in the place of another, to see [these consequences] from the standpoint of his aims and values" (*See* Saltmarsh 1996, 18). My point is that it is possible for an agent to go through all of this and still deliberately harm his victim. A dysfunctional married couple know precisely how to torment each other; each imagines vividly and in detail, from the other's point of view, the pain that he or she will cause, which does not prevent the torturing but urges it onward. What is necessary from a Kantian point of view is not just this kind of three-stage reflection, but the *will* to make the other person's ends my own. The question of how to acquire this will is just what remains mysterious.

In this context, I want to mention two social-scientific studies of the effectiveness of service-learning in moral education at the undergraduate level. The first is a report of a study at Vanderbilt (Giles and Eyler 1994). The second is a report of a study at the University of Rhode Island (Boss 1994). Giles and Eyler measure students' responses to certain questions before and after a one-credit "community service laboratory." It is important that they record no significant change in responses to the question whether we should help those in need or whether it is important to volunteer time in such service (though they do report a small, but significant, increase in the view that we should aspire to be community leaders and that it is important to influence the political system). They report that there was a significant increase in the intention to do more community service. There was, however, no control group (to check whether it was the community-service component that produced this effect) and no follow-up study on whether the intention was carried out (though they project such a study). They report a significant increase in the view that the people being served "are just like anyone else," and nearly all the students attributed this change to their personal involvement with the people they were assisting. They reach an optimistic conclusion about the intended, positive impact of a limited service-learning intervention where this impact is an increased social responsibility and orientation toward others as the basis of citizenship.

Boss taught an ethics course, as I did, with two sections, one including a service-learning component and the other not. Her conclusion is also optimistic. Relying on a test devised by a student of Kohlberg, which she administered both before and after the course, she reports that the students who had the service-learning component were more successful at reaching "moral reasoning at a higher stage." There was, however, no significant correlation between participation in community service work in the past (prior to the beginning of the semester) and a student's initial score on the test. Boss attributes this to the lack of reflection accompanying the previous community service that students had done. There is, however, another uncomfortable possibility. It is that students learn in an ethics course taught with Kohlberg's schema as content how they are expected to perform. They can then gear their service-learning into this model and score more highly as a result. The question for my purposes is whether we can use the score as a measure of virtue or as progress toward it. Boss tells a significant anecdote about a student "who on his self-ratings reported that he had improved a lot and regarded himself as a highly moral person." Boss says that she agrees with his assessment, though this student showed no difference on his pretest and posttest scores. In this case, I imagine there was genuine moral improvement but not in the specific skill of demonstrating the kind of reasoning that the test scored highly.

It is significant that it is a Kohlberg-type test that Boss administers because Kohlberg's highest stage is, as he acknowledges, drawn straight from Kant's universalization procedure for testing a proposal for action. Boss assumes "that an ethics class should foster independent or autonomous analytical thinking of the type found at the post-conventional stage of moral reasoning. . . . This assumption is based in part on a progressive philosophy of education in which the purpose of education is to stimulate the natural development of the students' moral capacities and judgements." For Kant there is not a natural progression or development toward living by the categorical imperative. Instead, there is a revolution of the will. For Kant, this is a revolution that we cannot experience either by examining the lives of others or even by introspection. It is certainly not a progression that we could measure empirically.

As with Giles and Eyler, Boss reports an improvement in moral sensitivity (in addition to the greater ability to reason well) as a result of the service-learning component of her course. I do not at all want to deny this, and it is quite consistent with my own experience of teaching a service-learning component. Boss gives a number of powerful examples of how her students changed—often in their own words. One key change was a decrease of stereotyping that resulted from dealing with people rather than abstract issues. Again, this is consistent with what I experienced. However, the only way she claims to *measure* this increase in sensitivity is by higher ratings that the students gave themselves both as moral people and as having made moral improvement. For my purposes, what would be necessary is a rating of actual moral improvement because (as Kant says) we are never more easily deceived than in the opinion we have of ourselves. This is likely to be especially true when students are rating themselves for an ethics course. Kant's view is that we do not see our own fundamental motivation, however hard we introspect, though God can see it and judge us on that basis.

I do not, however, want to end with the negative but with the positive. One of the standards I try to apply to my teaching is to ask, "Is there anything the students have learned today that will be helpful to their lives in ten years' time?" This question can be rather demoralizing, and needs to be handled with care. When I am teaching Descartes's third meditation, for example, with all its complex detail about formal reality and objective reality, I find it hard to sustain the sense that much will be retained beyond the exam. Nonetheless, it is appropriate to teach Descartes's third meditation, even to those who will only have one course in philosophy. What counts as "helpful" needs to be distinguished into many different categories, and I will not try to do that here. What I am convinced about, however, is that this service-learning component that I have described will be remembered and will be helpful to my students' ethical lives, if they choose to use it, long after they have left college. There is not much of my teaching that I can be so sure about, but I have to retain the recognition that the choice is theirs, together with God's, in some combination that I do not claim to understand.

References

Bok, Derek. 1986. *Higher learning*. Cambridge: Harvard University Press.

Boss, Judith A. 1994. The effect of community service work on the moral development of college ethics students. *Journal of Moral Education* 23 (2): 183-97.

Boyer, E. 1987. *College: The undergraduate experience in America*. New York: Harper & Row.

Dewey, John. 1908. *Ethics*. New York: Columbia University Press.

———. 1933. A humanist manifesto. In *The new humanist*, vol. VI, no. 3.

———. 1959. *Dewey on education: Selections with an introduction and notes by M. S. Dworkin*. New York: Bureau of Publications, Teachers' College, Columbia University.

———. 1981. *The later works, 1925-1953*. Edited by Jo Ann Boydston. Carbondale: Southern Illinois University Press.

Erlich, Thomas. 1996. Foreword to *Service-learning in higher education: Concepts and practices*, edited by B. Jacoboby et al. San Francisco: Jossey-Bass.

Frankena, William K. 1965. *Three historical philosophies of education*. Chicago: Scott, Foresman and Co.

Giles, Dwight E., Jr., 1991. Dewey's theory of experience: Implications for service-learning. *Journal of Cooperative Education* 27:87-90.

Giles, Dwight E., Jr. and Eyler, Janet. 1994. The impact of a college community service laboratory on a student's personal, social, and cognitive outcomes, *Journal of Adolescence* 17:327-39.

Hare, John. 1995. Same-sex relations and the argument from complementarity. Paper delivered to the Midwest regional meeting of the Society of Christian Philosophers.

———. 1996. *The moral gap*. Oxford: Clarendon Press.

———. 1999. Augustine, Kant and the moral gap. In *The Augustinian tradition*, edited by. Gareth B. Matthews. Berkeley: University of California Press.

Harkavy, Ira, and Lee Benson. 1998. De-Platonizing and democratizing education as the basis of service-learning. In *Academic service-learning: A pedagogy of action and reflection*, edited by Robert A. Rhoads and Jeffrey P. F. Howard. San Francisco: Jossey Bass.

Hatcher, Julie A. 1997. The moral dimensions of John Dewey's philosophy: Implications for undergraduate education. *Michigan Journal of Community Service-learning* 4:22-29.

Hauerwas, Stanley, and Charles Pinches. 1997. *Christians among the virtues.* Notre Dame: University of Notre Dame Press.

McPherson, K., and M. K Nebgen. 1991. School reform and community service. *Network* 2:1-4.

Meilaender, Gilbert C. 1984. *The theory and practice of virtue.* Notre Dame: University of Notre Dame Press.

Olthuis, James. 1995. When is sex against nature? In *An ethos of compassion and the integrity of creation*, edited by Brian J. Walsh et al. Lanham, Md: University Press of America.

Penn, William J., Jr. 1990. Teaching ethics—a direct approach. *Journal of Moral Education* 19 (2): 24-38.

Saltmarsh, John. 1996. Education for critical citizenship: John Dewey's contribution to the pedagogy of community service-learning. *Michigan Journal of Community Service Learning* 3:13-21.

Stanton, T. K. 1990. Liberal arts, experiential learning and public service: Necessary ingredients for socially responsible undergraduate education. In *Combining service and learning*, edited by J. C. Kendall, Vol. 1. Raleigh, N. C.: Society for Internships and Experiential Education.

Synod of the Christian Reformed Church of North America. 1973. Report 42 of the committee to study homosexuality.

Zigler, Ronald Lee. 1998. The four domains of moral education: The contributions of Dewey, Alexander and Goleman to the comprehensive taxonomy. *Journal of Moral Education* 27 (1):19-33.

Chapter 7

PERFORMANCE STUDIES, ACADEMICALLY BASED SERVICE-LEARNING, AND THE STAGING OF COMMUNITY

Robert J. Hubbard

Prologue

TRYING TO EXPLAIN what I do for a living to my father-in-law sometime leads to an awkward conversation.

"Yes, I teach three courses."

"How often do they meet?"

"About three times a week."

From the other side of the kitchen table, the hard-working farmer and truck driver from the upper Midwest crumples his forehead as he sips his coffee. I self-consciously stare at the floral print on the tablecloth. He does not say anything, but I can tell that he is wondering what I do with the remaining forty to fifty hours of the workweek. Without being asked, I interject, "Preparation takes a lot of time . . . ah . . . I also serve on committees, advise students, and do some research."

"Oh," he says politely. The research part clearly does not go over well. He knows that I am not working on a cure for cancer, or arthritis, or a way to finally put an end to quack grass. Through his politely dismissive facial expression, I hear him thinking: *The kid's got a Ph.D. in theatre for goodness sake.* I watch this sweet, intelligent, good-natured father-of-my-bride resist the temptation to roll his eyes.

Ernest Boyer's "The Scholarship of Engagement" helps put this awkward conversation into a larger context. Boyer observes that, after years of explosive growth, universities face the erosion of public confidence that stems from a perception that higher education no longer serves as a vital center for the work of a nation (Boyer 1996, 11). Boyer notes that this has not always been the case. For almost 350 years, higher education served the larger purposes of American life—from colonial colleges that prepared civic and religious leaders, to Abraham Lincoln's historical Land Grand Act that linked higher learning to the nation's agricultural revolution, to the G.I. Bill of the 1940s that raised the education expectations of a nation (11-12). This ability to connect intellectual pursuits with mainstream concerns seems distant in today's higher education. As recognized by Boyer, the university system currently suffers from perceptions that it is disconnected, elitist, indulgent, impractical, and deliberately confusing. (I can only imagine my father-in-law's response if he were to read a typical passage from a professional journal.) It is not surprising that this disconnect between educational institutions and everyday life, as argued by Boyer, creates "a growing feeling in this country that higher education is, in fact, part of the problem rather than the solution" (14).

Clearly, steps must be taken to reestablish higher education within the community. In "Lessons from Hull House for the Contemporary Urban University," I. Harkavy and J. L. Puckett call for scholarship to return to a mission orientation that advances the concept of academically based community service (Harkavy and Puckett 1994, 139). Several pedagogic strategies lumped under the title of service-learning or Academically Based Service-Learning (ABSL),[1] aspire to this purpose. In his preface to *Service Learning*, former U.S. commissioner of education and vice president of the Ford Foundation, Harold Howe, defines ABSL as "an educational activity, program, or curriculum that seeks to promote students' learning through experiences with volunteerism or community service" (Howe 1997, iv). Howe then offers a minor rewrite to Scripture, stating, "a briefer statement might go back to the Bible: 'Love thy neighbor' and learn by doing it" (Howe 1997, iv). In short, ABSL reestablishes higher education's connection to community by embracing ancient, holy, and tested forms of conduct. In a difficult time of shrinking budgets, rising tuition, and anti-intellectual backlash, ABSL scholarship may offer the best available means of restoring community faith in the work of higher education.

---

[1] Many scholars and practitioners use service-learning and academically based service learning interchangeably. For the purposes of this study, I prefer the latter because it implies a direct connection between a service project and a curricular goal.

ABSL and Performance Studies: A Statement of Purpose

Boyer's lament concerning the lack of connection between higher education and community sounds strange to a performance-studies audience.[2] Current trends in performance studies emphasize cross-cultural communication and performance as a tool in the creation of empathy. In his seminal essay, "Performing as a Moral Act: Ethical Dimensions of the Ethnography of Performance," Dwight Conquergood extols "dialogical" performance as a hopeful means of cross-cultural communication (Conquergood 1985, 10). Similarly, in "Empathy and the Ethics of Entitlement," Ronald Pelias eloquently states, "Empathy allows performers to escape their solipsistic worlds, to make human contact, to be members of the human community" (Pelias 1991, 151). An increased emphasis on community engagement also shows itself in the widespread appropriation by performance-studies practitioners of the theatre of social change theories and techniques of Augusto Boal and Jeff Wirth. Indeed, both in terms of philosophical and curricular goals, performance studies shares a great deal in common with the community-centered emphasis of service-learning pedagogy.

Regrettably, this shared emphasis of preserving and serving community has yet to translate into much cross-fertilization between performance studies and ABSL pedagogy. As illustrated by the recent National Communication Associations sponsorship of Bren Murphy and David Droge's *Voices of Strong Democracy: Concepts and Models for Service Learning in Communication Studies* (2000), many focus groups within the larger discipline of communication actively embrace service-learning. Unfortunately, performance-studies practitioners seem slow to make the connection.[3] Perhaps this reluctance

---

[2] Performance studies, formally known as oral interpretation, is an field within the disciplines of communication and theatre. The name change occurred in the 1980s as part of a larger effort to keep pace with rapid increase of scholarship by practitioners within the field in the areas of ethnography, oral history, and cultural studies. Currently, performance studies focus groups exist in both National Communication Associations and the Association of Theatre in Higher Education. Comprised of hundreds of active and diverse members, these focus groups ride the cutting edge of communication scholarship and produce several nationally referred journals. For a more complete definition and discussion of the emergence of performance studies as a field of study, see (HopKins 1996) and (Park-Fuller and Pelias 1996).

[3] Many teachers and scholars within the various disciplines of communication studies embrace service-learning in their teaching. Applications are particularly active in the areas of small-group theory, interpersonal, and intercultural communication. Performance studies lags behind its companion divisions in communication studies. At the 1998

stems from the belief that they are already doing service-learning, that performance studies at its core is a service-learning activity. Unfortunately, this reasonable if narrow view fails to acknowledge the ways in which a well-articulated ABSL framework might enhance a performance-studies classroom project. The following narrative is designed to unite two should-be bedfellows. The chapter divides into three parts. Part one addresses ethical questions involved with selecting a service-learning project. Part two consists of a project description, or a "thick description," of two successful service-learning projects; both projects took place in an introductory performance-studies course and were integrated smoothly into existing curriculum. Part three contains a reflection upon the value and challenges that accompany the use of ABSL within a performance-studies context. As an overall approach, this study corresponds with Peter Scales and Donna Koppelman's appeal that the cause of service-learning can best be advanced if teachers are "exposed to examples of successful service-learning programs" (Scales and Koppelman 1997, 132). Ideally, this process will spawn additional applications, improvements, and uses for ABSL within a performance-studies context.

Thoughts on Getting Started

My first encounter with ABSL began in near ignorance. While attending faculty orientation at Calvin College, I listened to the coordinator of ABSL at Calvin College give a presentation on possible applications of service-learning in the college classroom.[4] Wheels immediately began turning regarding a possible

---

National Communication Association (NCA) annual conference in New York City, I chaired a panel dealing with service-learning applications in the performance studies classroom. After an extensive search among people active in both the performance studies and service-learning NCA focus groups, I could only identify four NCA members who used service-learning in their teaching. Two of these members presented on the panel.

[4] On this point, a disclaimer is appropriate. I teach at an institution very supportive of ABSL, both in terms of resources and credit given to faculty. The ABSL staff at Calvin College help to facilitate many of the difficult logistical concerns such as first contacts and student transportation. As the visibility and institutional support of ABSL programs continue to increase, more and more colleges and universities will likely institute similar resources for faculty. The point cannot be denied, however, that ABSL does increase faculty workload, especially if institutional support is lacking. It is my opinion, however, that the positives far outweigh the negatives.

application with an existing oral-history assignment in my performance-studies course. For this assignment, students conduct and tape-record interviews, create transcripts from one or more of the stories, then "restore" the original performance into the form of a dramatic monologue. Through repetition, I learned that the assignment works best when the oral histories share a common theme. For example, one semester, students collected "holiday stories"; another semester, the project centered on stories dealing with family rules; on another occasion, students collected and performed religious conversion stories. From these experiences, I observed that a common assignment adds cohesion and unity to the overall exercise while also yielding noticeably richer performances. By the final performance of a semester, all class participants seem to understand considerably more about the given topic or type of experience. Because of its tendency to focus on a given community, using ABSL in conjunction with the oral-history assignment appeared to be an ideal way to generate a common pool of interview subjects. Furthermore, as a student of performance studies, I found the ethnographic and community focus of such an assignment intriguing.

In my first meeting with the representative from the service-learning center, I energetically explained all of the ways a service-learning component would strengthen my oral-history assignment. After patiently listening to my comments, the representative politely asked how the project would benefit the community. To my embarrassment, I had never directly considered this question! I had fallen into perhaps the most common pitfall of ABSL: focusing on the curricular benefits ahead of the actual service component. In "What Is Community Service Learning?" Carol Kinsley firmly prescribes that student's service-learning experiences should center around "two firm anchors." First, the service experience should be "directly related to academic subject matter," and second, students must make "*positive contributions to individuals and community institutions*" (Kinsley 1994, 14 [emphasis mine]). Similarly, in "Encouraging Cultural Competence," Janie Ward laments that poor planning and short-term thinking often result in a condition in which "service-learning recipients end up getting less out of the service relationship than do the students" (Ward 1997, 140). My oversight also raises provocative questions concerning the ways in which many of us in performance studies address the topic of cross-cultural engagement; I return to these questions in the "Reflections" portion of the chapter.

After further discussion, we decided that a theatrical performance of the students' oral-history monologues in honor of the participating community might serve as an appropriate way of accomplishing the service element of the assignment. The concept of performing as a sign of tribute or as a living offering dates back to the very origins of art: It can be seen in everything from prehistoric cave paintings, to court performances in Shakespeare's England, to free concerts in Central Park. Our hope was that this same spirit of homage and community engagement would translate into the performance of oral history.[5] Admittedly, the motive of celebrating a community through performance poses ethical questions. While the individual lives of community members are surely worth celebrating (as would be any individual life), is it always responsible to celebrate a community? What if the community is victimized and decimated by dominant power structures? To what degree does celebrating the community celebrate the victimization? Again, aided by information from the following project descriptions, I return to these questions in the "Reflections" portion of the chapter.

In the spring of 1997, my students collected oral histories from volunteers at Holland Home, an extended-care facility in the city of Grand Rapids. Every spring, the administration of Holland Home holds a luncheon at a local church to recognize the eighty or so volunteers who contribute to the successful operations of the facility. As part of the festivities, my students performed a compiled script consisting of the oral histories centered on the theme of volunteerism. In addition to providing the entertainment for the luncheon, the thirty-minute production served as a means of recognizing and celebrating the contributions of the volunteers. The second oral history service-learning project took place in the spring of 1998. In this instance, students collected oral histories from residents of an economically depressed section in downtown Grand Rapids known as the Heartside neighborhood. The residents who participated all shared a connection with Heartside Ministries, a local Christian nonprofit organization that, among other things, provides Christian ministry, addiction counseling, and vocational training to the Heartside community. Guided by the desire to give voice to the

---

[5] I should point out that, although the idea of a performance for the participating community originated in the meeting with the service-learning center, we did discuss our proposals with qualified representatives acting on behalf of the respective communities before initiating each project. In hindsight, we may have served the participating communities better by involving them in the initial discussion. Unfortunately, the logistics of brainstorming often prohibit such involvement.

struggles, triumphs, and persevering spirit of the Heartside residents, students organized oral histories into a complied script and performed the script at a luncheon given for members of the Heartside community at a coffee house in the neighborhood.

In addition to making sure the service-learning project enhances curricular goals while genuinely serving the community, a conscientious instructor should also devise his or her project with a strong reflective component. In "Learning from Qualitative Research," Robert D. Shumer argues that "reflective practices need to be important and intentional elements of sound ABSL projects" (Shumer 1997, 28). Similarly, in *Combining Service and Learning*, Jane C. Kendall addresses the student directly. She states: "The highly individualized learning that you're doing in the community requires time for reflection so that you can take a look at what you're doing, relate it to yourself, and generalize from it to other experiences" (Kendall 1990, 85). Kendall then lists three primary strategies to bring about reflection. These strategies include requiring students to keep journals of the experience, regular meetings with supervisors and faculty advisors, and frequent interaction with other service-learners (Kendall 1990, 85). Ideally, a reflective component similar to Kendall's model should run through an entire service-learning project. At the outset, the instructor should determine methods of reflection that best service the "highly individualized" demands of his or her project.

Project Descriptions

As a method of systematizing and clarifying an often organic and chaotic process, I have mapped my attempts to merge ABSL with oral-history performance into four stages. These stages include "Coming Together," "Collection and Incubation," "Classroom Performance," and "Community Performance." Far from a prescriptive regimen, I offer this model only as a rough guide for future service-learning applications. Indeed, since every ABSL project is unique, successful applications rely on the virtue of flexibility. This said, the first stage describes two examples of coming together that may serve as helpful strategies. The first example involves contact initiated by the instructor with a community representative while the second describes the delicate task of introducing students to their community partners.

Stage One: Coming Together

After deciding on a service-learning project that enhances curricular goals and makes positive contributions to the community, the next step becomes introducing the project to the students and to the participating community members. This step should be performed thoughtfully, as a certain degree of skepticism and uneasiness may run through both groups. In some cases, the special qualities and needs of individual projects may dictate the method of introduction. For example, in the Holland Home project, I carefully explained the service-learning component to my students on the first day of class. The next class period, a service-learning representative gave a short overview of the service-learning program at Calvin College, including such things as how to record hours for a transcript record and methods of transportation the students could use to visit the field site. Following this presentation, the volunteer coordinator from Holland Home gave a short presentation documenting the history and mission of the institution, the types of volunteer work performed there, and the kinds of people who serve as volunteers. The project began taking shape two weeks later when an energetic group of Holland Home volunteers visited the classroom. Warmed by introductions, explanations, and refreshments, volunteers paired with students. This initial meeting provided them an opportunity to introduce themselves to one another. I also instructed both parties to use this time to schedule a second meeting in which students could accompany volunteers in whatever service they provide for Holland Home.

The Heartside orientation began similarly with short presentations to the students early in the semester by the service-learning center and the director of Heartside Ministries. The director anticipated that he would be able to field approximately ten residents willing to participate in the project. As a result, we decided to double-up and assign two students to each resident. This choice led to substantial changes in the process elaborated in the "Classroom Performance" section of the chapter. Instead of meeting on the college campus as was the case with the Holland Home project, Heartside residents and students met in the fellowship room of Heartside Ministries. This location provided the residents the security of a familiar setting and allowed the students the opportunity to visit the unfamiliar neighborhood. When only three residents initially attended the meeting, I questioned the viability of the assignment. But, as the hour progressed, several more arrived. In the end, all but one group (two out of twenty-two students) found partners. Although the overall reception to the project met with positive response, a few residents did express concerns. One middle-aged man wanted assurance that no medical experiments would be performed on him. Another younger and angrier man wondered why he should give his stories away to "a bunch of kids who have no idea what I'm going through." Such questions were useful in that they helped clarify the assignment, as well as force both the students and me to continually reevaluate our purposes and motives. By the end of the session, everyone shared a clearer sense of the project, and all but one resident agreed to participate. We then divided into project groups with just enough time for students and residents to introduce themselves and schedule a second meeting. With everyone possessing a better idea of whom, where, and why, the meeting concluded, and I drove my students back to campus.

Stage Two: Collection and Incubation

The intention guiding the second stage of this chapter, Collection and Incubation, is to provide the reader with hard-earned insights into logistical and ethical issues that may arise during an ABSL project. Initially, my discussion forms the backdrop for the intricacy of scheduling meetings between students and their community partners. The discussion quickly shifts, however, from logistical to ethical concerns as I chronicle examples of complications that first showed themselves during this phase of the service-learning projects.

After introducing the ABSL component, the course as a whole temporarily swerves away from the oral-history assignment in favor of a unit on poetry. During this three-to-four-week period, students meet with their community partners on their own time, record interviews, and select possible stories from the audiotapes. In the case of the Holland Home project, students accompanied volunteers on their service work. These visits included everything from spending time in the Holland Home beauty shop to observing pet therapy in action. Conversely, students involved in the Heartside project used this initial period of the project to interview residents either at Heartside Ministries or at a coffee shop in the neighborhood. Some students chose to attend religious services with their residents at the chapel located at Heartside Ministries. During this phase of both projects, I kept up with the developments by asking for progress reports at the beginning of classes and by monitoring journal reflections. For the most part, however, students functioned independently during this portion of the assignment.

Based on my experiences with ABSL projects to date, the highest percentage of "unplanned" events take place during this incubation period. For example, one student involved in the Holland Home project expressed concern that the content of the oral history he collected did not meet the "goals" of the assignment. When I asked him what he meant by this, he told me that a large portion of the oral history revolved around the fact that the volunteer, a retired woman in her seventies, did not feel appreciated for her efforts. She told him how certain residents of the home cruelly criticized her clothing and her overall personal appearance, and how this behavior often caused her to leave her desk in tears. The Heartside project also generated some difficult questions when two students working together collected an oral history from a man who confided to them that he struggles with an addiction to pornography.

Understandably, these students wondered if they should include these aspects of the narratives in their transcripts. Indeed, the degree to which either of these difficult issues should appear in the final performance text symbolizes the ethical dimensions accompanying an assignment of this type. In such cases, a service-learning facilitator must carefully weigh the service components of the final performance against the curricular goals of the assignment. In the case of the Holland Home volunteer, we decided to include the difficult portion of the interview. We did so because the volunteer wished it and because her negative experiences in many ways defined her overall feelings about service. In the case of the Heartside resident, we chose not to include his struggles with pornography in our final script. We based this decision on a concern for the resident. When the students brought up his addiction in a later meeting, he appeared shy and embarrassed, as if he felt that, in an unrestrained moment, he had revealed too much of himself. The fact that the discussion of pornography composed a relatively small portion of the overall interview helped in the decision. Still, such choices are not easy, nor should they be. As Conquergood wisely warns us, "performance does not proceed in ideological innocence and axiological purity" (Conquergood 1985, 2).

Another set of unplanned events involved the scheduling of meetings with the Heartside residents, many of whom were homeless and could not be reached other than through Heartside Ministries. Of the ten groups of students and residents who initially set up second meetings in the Coming Together stage, only five successfully met during their scheduled times. Working with the Heartside staff, students scheduled new meetings with some of the residents. Still, a total of three groups (six students and three residents) never successfully met. This placed me in the awkward situation of having to quickly devise alternative assignments for these students. Predictably, student morale dropped with each unforeseen obstacle.

Although awkward and frustrating, an argument can be made that these types of complications actually strengthen the case for using ABSL. In "Service Learning: A Theoretical Model" Barry G. Schekley and Morris T. Keeton argue that students gain "knowledge-about-the-world" from a service-learning experience in two ways: "confirmation" and "disconfirmation" (Schekley and Keeton 1997, 38). "A testament to the strength of the process in which learners preshape experience," confirmation occurs when learners' experiences "conveniently match the expectations they have for these experiences." Conversely, disconfirmation involves those cases when learners' expectations do not match their experiences. Sheckley and Keeton report that adult students "learn more from experiences in which their expectations were disconfirmed than from experiences where expectations were confirmed, even though disconfirming learning projects were more frustrating, anxiety producing, and stressful" (Schekley and Keeton 1997, 39).

It follows that students become uncomfortable when collecting oral histories that reveal less-than-rosy portraits of volunteerism or depict troubling revelations about their subjects. Even the inability to do something as seemingly simple as set up a meeting may frustrate them enough for them to consider academic mutiny. During the anxious moments, we must remember that, through disconfirmation, learning still takes place. In his attempt to articulate the ideal motives behind performance ethnography, Pelias stumbles upon a theme of disconfirmation. He writes: "Instead of reifying performers' personal ideologies or institutional values, [performers] strive for social consciousness in which others are not rendered invisible (de-realized) or assumed known (over-realized), but are closely regarded, familiarized" (Pelias 1991, 150). In short, through disconfirmation, students gain a richer, more complex, and empathetic understanding that far surpasses simplistic, idealized, and one-dimensional views often carried into the project.

Stage Three: Classroom Performances

Having completed their initial fieldwork, students now enter the Classroom Performance phase of the oral-history assignment. This stage begins with a discussion of literature as an oral phenomenon followed by techniques used in the creation of oral-history transcripts. The emphasis then evolves into strategies for enhancing live performance. These strategies center on the value of performance workshops of the oral-history transcripts, both as solo pieces and as dramatic duos.

For approximately three to four class periods, I discuss the oral history assignment in the context of "dialogic performance" (Conquergood 1985), "natural performance" (Stucky 1993), and personal narrative structure (Langellier 1989; Langellier and Peterson, 1997). Showing and discussing selections from the videotape of Anna Deveare Smith's *Fires in the Mirror* (1997)[6] helps students envision the kinds of performance possible from this assignment. I give students the option of a traditional transcription style, or a more poetic approach that utilizes the principles of prosody and graphemics discussed in the earlier unit on poetry and utilized by Smith in her scripts. After working through the above material, the class moves into series of workshop performances followed by a round of final performances. With or without a service-learning component, this basic approach works well as a means of generating meaningful and nuanced oral-history performances.

The fact that students who participated in the Heartside project worked in groups of two forced a modification of the above approach. Instead of performing solo pieces, students explored techniques of bifurcating their oral-history narratives. To help this process, I introduced different options for

---

[6] Anna Deveare Smith is an internationally known actress, playwright, and performance artist. She is best known for her series of one-woman shows based on oral-history interviews. Smith began her unique style of theatre in the 1980s with her "On the Road" series. In an attempt to use performance to document the American experience, Smith traveled the country interviewing people and then performing the interviews verbatim. Her plays include *Fires in the Mirror* (1991), a play about the riots between blacks and Jews in Crown Heights, Brooklyn; *Twilight: Los Angeles* (1994), a play about the Los Angeles riots; and *House Arrest: First Edition*, a group piece centering themes of politics and celebrity. Smith's blend of theatrical art, journalism, and social commentary won her a $280,000 "genius" grant from the MacArthur Foundation in 1996. The obvious similarities between Smith's work and my oral-history assignment make her a valuable resource for this assignment.

dividing the single narrative into two voices common in chamber-theatre style scripting. In *Experimental Theatre: Creating and Staging Texts*, Judy Yordon offers useful pointers in this area, particularly in her chapter on creating chamber-theatre scripts (Yordon 1997, 99-153). One option involves dividing the narrative as settings change. In other words, students simply change the speaker when the story moves to a new location. Another approach involves switching speakers based on shifts in time. This method essentially creates a narrator's anchoring a story in the present while the second performer plays both the past and the future. In yet another possible approach, students divide narrative along the Labovian model of "abstract," "orientation," "complicating action," "evaluation," and "resolution" (Labov and Waletsky 1967, 12-44). By far the most intricate approach, this option offers the added benefit of helping students recognize and appreciate the structural components of oral history. Armed with one or more of these methods, students become better equipped to approach the dual task of turning one voice into two and two voices into one.

Comparing the Holland Home and the Heartside classroom performances, I observed that the bifurcated Heartside oral histories pushed students away from mimetic/imitative movement choices that typically complement oral-history performance (i.e., the Anna Deveare Smith performance) and toward a more suggestive aesthetic common in readers-theatre and chamber-theatre staging. A number of choral-reading style scripting choices—such as speaking words simultaneously, echoing phrases, overlapping dialogue—also emerged as prominent scripting choices. With only a few exceptions, the classroom performances of the Heartside residents far exceeded my expectations as students produced exciting, creative, and often unexpected performances.

Stage Four: Community Performance

All of the components of a semester-long oral-history project merge into one with the creation and performance of a compiled script. Based on first impressions, the Community Performance stage appears to be the most challenging and seemingly the most overwhelming sequence of the project. In this stage, the instructor divides students into project groups, introduces the genre of the compiled script, discusses and illustrates presentational staging techniques, devises introductory, transitional, and concluding material to connect group projects, and, finally, facilitates a community performance of the newly created compiled script. In spite of the seemingly large number of steps, I have found that the design of the assignment establishes a momentum that propels the project reasonably effortlessly toward a successful and rewarding conclusion.

Key to the success of this assignment is the decision to divide students into small groups. Imagine the task of composing and staging a thirty-minute, multigenre script that involves twenty student performers equally—a sizable project for a seasonal directing slot, much less one project within a 3 credit-semester-hour course. Placing students in small groups of four to five makes the project manageable and increases student ownership. Instead of one producer/adapter/director, each group compiles its own five-to-seven-minute script. As part of the compilation process, I require students to incorporate selections from the oral-history assignment as well as at least two other genres of literature into their compiled scripts.

As a primer to the group work, I spend a class period introducing students to various techniques of compiled script formation, focusing specifically on the range existing between assemblage- and collage-scripting techniques. I then spend a second class period introducing basic presentational staging techniques useful in group performance. Material from Marion Klienau and Janet McHugues' *Theatres for Literature* (1980), as well as Yordon's *Experimental Theatre* (1997) serve as useful guides for these discussions and demonstrations. Students generally appreciate having time to explore and experiment with the new material in their project groups. Armed with practical information on scripting and staging, students spend the next three to four class periods scripting and staging their group projects. We then perform in a workshop style each piece in front of the rest of the class. Together, we use this time to polish and refine student-generated scripting and staging choices.

Suddenly, we now have about twenty-five minutes of scripted and staged material. The final step in the process involves connecting the four to five short group performances into one master script. First, the production needs an introduction. With both the Holland Home and Heartside performances, students began the performance by introducing themselves as if they were their community partners. This simple framing device both established the relationship between the students and their community partners and introduced the audience to the basic convention guiding the performance as a whole. To make the frame visually interesting, I directed students to meet center stage in groups of two in lines that circle back to the center. In both performances, members of the audience applauded or cheered as they heard their name or the name of someone they knew. When the final two performers introduced themselves, the line opened to reveal the configuration of the first performance group. With the Heartside performance, I instructed one student to shout out, "voices of Heartside" with the rest of the students responding in unison, "in celebration of community."

After devising an appropriate method of introduction, the next step involves deciding how to deal with transitions. I learned the hard way the importance of filling in the gaps between each of the small-group pieces during the Holland Home performance. In this case, I neglected transitions almost completely and the overall performance suffered. Audience members appeared confused as to when to applaud or how to react to the dead spots between each of the small-group performances. The absence of transition-friendly technical theatre equipment (light boards, sound equipment) further complicated matters. With the Heartside performance, I found a low-tech solution. Two students, one on piano and one on guitar, played music during the transitions gaps. The music came from a Christian hymn used as part of the compiled script by one of the groups. Although countless options exist for transition material, the use of live music filled gaps in the script needed for set-up time while successfully unifying the performance as a whole.

Finally, the performance needs some kind of concluding statement. Several possibilities exist. With the Holland Home project, I added a recognizable frame to the performance by ending it as it began, with the students introducing themselves two by two. As a way of symbolizing the connections made during the performance, students recited their own name along with the name of their community partner. With the Heartside project, I tried a different approach. Near the end of the final group's performance, the rest of the performers, who had been sitting near the periphery of the small coffee house stage, slowly filled in all of the spaces not taken by members of the group that was performing. This action symbolized a community coming together. By the final line of the script, every student performer and, by implication, every community partner, owned a place on stage. At this time, the same student who began the performance again reached his arms toward the audience and shouted, "the voices of Heartside," followed by a unison repetition of the line, "in celebration of community" from the rest of the performers. I was happy to notice that several of the Heartside residents participated in this call-and-response moment of dialogue.

Reflections

The marriage of performance studies with ABSL holds the potential to increase student learning and to make positive contributions to the community. Benefits to students emerge in predictable and unpredictable ways. At the very least, students get to know people they otherwise would not. At best, a transcendent joining takes place. Pelias describes this joining: "They become a part of the community of voices seeking meaningful contact and struggling to make sense of the world" (Pelias 1991, 150). Prior to turning in their journals for the Heartside project, students responded to three questions: What do I have in common with my resident? What don't I have in common with my resident? And what did I learn from my resident that I can use as "equipment for living"? Predictably, many students addressed the third question with responses such as, "I realize how easy my life is compared to Jim's," and "Mary taught me to stop taking things for granted." Occasionally, however, the reflections took less expected turns. One student wrote, "I learned the importance of joy and laughter. It is so important to smile and find joy in life, whatever the circumstance. Geoff reminded of this." Another student wrote, "Helping people is how Rick defines himself. He sees everyone as image bearers of God. I hope someday, I can do the same, especially if I'm ever in a position like his." Finally, a third student reflects, "The quality I most want to imitate in Marlene is her ability to keep going when most of us would crumble. She is a tower." These qualities—optimism, selflessness, and perseverance—stand as worthy goals in any curriculum.

In a 1997 National Public Radio interview, Anna Deveare Smith discussed the differences between journalists and performers. Both collect stories, but whereas journalists strive to remain disconnected and objective toward their subjects, Smith states, "my job as an actor is to *love* the characters I play." Merging ABSL and the performance of oral history forces students to lose a bit of their journalistic objectivity. Through the act of performance, vocal patterns and experiences commingle into one—a relationship forms. Certainly, to claim that cultural understanding automatically results from a five-minute performance of an oral-history transcript shows a disturbing naïveté. Yet, on some level, student performers must learn care for their subjects in order to connect with their words. To echo Smith, they must learn to love them, if only a little. Considering the alternatives of ignorance, apathy, or hatred, integrating ABSL into a performance studies classroom exists as a worthwhile, helpful, and affirming pedagogic tool.

The oral history assignments described above also offer something useful and affirming to their participating communities. True, a skeptic might argue that, despite the positive efforts of volunteers, our systems for aiding the elderly are less than ideal and therefore should not be glorified in performance. A likeminded voice might argue that our homeless communities inspire anything but communal celebration. Ultimately, these positions neglect the empowering capabilities of community performance. In *The Ritual Process*, Victor Turner celebrates the efficacy of the performance event as a tool for building community. Turner posits that, for many communities, experience becomes meaningful when "expressed" or "pressed out" through performance. He argues that public performance of narratives and rituals structure and create meaning for a society (Turner 1960, 13-14). It is certainly true that traditional forms of discourse generally do not privilege stories from groups such as Holland Home volunteers or Heartside residents. In keeping with Turner's observations, oral-history performances highlight communities who might otherwise see themselves as voiceless. Such performances do not endorse the process that led to a community's standing in the world so much as they bear witness to it. By sharing their stories with students, participating community members create a record, a transmission of life experience, that places them within the fabric of a group of people united by symbolic beliefs and shared experience. Indeed, in his discussion of the challenges of performing oral history, Pelias outlines the ideal outcome of performance ethnography. He states: "When performers speak 'with' or 'beside' others, they share the stage, giving others equal opportunity to be heard" (Pelias 1991, 150).

Experience supports these conclusions. Sitting in the audience at the Holland Home and Heartside performances, an observer could witness several community participants turning and smiling to the people around them when they saw themselves portrayed. One young man at the Heartside performance could not contain himself, joyfully shouting, "That's me! That's me," whenever his student partners spoke his words. Similarly, after the Heartside performance, a middle-aged woman walked up to me and asked for a copy of the script.

Moments before, she watched students perform her stories of struggling with drug addiction and of being a homeless, single mother. With an expression of confident gratitude, she said, "I want my kids to have this script. Other people have got to know our stories."

Finally, beyond the attributes of community service and improved pedagogy, the use of ABSL promises something of practical and great importance to performance-studies practitioners: accountability. In the 1980s, members of what was then a discipline known as "oral interpretation" changed its name to performance studies. Although a complicated issue, the change grew out of a desire to expand the definition of what constitutes performance, to widen the lens of investigation from literary to cultural texts, to be, in short, more inclusive of otherness. Inherent in all of the debates and discussion of this time lurked a subtle altruism, a belief that a symbolic renaming might somehow contribute to a better understanding of difference in the world. The logic is simple: replication of life performances, when done responsibly (Conquergood's dialogical performance, Pelias' dialogic embodiment, Stucky's natural performance) leads to empathy and increased understanding of otherness. We then assume that this empathy and understanding will translate into better communication and, when applicable, reconciliation. ABSL puts teeth into these assumptions. Beyond simply being respectful and ethical of otherness, ABSL forces students and teachers to devise and direct projects that will contribute positively to the participating community. As a final thought, I hope this chapter gives the reader an example of how the idealism of performance studies can be approached through the humble efficiency of ABSL.

Epilogue

Now when I look across the floral print tablecloth at my hard-working farmer and truck driver father-in-law, I feel less awkward.

"So, what kind of 'research' are you working on now?"

"Well, I'm writing up some work that I've done recently in an area called academically based service-learning."

"What's that?"

"Well, let me tell you. . . ."

References

Boyer, Ernest. L. 1996. The scholarship of engagement. *Journal of Public Service and Outreach* 1:11-20.

Conquergood, Dwight. 1985. Performing as a moral act: Ethical dimensions of the ethnography of performance. *Literature in Performance* 5:1-13.

Droge, David, and Bren Murphy, eds. 2000. *Voices of a strong democracy: Concepts and models for service-learning in communication studies.* Washington D.C.: American Association of Higher Education in cooperation with the National Communication Association.

Harkavy, I. and J. L. Puckett. 1994. Lessons from Hull House for the contemporary urban university. *Social Science Review* 68:134-41.

HopKins, Mary Frances. 1996. Cultural capital in the academic market: The place of literature in performance studies. *Communication Education* 45:89-95.

Howe, Harold. 1997. Preface. In *Service learning*, edited by Joan Schine. Chicago: University of Chicago Press.

Kendall, Jane. C., and Associates. 1990. *Combining service and learning: A resource book for community and public service.* Raleigh, N.C.: National Society for Internships and Experiential Education.

Kinsley, Carol. W. 1994. What is community service learning? *Vital Speeches of the Day* 61:14.

Kleinau, Marion L., and Janet Larsen McHughes. 1980. *Theatres for literature.* Sherman Oaks, Calif.: Alfred Publishing Co.

Labov, William, and Joschua Waletsky. 1967. Narrative analysis: Oral versions of personal experience. In *Essays in the Verbal and Visual Arts*, edited by J. Helms. Seattle: University of Washington.

Langellier, Kristin. M. 1989. Personal narratives: Perspectives on theory and research. *Text and Performance Quarterly* 9:243-76.

Langellier, Kristin. M., and Eric Peterson. 1997. The politics of personal narrative methodology. *Text and Performance Quarterly* 17:135-152.

Pelias, Ronald J. 1991. Empathy and the ethics of entitlement. In *Theatre Research International* 16, edited by Claude Schumacher. Belfast: Oxford University Press.

Park-Fuller, Linda, and Ronald. J. Pelias. 1996. Charting alternative performance and evaluative practices. *Communication Education* 45:126-39.

Scales, Peter C., and Donna J. Koppelman. 1997. Service learning in teacher preparation. In *Service Learning*, edited by Joan Schine. Chicago: University of Chicago Press.

Schekley, Barry G., and Morris T. Keeton. 1997. Service learning: A theoretical model. In *Service Learning*, edited by Joan Schine. Chicago: University of Chicago Press.

Shumer, Robert D. 1997. Learning from qualitative research. In *Service-learning applications from research*, edited by Alan S. Waterman. Mahwah, N.J.: Lawrence Erlbaum Associates, Inc.

Smith, Anna DeVeare. 1997. Interview on "Morning Edition." *National Public Radio*. November 26.

Stucky, Nathan. 1993. Toward an aesthetics of natural performance. *Text and Performance Quarterly* 13:168-80.

Turner, Victor Witter. 1969. *The ritual process*. Chicago: Aldine.

Ward, Janie Victoria. 1997. Encouraging cultural competence in service learning practice. In *Service learning*, edited by Joan Schine. Chicago: University of Chicago Press.

Yordon, Judy. 1997. *Experimental theatre: Creating and staging texts*. Prospect Heights, Illinois: Waveland Press.

Chapter 8

LESSONS IN SERVICE-LEARNING: DILEMMA OF GUILT, LESSON IN RECIPROCITY

Laura Hoeksema Cebulski

WIDE-EYED AND TOOTHLESS, Jesus Vargas was my favorite day-camper. A waist-high bundle of creamy colored skin and scraped knees, his boundless energy greeted me every morning at 8 A.M., a full hour before camp began. As his counselor, I had the daily privilege of gathering him up into my arms and spinning us around until we were both too dizzy to stand, and too tired from laughing. Growing up in the inner-city of Philadelphia's northeast side, Jesus saw and experienced more than a six-year-old's body and soul could possibly hold within itself. Not knowing anything different, not yet knowing how to express cynicism and hate and pure anger, Jesus somehow let go of the drugs, the AIDS, the violence, and the sexual abuse in a huge spacey smile and a spirit almost too-ready to give hugs. His innocence and his energy sometimes inspired me, sometimes hurt me, but always left me baffled and questioning.

One day as the loud and restless six-year-olds had their turn at the craft table, I wandered over to Jesus who was very uncharacteristically concentrating over a piece of paper. "How do you spell *window*?" he asked me somewhat urgently. After patiently helping him with the two syllable word, I asked him if he would share what he was writing about. He pulled out a piece of torn construction paper on which he had drawn a house—a simple elementary-school drawing with a centered front door, a triangular roof, and even smoke coming out of the chimney. Right away I noticed that the typically symmetrical windows were, on Jesus' house, greatly differing in size: one was decidedly large while the other was small and insignificant.

He then pulled out the paper he had been writing on, in sloppy, unpracticed script, misspelled and mispunctuated: "Through this window, I see my city,

117

Philadelphia," he read aloud to me as he pointed to the small window. I thought about Jesus' city—the bloody syringes on the church steps; his mother, dying at home from a life of prostitution; his residence above the most dangerous drug-trafficking corner in the city. "And through this window," he said, moving his finger to the big window, "I see God." I do not think Jesus knew exactly what he had drawn or written or why it made me want to cry. Was his little mind capable of the theological statement he had so carefully spelled out?

Looking back, I realize that Jesus Vargas taught me one of my first lessons in service-learning. Even though my involvement with him was during the summer and really separate from my college's service-learning projects, he was part of a seed that was planted in me. I developed a desire for more involvement in service. Jesus taught me that no matter what the economic, racial, social, or even age difference between the one being served and the one serving, you cannot escape the reciprocity. Nor would you want to. Jesus gave to me that summer—he gave me love and showed me courage. Thus, like many others involved in service activities, I began to ask myself: Who is being served more from this deal?

That summer, the one between my freshman and sophomore years, was steeped in growth for me at every level: relationally, emotionally, spiritually. It was impossible to separate that growth from the foundation of my activity: serving at a day-camp during my summer off. It was more than the deep things that the kids happened to say or the unabashed love and affirmation they gave me. It was the way that serving brought me to my senses, the way it opened me to the world—to the reality of violence and pain, to my own ignorance.

I knew that I had touched some children's lives, and through them, some parents' lives as well. Still, there was this nagging sense of guilt that I had benefited most from the experience, and that I could leave that summer in Philadelphia with some pious sense of servanthood.

One thing was for sure, I was going to visit the Service-Learning Center when school started in the fall. The very wording of the office intrigued me and made me think that maybe there I could find an answer to my dilemma of guilt. Was it possible that *learning* was a legitimate part of *serving*?

Dilemma of Not Doing Enough, Lesson in Relationships

Ransom Towers is a low-income apartment building in downtown Grand Rapids. Most of the residents are elderly people, most without many visitors, most without ever experiencing a sense of community from family or anywhere else. As an idealistic college student taking a class on how music could build community, I figured that I could translate that for the friends I had made while volunteering at Ransom Towers. So I gathered up a group: twenty-odd elderly people and a few college-aged friends I had conned into coming. Some of the elderly residents were in wheelchairs or standing unsteadily, some smiling nicely without hearing a word that was said, some nodding in and out from sleepiness—and all of us learning and teaching each other somewhat childish songs designed to build community.

"Bumpity, bumpity, yellow bus," we all sang, "will you say your name for us!" We would point to a person, listen to their name, and repeat the name together in chorus. For someone who receives very little attention in life, for someone who seldom feels really special to anyone else, it is amazing how powerful it can be to hear your name sung by a room full of people, because the name is not just sung, it is carefully mimicked, intonation and all, and delivered with a smile and maybe even a pat on the back. I admit, a whole lot of community was built in those singing sessions. Once again, I did not know who felt better at the end of the night, the old men and women who had been hugged and affirmed by the knowing of their name, or me, who had felt the same sense of encouragement and community.

This time though, I had a framework in which to deal with my quandary. I had begun serving at Ransom Towers through a social work class I was taking. Working with old people was my last choice for a service opportunity. When the Service-Learning Center placed me there, I was not happy. Is it not true, however, that sometimes we learn more from things we do not want to do? Indeed, I ended up loving it—not only because of the emotion-filled singing sessions and the one-on-one interaction that I did there every week, but also because I learned to see its worth not just in the benefit to the people I helped but equally as much by my own learning and growth. The Service-Learning Center had taught me well: Service was a part of learning as much as learning was a part of service. The reciprocity of serving no longer made me feel guilty. Rather, it made me feel whole and challenged and humbled.

Still, there were days when I wanted to "do" more. The battle cry of any good young Reformer is always wanting to do more! Sure, the odd jobs I would perform for the people at Ransom Towers were helpful; they needed those checks signed and mailed, they needed the dust removed from the top of their ceiling fans, but the majority of my time was spent in talking and listening. Just the basics of human relationship. Again, that guilty feeling haunted me. Was I "serving" enough? Could my efforts be recorded and used in some important statistic? Was my service quantifiable?

Another service-learning lesson was in the works. Through the daily task of reflection (a requirement for my class was to keep a journal), I managed to respond to most of my doubts. Perhaps my idea or definition of service was too narrow. Perhaps I needed to allow for some creativity. I had to recognize the importance of human relationship—to affirm it as a worthwhile form of service. I am still learning this, but the schemata of service-learning will forever guide my wandering assumptions about what qualifies as service.

Dilemma of Ignorance, Lesson in Learning

While spending a semester in Honduras studying development, I learned about a project that had gone amuck. There was a group working on a water project in a small village in the mountains of South America. Prior to this agency's involvement, the women would spend between one and two hours each morning lugging containers up from the river to use for daily cooking and cleaning. The trip for water was long and difficult—steep downhill to the river and steep back up. When the development group evaluated that particular village, it was clear that something had to be done about the water issue. It was simply too inefficient. Certainly more important tasks could be completed if the women did not need to worry about water each morning. So, for two years, they designed and installed a water-routing system that brought water up from the river right into the middle of the village. The development agency took time to teach the local people how to use and maintain the system. They left feeling successful and confident that the project would be timesaving and community-run.

Two years later, when that same development agency returned to the little village to do a follow-up evaluation, they were alarmed to find the water system dried up and not in use. Had they not taught proper maintenance? They began to ask around the village to find out. It soon became clear why the village had not maintained the water system. The women, it seems, viewed their daily water retrieval as an important social time. Because they went to the river in groups, it was a time to laugh and talk and have privacy from any curious men or children. The hour or two it took every morning was far from inefficient or tedious—it was essential to their social lives. They did not dread it—it was a favorite time of the day.

Why had no one asked the village what they thought of a water system to begin with?

If my time at Ransom Towers showed me the value of reciprocity and human relationships in service-learning, then Honduras taught me the value, no the necessity, of the *learning* component in service-learning. My idea of learning was expanding beyond the nice feeling of reciprocity. Certainly learning had to do with personal growth and realizations as a result of the service, but it had to be more intentional than just that. The lack of sensitivity in many overseas development work challenged me on this. There is this sense that a genuine desire to serve can supersede the necessity of knowing the people or group you are seeking to serve—a sense that a rightness of heart or good intention can cover for a lack of cultural understanding. In Honduras, I learned that a degree of *learning*, in deepest and sincerest humility, had to precede any successful service situation.

Now this learning can include becoming familiar with a culture or people group (even for service done domestically!) learning a new language, researching their history, talking to people who have been there, knowing societal values or expectations, but this learning also entails a state of mind, a preparedness of spirit—before, during, and after the service.

The time that I spent in Honduras was for a semester class called Third World Development Studies. The classes were set up to focus solely on learning. Any serving that was done in Honduras was self-initiated. I believe that the professors took some questioning from the Calvin community for leading a semester in Honduras and not doing any "missions" work. I also believe that many in the Calvin community were under the impression that that is what we were doing! On the contrary, our classes were set up to familiarize us with the culture, history, and contemporary issues facing Honduras and then to study why poverty existed and what the solutions were. As our semester progressed, it was clear how complicated the problem of poverty was and how complicated an outsiders' solution fit in.

We studied the ineffectiveness of some service work. Like the water project left un-used. We also studied and discussed the harmfulness of some service work. Missions work, for example, done in the name of spreading the Word of the Lord, and instead, messing with some basic functions of a particular culture. We studied how money is given, and we looked at the dilemma of international aid given to corrupt governments—the difficulty of getting money into the hands that will help people.

An important skill for service that I learned in Honduras was the ability to think critically. Coupled with a sense of humility, the ability to think thoroughly through a situation of service is invaluable. To discern when help is really helpful, to be deliberate about methods used with a certain people group, to reflect on potentially harmful actions, to critique a project as it is carried out, to change what is inefficient or ineffective—all these and more are evidence of a program geared toward thoughtful service, toward service that is as much learning as it is meeting a need for an organization or individual.

Service-Learning: Bringing It All Together

As if the character of service-learning through classes were not enough to challenge and grow my person, Calvin also provided me with a program called Service-Learning Scholars. The Service-Learning Center is a department on campus where students and professors can explore service possibilities in the community. It is where all the communication with local agencies is made, where students are placed to perform service work, and where local needs are felt. The center is run by two full-time directors and a dozen students. These student workers are part of a program called Service-Learning Scholars.

Working at the Service-Learning Center is not just a job. It is, in and of itself, an experience in service *and* learning. The students are chosen because of leadership skills and a strong interest in service opportunities. The scholars, as they are called, spend the year encouraging and recruiting other student servers, providing placements at local community organizations, and maintaining all the paperwork necessary to track over a thousand students involved in service!

The work certainly provides a service to the students, faculty, and classes of our college, as well as to the local organizations who receive our student volunteers. However, a great deal of the value in being a Service-Learning Scholar is in the learning process. The program is intricately set up by the office's two directors to encourage scholar leadership, decision making, interpersonal skills, program development, creativity, vision, and organizational skills, all of which are abilities that are easily applicable to professional work in any field.

Gaining experience specifically in a nonprofit organization is a big part of the learning process as a Service-Learning Scholar. The labor of recruiting and tracking volunteers, the continual need for networking and partnering with other organizations, the communication required for quality relationships, and the tediousness of organizing forms and paperwork are all just a part of what is learned as a Service-Learning Scholar.

The rest of the learning comes in careful mentoring by the two program directors; guiding us through reflection, leading us through problem solving, steering us toward effective project planning, and escorting us through the fear of classroom presentations or organizational contacts. This mentoring relationship gives great responsibility and trust to the scholar, yet also nurtures in a way that serves as a transition from being a college student to being in the workforce.

Personal Service-Learning Reflections

Participating in service-learning has shaped my worldview and specifically, my view of service in ways that I have found to be not only unique but also valuable postcollege. I have a sensitivity to service—to the pitfalls of patronizing service, to the abuse of exploiting recipients of service, to the value of respect and humility in service—that challenges my contemporaries and older generations alike. My experiences and sensitivities have proved to be valuable to my work in directing programs for a community-based nonprofit organization. I have continually been called to stand up for a more thoughtful form of service or speak out against an improper or misplaced idea of service.

Not surprisingly, service-learning has impacted my decision making, particularly involving career choices. While it is not likely that I will remain in one job for my entire adult life, I know for certain that my work will always in some way be serving people. I have been trained to never stop seeking to learn from my service; and never to stop seeking creative ways to view service, or to create it in my life wherever I may be. For me, it is about loving people. Whether they are kids or young mothers or mentally disabled or homeless or elderly, I want to love people with all that is in me. With my mind, yes, but also with my ears and arms and hands and feet.

Attending a college with an ethos of service shaped me and continues to shape me in ways I will forever be discovering. Intellectualism rules in college. There is a necessary focus on training the mind. With noses in books and fingers on keyboards, students are led to believe that a sharp and full mind is the ticket to a good life. A college that places emphasis on service takes that training of the mind and synthesizes it with training of the heart. Not emotionalism devoid of reason, but rather thoughtful, meaningful, useful compassion to the community it exists within. This intersection of mind and heart is what I found in my service-learning experiences. Never did I find service experiences to mock my intellectual pursuits, rather they complemented my study with a good dose of reality, with a good dose of heart. It is a worthy goal of any college to produce graduates who can not only think well but also love well.

Chapter 9

FROM TOLERANCE TO M.I.N.D. RENEWAL: SERVICE-LEARNING AS AN EXPERIENTIAL BASIS FOR THINKING ABOUT DIVERSITY

Michelle R. Loyd-Paige

THE MISSION STATEMENT of the Department of Sociology, Social Work, and Criminal Justice at Calvin College reads that it exists "to prepare students to function effectively in the restoration of social and cultural relationships from a Reformed, Christian perspective." This mission declaration in conjunction with the accrediting guidelines of the National Council of Social Work that demands a program component focused upon oppressed and vulnerable populations, led to the development of a required three-hour course called Diversity and Inequality in North American Society.

The course, since its inception in 1993, has undergone several revisions. The path of these revisions could be described as "from tolerance to mind renewal." While the content and the learning objectives of the course have essentially stayed the same, two factors have led to a welcomed transformation of the course by both students and the instructor. The introduction of an academically based service-learning option and the integration of a biblically based theme of reconciliation have enabled students to move from a state of tolerance of diversity to one of engagement; and from a sense of hopelessness in the face of staggering social inequities to feelings of empowerment. This chapter examines how students who participated in academically based service-learning placements have practiced MIND renewal and experienced empowering relationships while considering the conceptual content of a diversity course in their reflective papers.

This chapter begins with a description of academically based service-learning. Next, a description of the diversity course is provided as context for

125

the student statements that relate MIND renewal with the empowerment of relationships. Afterward, follows an examination of the concept of reconciliation with attention to the principles of MIND renewal and relationship empowerment. Subsequently, the focus of the chapter moves from description to student voices. In this section, excerpts from student reflection papers are provided to illustrate the concepts of MIND renewal and relationship empowerment. Finally, this chapter concludes with a brief statement of the movement from tolerance to a reconciliation mind-set.

Academically Based Service-Learning

Service-learning at its best is reciprocal in nature. It links opportunities to address community issues with equally sound educational experiences for students. It aims at fostering critical thinking and problem solving, civic and community responsibility, and making a contribution to the common good. The goals for service-learning at Calvin College are fourfold: to learn to relate to others as bearers of God's image—even the poor, the sick, and the old; to bridge social and economic barriers between people; to understand the broader context and causes of the needs that exist; and to discover and develop a personal vision and capacity for service in a broken world.

The goals of service-learning at Calvin College make it a natural for a course that surveys the nature and consequences of diversity and inequality. However, service-learning without being academically based tends only to increase awareness of societal ills and social differences. Increased awareness is foundational for tolerance of differences, but awareness alone does not demand social action or self-examination. Awareness alone allows a person to blame the victim for their social distress without a critique of the victim's relationship to the environment, social institutions, cultural patterns, or prevailing social forces. Awareness alone also allows a student, or any other person, to neglect examining his or her own role both in the continuation of social distress and in initiating change. In the context of a class on social diversity and reconciliation, the maximum benefit of a service-learning placement is experienced through exposure to cultural differences *and* concrete connections to the course content *and* self-examination.

Academically based service-learning may be simply defined as service performed within the context of a course in the curriculum. Academically based service-learning differs from volunteering in that service activities are related to and integrated with the conceptual content of a college course. Academically based service-learning is an exemplar of critical pedagogy. Critical pedagogy is the art of teaching for transformation, not just for the accumulation of knowledge. Critical pedagogy views the purpose of education as a catalyst to bring about equality and justice in a world of structured inequality. Critical pedagogy, as with service-learning, involves students as active participants in the learning process (Derman-Sparks, 1998).

Course Background

The course description from the syllabus of the Diversity and Inequality in North American Society course taught at Calvin College each semester describes the course as: An analysis of the social structure of diversity and the social processes of inequality in contemporary North American Society. The major objectives of the course are to study the interrelationships of gender, race, and class and to develop an understanding of current social conditions through inclusive analysis of gender, race/ethnic, and class relations. Emphasis is placed on patterns and consequences of discrimination and oppression.

The course begins with a review of the concept of diversity and its relationship to inequality and stratification. From there the focus of study turns toward a biblical understanding of the promise and challenge of reconciliation. Four spheres of human diversity and inequality are covered to increase a student's knowledge of the nature and positive value of diversity, the forms and mechanisms of oppression and discrimination, and the impact of social policies on the lives of oppressed and marginalized populations of North America. These four spheres include disabilities, gender, economic stratification, and race/ethnicity.

The students who take the diversity and inequality course are predominately white and middle-class. Approximately 60 percent of the students are sophomores who aspire to be social workers. On average, nearly half have Dutch origins and/or Christian Reformed religious backgrounds; however approximately 80 percent affirm some expression of the Christian faith. The religious and ethnic background of the students is significant because it tends to be associated with distancing behaviors and the "color-blind syndrome." Distancing and the maintenance of a color-blind stance are associated with tolerance of diversity, but hinder movement toward wanting to do something about the social distresses related to diversity.

Distancing behaviors, as described by Edler and Irons (1998), are those conscious or unconscious attitudes and positioning that tend to remove whites (or any other dominant group) from accountability, guilt, or the discomfort associated with discussions of racism or other social inequities. Whites act out distancing behaviors in several different ways. One way is to emphasize the changes that have occurred in race relations and to downplay the existence or any negative consequences of racial inequality. This kind of emphasis tends to slow down or prevent whites from acknowledging and moving on to what still needs to be done to bring about racial parity. Another distancing behavior involves whites' labeling one another as racist. Labeling an individual or group as racist tends to ignore the institutional influences of social distresses. One final illustration of distancing behavior is called being the expert. Being an expert occurs when whites deceive themselves into thinking that they are experts on race relations because they have a "friend who is black" or they have lived in a multiracial community. This form of distancing usually manifests itself in this diversity class by sayings such as "I went on a mission trip last spring to help the poor in Arkansas, and those poor people . . ." or "A black family lived in my neighborhood and I think blacks are. . . ." In and of themselves these experiences are fine, but, they often accompany an attitude of, "I know how those people are, there is nothing else for me to learn about them."

The color-blind syndrome is perhaps more prevalent than the distancing behavior; if not, it is definitely more manifest. It shows up every first week of a new semester and usually takes a few weeks to dissipate. The color-blind syndrome demonstrates itself whenever students say, "I do not see color, I only see people." This usually happens because students often confuse being color conscious with being a racist. In the minds of many students, to see the color of a person is to be prejudiced. Students with color-blind syndrome generally see themselves as being sensitive, and in fact many would describe themselves as trying not to be offensive. The reality is, however, that when we dismiss the social significance of race in our society, we are actually clouding our understanding of the lives of people who are racially different from ourselves.

The early versions of class often ended with student "despair." The course had accomplished the knowledge goals of the course all too well. The reality of the depth of the brokenness of our nation's communities left the students feeling paralyzed and doubting their own abilities to make a difference . . . like a pebble thrown in the ocean. Students felt as if there was no hope of a remedy for the prevalent inequalities and injustices, usually more prevalent than they realized—that we really could not "all just get along."

Actually, mere awareness of problems—inequalities, exploitations, the suffering of others—is not supposed to inspire hope. It is supposed to create outrage and a desire to change things. Unfortunately, where awareness of problems is combined with feelings of powerlessness, the result is often despair (Schwalbe 1998, 206).

In the beginning, pedagogically the class was lecture based, had no experiential piece, and asked questions but provided few answers. This strategy was intended to support critical thinking, but it had the latent effect of leaving the students without a context for viewing themselves as agents of change. To remedy this, a theme of biblical reconciliation was added in conjunction with an optional service-learning component.

The biblical theme of reconciliation, described in Curtiss DeYoung's book *Reconciliation: Our Greatest Challenge—Our Only Hope* (1997), a required text for the course, provided a theoretical understanding of the process of reconciliation. Being able to see that hope was possible in the face of challenges associated with diversity and inequality helped to alleviate the sense to despair that usually accompanied the end of a semester. It was the service-learning experiences that allowed students to experience the reconciliation process they were reading about.

The addition of the service-learning component can be described as a pedagogical tool that empowers students to explore multicultural relationships and allows students to see firsthand both the simplicity of reconciliation (it is centered in relationships) and the complexity of reconciliation (it is a process that demands time and is not always rewarding). Service-learning requires students to ask questions about themselves, about why they view the world as they do, and about how they will negotiate multicultural relationships.

Once we ask those questions, we need tools to help make sense of where it leads and to imagine how we might go from there to something better. We cannot help but be a part of the problem; practicing sociology is a way to also be a part of the solution. This not only helps the world, but makes it easier to live in the world, especially given how crazy a place it can seem. It helps to be able to see how one thing is connected to another, and, in that, how to find ways to make some small difference. We cannot change the world all by ourselves, but we can make informed decisions about how to participate in it and how that help can turn the world toward something better—even if its just in our neighborhoods and in our families or in where we work (Johnson 1997, 2).

Reconciliation

Reconciliation is a word we are hearing more and more. We hear it in news reports of peace negotiations in the Middle East. We hear it in reference to religious movements such as the Promise Keepers. We even hear of it on TV talk shows in reference to the settling of long-standing family disputes. But, what does the word actually mean?

The word "reconciliation or reconcile . . . in the classical Greek denotes a change from a state of enmity to one of friendship, the healing of a quarrel . . . a radical change occurs in which intimate and personal relationships are renewed" (DeYoung, 1997, 44). Using the term *reconciliation* acknowledges that there are preexisting barriers to relationships. So, reconciliation signals the reconnecting of those who have parted. Silas Johnson, in his book, *From One Light Many Colors*, further describes reconciliation as the process of comparing differences, making adjustments, bringing differences into balance, and either making things right or justifying the differences—justifying in this sense refers to restitution or making up for the differences.

Reconciliation is multifaceted. It involves making adjustments within us and with other people. It also involves making adjustments to heal broken relationships. Making adjustments within ourselves begins with honest self-examination and continues as our understanding of who we really are and what has shaped us increases through our contact with others. Making adjustments with other people involves becoming aware of other people and becoming skilled in the ability to listen to and interact with people who are different from us. Making adjustments to heal broken relationships requires changed thinking, changed feelings, changed purpose, and changed will.

Reconciliation requires a reconciliation mind-set and the empowering of relationships.

A reconciliation mind-set is the foundation for MIND renewal based on motivation, internalization, normalization, and determination.

- **Motivation** is our reason for involvement. Our motivation must change from being cultural tourists (simple awareness, no involvement) to a desire to grow from interactions and see a difference being made in the lives of others.
- **Internalization** is taking personal responsibility for moving from a "them and me" to an "us" state of mind. It requires learning the facts about others.
- **Normalization** is releasing one's self and others from the past and being intentional about relationships and justice.
- **Determination** is becoming committed to the process and being hopeful for change.

MIND renewal is the hope of reconciliation, a formula of self and community examination, and a process of becoming change agents. Essentially it involves renewing or changing the way we think about our involvement with others, especially people who are different from ourselves.

The empowering process has four principles:

1. It is a process, which means that it occurs between equals who acknowledge that they need each other.
2. It sets people free, which means becoming less influenced by stereotypes and taking sides on behalf of the weak and vulnerable.
3. It includes all voices and viewpoints, which means learning to listen to people from outside our experience describe their experiences.
4. It involves taking the risk of trusting, which means trusting others and trusting that your purpose and talents will make a difference.

The empowering process is not the whole of the reconciliation process, but it is a critical element because it sets the guidelines for relationships that will have a lasting impact. Guidelines for multicultural relationships empower all participants. It empowers us to look at how we participate in social life and to see ways to take some small share of responsibility for the consequences that social life produces. It gives us a way to be not simply a part of the problem but also a part of the solution (Johnson 1997, 190).

Student Voices

> As a volunteer and student I was able to use this service-learning experience to strengthen my faith and broaden my knowledge on looking for inequality and correcting it with reconciliation. This experience has been an incredibly challenging one. I would recommend the Recuperation Center to anyone looking for a challenging experience of diversity with room for reconciliation.

The service-learning experiences that the students were involved in required that they form relationships with people—people who were unlike themselves in many ways but similar in some important areas. Both were in positions to help one another, both were vulnerable, and were both looking for solutions. Students were placed at Degagě—a drop-in center for the homeless, Park School—a school for pregnant and parenting teens, Ramoth House—a residential shelter for battered women and their children, Franklin Schools—offering an after-school tutorial program for Spanish-speaking children, and Madison Youth—a church run after-school program.

Through these experiences, students went from basic knowledge of human behavior (through class readings, lectures, and personal experiences); to knowledge and skill in agency policy and services; to greater self-awareness, including insights into their own identities and an understanding of how those identities may influence their place in life; to an understanding of the social reality of minority (majority) status upon the lives of others; to an understanding of the social factors that affect the pace of reconciliation.

Service-Learning as Empowerment

Comments on empowerment occurring between equals who acknowledge that they need each other:

A female student, reflecting on the goal of Degagě, wrote: The other essential strategy of reconciliation present at Degagě is centering reconciliation in relationships. The goal of Degagě is to build relationships and foster community. Not only is it based on relationships, but also it is based on the premise that everyone is made in the image of God, and therefore everyone is deserving of respect and dignity. The relationships that are formed between volunteers and patrons of Degagě are based on equality and not a hierarchy of power.

Another female, involved at Degagě, wrote: There is a lot to learn from going and volunteering at Degagě. I've learned that poverty could happen to any of us, so why should we act any better than the guests who come to Degagě? In all I've learned a lot about myself, and I feel bad that although I go to serve the guests, they're the ones really "feeding" me.

Comments on empowerment as setting people free:

Writing about her experience at Park School, a female comments: Knowing this, I feel rather ashamed at the stigmas the world puts on single, black teenage mothers. I have even felt that many of them fit the stereotype of being unreliable and unwilling to work hard. However, I realized while helping the student who wrote the paper that many of these young mothers are willing to work hard, they want to be successful in life, and they desire to be a good parent. They are not taking the easy way out, but they are fighting the injustices and prejudices of society.

Reflecting on a conversation she had had with a resident of Ramoth House, a student wrote: One woman told me the moment she walked in the door of one supposedly Christian agency that she felt like she had already been characterized as just another "poor-single-ghettofied-crackhead-mom who couldn't take care of her kids and was looking for a handout." What she was, in fact, was a woman who, for the first time in her life, made a courageous commitment to independence and decided out of love for her children to leave a man who had abused her for years.

Another female wrote: For some of them, Park School is the only environment in their lives where they feel respect and self-worth. I can only imagine how disheartening it must be to feel acceptance and understanding when they are at school, only to go back to the prejudices of the world once they leave the building.

Comments on the inclusion of all viewpoints and voices:

A white student reflecting about her encounter with black teens at Park School, wrote: They could not believe that I had never had pig's feet or had tried chitlins. We ended up talking back and forth about family traditions, and it was interesting to find out new things about each other.

A female, journaling about the children she met at Ramoth House, wrote: One of the things that struck me was the presence of children at the shelter. I have often taken for granted the safe and secure environment that I called home. These children have had no stable and safe place to call home. I will never forget the little boy who told me out of the blue one day that he never wanted to go home ever again. He told me that he got stomach aches just thinking about having to go there and having to "hide again."

Another female, working at Ramoth House, wrote: When you have it good all your life, it is hard to imagine the reality of these children's lives. It seems more like something you hear on television, not something that someone you care about is facing. I know that I would like to deny that crime, drugs, gangs, poverty, and broken homes that the youth face is as bad as it seems, but being a criminal justice major, I know that it is out there and is even worse than I would like to imagine.

A female, concerning her experiences at Degagě, wrote: My experience at Degagě has been very enlightening and an eye opener. I learned that all people no matter what they look like on the outside cannot be put into one group. Time needs to be taken to get to know each individual and to listen to each person's story. By informing ourselves of another's life we are moving in the right direction toward reconciliation.

Comments on taking the risk of trusting:

A female student, reflecting on a conversation she had at Degagě, wrote: He joked with me and asked if my mother hadn't warned me to stay away from strange men like him! She has of course, but my time conversing with Jeff-Kathy was quite enjoyable, and it was good for me to get to know a transvestite, even to such a tiny extent. I think he was glad that someone was listening to him, but it was hard to see how lonely he was. He made a grand exit, and I may never see him again, but he taught me that it does not hurt to accept the beautiful person God created no matter how they differ from you.

A female student, working with children at Madison Youth, wrote: I found this experience to be very good for me. At first it was very difficult because I did not know how to relate to these youth. The reason I say that is because when I was in junior high, I was very well behaved and innocent (the opposite of the majority of my talent team kids). I also had a hard time building trust with the girls in my talent team, so I was frustrated. I prayed a lot that God would help me. Finally, I realized, that I was trying too hard.

A female student, remembering a special friend she had made at Park School, wrote: Michelle has become a close friend of mine. From the moment I began talking to her I liked her and we "clicked" almost immediately. We can talk freely together and we share many common likes and dislikes. Michelle and I also have differences. She is of Latin origin, from a lower-income family and is a mother at sixteen. A year ago I may not have chosen a friend like Michelle at first glance. I grew up within a peer group that was very similar to me in all areas: race, social class, religion, and background. It is not that I was opposed to being with people who were different, it was just that it was unfamiliar to me. Since becoming Michelle's friend and tutor at Park School, my eyes have been significantly opened because of my positive experiences there.

Service-Learning as MIND Renewal

Comments on motivation:

A student, working at a drop-in center for the homeless, wrote: While working at Degagé, Christ has really opened my eyes to the needs of our society as well as to the need to put faces on the issues that are going on in our community. I have been encouraged to make a difference in our society. It is so hard to come away from this course, from discussions, even from newscasts, and have a hope that change can be made and reconciliation be brought to fruition. But by my experience at Degagĕ, I have learned that God does not ask for your ability but only your availability. I have learned that if there are willing hearts, barriers can be broken down, and we can get to know one another as brothers and sisters in Christ.

A female student, recalling what she had learned about reconcilation at Park School, wrote: Being open to a new experience and to learning more about others and myself also helped me to come away feeling more enriched. What I know I enjoyed most of all though was breaking down some walls and developing relationships with new people and having created what will be lasting memories for me.

Comments on internalization:

A male student, reporting on a conversation with a teacher at a tutorial program, wrote: After spending time in Mrs. V's class I learned that I have a responsibility to contribute to the lives of children in society, through financial aid or by giving of my time. I asked Mrs. V what I could do as a white male in a school that reaches out for the most part to minority children. She said that I can and should remain involved in learning more about the plight of these children and invest in their lives. As the one with power, I must be the one who gives it up. No one will take it from me; I must humbly give it up. I hope I will be able to be a better agent of reconciliation as a result of my participation in this experience and that I will continue to learn about others.

A student, thinking about her experiences at Park School, wrote: Overall this was a great experience for me to be involved in because I got to witness reconciliation at work outside of the textbook. It also gave me insight into dividing walls, my insecurities, my weaknesses, my strengths, and myself. I think what helped make this a positive experience for me was the girls' willingness to trust me and to let me get to know them.

Comments on normalization:

A student who worked at Degagě wrote: Despite experiencing the hostility embedded in "classism" while I volunteered at Degagě, I left the experience feeling hopeful. Each human interaction made my work feel less like a service to others, and more like an experience that taught and benefited me. I realized that this is what true reconciliation is: interacting with those of a different group on a mutual level, all people involved benefiting from it and all walking away from the interaction with a deeper peace and hope in the unity of all peoples. This experience convinced me that I need to make volunteering a part of my weekly life.

Another female student at Degagě also wrote about how her view of the homeless changed: It was easy in the beginning to think that the overwhelming majority of the people were homeless; I was wrong. Most of the people I have gotten to know do have a permanent place to stay and many have decent paying jobs. Assuming that all the people could be lumped together was wrong on my part and was a barrier to reconciliation.

Yet another student wrote of her Degagě experience: The mutuality of doing the same work puts volunteers (students) and patrons (the homeless) on the same level—they are both reaching hands out to help each other, as opposed to volunteers reaching a hand down to pull up people who can do nothing for themselves. One of the latent functions of Degagě is that the volunteers are no longer isolated. They (the volunteers) are in the Heartside area playing games with Heartside residents and hearing and sharing stories.

Comments on determination:

A student, working with marginalized people through a program to assist the homeless and other low-income people wrote: The Other Way Ministries is making a difference though. I am making a difference as well. It does not always seem like it, and often it has been exhausting, but when M's face lights up and I get a big hug when I walk in the door, I know everything I have done has been worth it because of that one thing. That is all it takes to know that you have made a difference. It does not take moving a mountain, it may just mean you put a dent in it.

A female, reflecting on her relationship with the students at Park School, wrote: I am getting kind of sad knowing that my time spent here is almost done. I know that I could come back next year if I wanted to, but now I am getting so comfortable with many of the girls it is going to be hard to say goodbye. I have begun to really look forward to coming every week, and when this class is over I am going to keep coming until their school (Park School) is out.

A student at Degagĕ wrote about a rekindled passion: My eyes have also been opened even more to the problems that those who are impoverished or who fell on hard times are facing, and I feel much more passionately about taking action.

A female student at Ramoth House wrote: I will continue to help out at Ramoth House and hope someday to assist with a program that works to empower women who have experienced domestic violence.

Conclusions: From Tolerance to MIND Renewal

An increase in social responsibility is one of the most consistent findings of service-learning. Students are more likely to see themselves as connected to their community, to endorse systemic approaches to social problems, to believe that communities can solve their problems, and to have greater racial tolerance when involved in service-learning (Giles and Eyler, 1998, 66). Sociology classes, such as Diversity and Inequality in North American Society, can be enriched by the inclusion of academically based service-learning components. One of its greatest benefits is that students get to experience cultural differences and concrete connections along with course content. As mentioned earlier in this chapter, one of the greatest challenges of these types of courses is moving students from a tourist mind-set to one of engagement. Part of such a move involves overcoming the distancing behaviors of students.

The first step to overcoming distancing behavior is to realize that one is in social relationships with other people—even people that are not well known. The second is to realize that many of these social relationships are constructed by the social norms of our times and have more to do with social institutions than personal knowledge. The third is to become involved in empowering relationships. Empowering relationships are made possible through making adjustments within one's self; through making adjustments in our view of relationships with others—especially with people who are unlike ourselves; and through resolving to heal broken relationships. However, having a broadened knowledge base about diversity issues and an understanding of the need for empowering relationships without corresponding action leads to frustration, and like faith without works, is dead and void of any lasting value. Academically based service-learning is a valuable tool for connecting knowledge and experience with empowering relationships. It is a tool with the potential of not only empowering students to see themselves as doing-something about the world in which they live but also of empowering the people they work with in the community to see themselves as teachers and as people with something valuable to contribute to the world in which they live. Academically based service-learning is a good pedagogical tool. Good pedagogical tools empower students to see beyond themselves and impact their worlds in ways they may have never before imagined.

Service-learning empowers us to look at how we participate in social life and to see ways to take some small share of responsibility for the consequences that social life produces. It gives us a way to be not simply a part of the problem, but also a part of the solution (Johnson 1997, 190).

This chapter was descriptive and anecdotal. It showed how a course on diversity and inequality went from a focus on the toleration of diversity to that which advocated MIND renewal. The MIND renewal the students experienced was made possible by the empowering relationships developed by the students with the participants in their service-learning placements. However, it was not just the relationships situated in these service-learning placements that brought about the desired understanding; it was the academic connection between the course work and the service placement. Service-learning is a valuable teaching tool, but more work is needed to study its effectiveness, more teachers need to be willing not only to incorporate service-learning but to take a critical look at how service-learning impacts the lives of their students and their disciplines.

References

Derman-Sparks, Louise. 1998. Educating for equality: Forging a shared vision. In *Beyond heroes and holidays,* edited by Lee, Menkart, and Okazawa-Rey, 2-6. Washington. D.C.: McArdle Printing, 1998. Network of Educators on the Americas.

DeYoung, Curtiss Paul. 1997. *Reconciliation: Our greatest challenge—our only hope.* Valley Forge: Judgson Press.

Edler, James and Bruce Irons. 1998. Distancing behaviors often used by white people. In *Beyond heroes and holidays*, edited by Lee, Menkart, and Okazawa-Rey, 114. Washington D.C.: McArdle Printing, 1998.

Giles, Jr., Dwight E. and Janet Eyler. 1998. A service-learning research agenda for the next five years, *New Directions for Teaching and Learning* 73:65-72.

Johnson, Allan G. 1997. *The forest and the trees: Sociology as life plus promise.* Philadelphia: Temple University Press.

Johnson, Silas. 1996. *From on light, many colors.* Tulsa, Okla.: Harrison House Inc.

Schwalbe, Michael. 1998. *The sociologically examined: Pieces of the conversation.* Mountain View: Mayfield Publishing.

Chapter 10

POWERFUL PARADIGMS AND COMMUNITY CONTEXTS: SERVICE-LEARNING IN TEACHER-EDUCATION PROGRAMS

Susan Schneider Hasseler

I TEACH AN INTRODUCTORY CLASS for freshman and sophomores that they take early in their college experience. The class includes a mandatory service-learning experience in an educational setting. Because one of the purposes of the class is to introduce students to multicultural perspectives on education, the prospective teachers are encouraged to work in school settings in which the majority of the students are from ethnic backgrounds other than their own. Due to the composition of our student body and the many opportunities to assist in schools in our local core-city area, most of the students are engaged in service-learning in schools that are located in low-income neighborhoods and that have large ethnic-minority populations.

For the most part, my students are sincere, conscientious, and well-intentioned. Most come from homes in which schooling was held in relatively high esteem and was viewed as a natural route to success. Most of their parents have the resources to support their learning in and out of school. Few of my students have suffered physical deprivation or material need. Many have spent the majority of their lives interacting with people highly similar to them. Most of them have engaged in some kind of community service through their church or school with very little support in understanding the communities in which they served and very little reflection on the service experience. They want to be effective teachers. They want to have an impact on their students. They want to live as committed Christians. They are usually completely unprepared for and overwhelmed by the complexities of the urban-school environments in which they serve.

141

I also work with some of these same students in the last semester of the teacher-education program. They are engaged in a full-time, semester-long student teaching experience in a K-8 school setting. The students with whom I work have chosen to student teach in ethnically diverse, urban-school settings. They have completed the required courses in our liberal arts core curriculum, subject matter majors and minors, and multiple professional classes. They have many tools now that will assist them in becoming effective teachers. They still want to have an impact on their students, they still want to live as committed Christians, and they are still unprepared for and overwhelmed by the complexities of the urban-school environments in which they serve.

How do we assist students in moving from bewildered spectators and frustrated participants to teachers who have the commitment and skills needed to understand and change the societal structures that so powerfully impact schools and children? How can we better prepare our students to bring healing to a broken world? What are the particular challenges we face in helping students develop these commitments and skills?

Powerful Perceptions

Prospective teachers come to teacher-education programs with many strongly held beliefs about teaching and learning based primarily on their prior experiences as students in K-12 classrooms. Their role as student often leads them to view education as an individual enterprise with little understanding of the complex contexts that impact teaching and learning in schools. In addition, the heavy preponderance of white, middle-class young people in teacher-education programs means that students have limited experience with and understanding of issues surrounding poverty and oppression in North America. These circumstances make it difficult for students to grasp the complexities of most urban-school settings and can cause them to make conclusions about students and parents that are misguided and hurtful. As Ivan Illich so eloquently argues in his article, "To Hell with Good Intentions" (1968), people who come to "help those in need" have the potential to do more harm than good when they are ill prepared for the task.

The students with whom I work closely match the description of white teacher-education students offered by Christine Sleeter (1999) and other multicultural educators. My students believe that the rules of society apply in the same way to everyone; and while individual progress might be hindered by prejudices and stereotypes as well as meager economic resources, these obstacles can be overcome by individual hard work. Many of the students in my institution come from second or third generation western European immigrant families who worked their way up in the North American economic system. With little understanding of the realities of North American history and economic and political systems, they try to apply the experience of Euro-Americans to all ethnic and social groups. These perspectives shape the assumptions they make about the motivation, commitment, and resources of the students and families with whom they work. Unfortunately, they often draw conclusions that focus on individual or family deficits.

None of this is surprising, given the experiences of my students prior to coming to college and the general emphasis of their college courses. The content of most secondary and college-level courses is shaped by a combination of American individualism and the western European canon (Fitzgerald and Lauter 1995). Even teacher-education programs tend to focus much more heavily on understanding individual development, cognition, disciplinary content, and pedagogy than on community, context, and societal structures. It is no wonder that perceptions about complex urban settings change little over the course of a teacher-education program. Unfortunately, this leaves the student teachers with negative perspectives about families and expectations for children that can be very destructive to the children with whom they will be working in the future. In addition, they are provided few resources to develop the commitment and skills needed to understand and change the societal structures that so powerfully impact schools.

Challenging the Assumptions

The literature on teacher learning makes it clear that changing tacit beliefs such as those described above is extremely difficult. Assumptions need to be made visible and examined in a way that challenges the learner to consider them carefully. A combination of creating disequilibrium and providing credible alternative perspectives is needed to initiate significant cognitive change. Learning within an authentic setting can provide the kinds of experiences needed to create disequilibrium and introduce alternative perspectives (Brown, Collins, and Diguid 1989). Simply having experiences in a school or community agency is not enough, however. Students in most teacher-education programs have multiple classroom experiences before they graduate, but many of their original beliefs about teaching and learning remain unchanged at the end of the experience. New information, abstract conceptualization, reflective observation, and active experimentation with new ideas need to be combined with experiences to assist teachers in learning alternative perspectives and practices (Schon 1983; Anderson and Erickson 1997). Well-constructed service-learning experiences have the potential to provide these instructional elements.

Service-learning is generally defined as a pedagogical strategy that requires students to meet authentic, meaningful community needs while engaging in study and reflection that will help them understand and learn from the experience (Anderson and Erickson 1997; LeSourd 1997). The combination of engagement in a community, academic study, and reflection seem to provide the necessary elements to challenge prospective teachers' beliefs and assumptions in an effective way. Wade and Anderson (1996) suggest that community-based service-learning moved their student teachers from a view of learning as an individualistic, academic activity to a view of learning as a process that involves the intellect, emotions, body, and context. The student teachers began to see the community as a powerful learning tool and developed a greater awareness of the impact that life outside of school had on children. They also developed a greater sense of self-efficacy regarding their ability to solve societal problems through taking action. Battisoni (1997) reports that service-learning challenged his students to think more critically and creatively about public issues. He also noted that the experiences helped his students overcome feelings of hopelessness and powerlessness by showing them a collaborative model of problem solving. It is evident that these experiences can accomplish many important goals in the teacher-education process. However, certain elements must be included in these service-learning experiences to help students understand the complexities of schooling in our society and become agents of transformation and reconciliation.

Constructing Powerful Service-Learning Experiences

When constructing service-learning experiences for teacher-education students, the knowledge bases and skills needed to understand school contexts, the structure of the service-learning setting and opportunities for reflection and reconceptualization, all need to be considered. A careful combination of these three elements has the potential to make prospective teachers' assumptions and beliefs explicit and to challenge the assumptions that get in the way of the equitable treatment of all children.

Essential Knowledge Bases

Effective service-learning experiences must include adequate opportunities for prospective teachers to gain a deeper understanding of the complex contexts of schools. The students need to have a clear understanding of the economic, political, and social structures in North America that affect schooling and individuals. They need to understand the particular impact of these structures on people of color and the poor. They also need to understand the history of cultural and racial oppression and the ways in which this history shapes current assumptions and decisions about children and schooling. They need to learn about the cultural backgrounds of the students with whom they are working and the ways in which these children and families view schools and learning. The college students also need an opportunity to examine their own beliefs about culture, poverty, and learning. They need to understand how their personal perceptions have been shaped by their own cultural background and by history. They need to understand how their responses to students can be shaped by a sense of cultural superiority and how these responses can impact their teaching. The concepts of "oneness" and "color-blindness" needs to be explored in the context of North American history and societal structures. Prospective teachers also need to understand the limitations and fallacies of an individualistic view of achievement and success both in relation to their own experiences and to those of others. When prospective teachers have a deeper understanding of the many factors surrounding school success and the impact of their assumptions on the students they teach, they can begin to relate to students and their families in more appropriate and equitable ways.

Students must also develop the skills needed to assess resources and build on cultural strengths. They need to understand the variety of support systems available to families and individuals that may look very different from their own support systems. They need to learn how to identify resources and assets of individuals and communities. They need to learn culturally appropriate communication and interaction skills. They need to learn the appropriate roles that people from dominant cultures should play when working to overcome problems associated with schools and achievement. They also need to become familiar with culturally responsive teaching strategies and materials. Gaining this knowledge and learning these skills while directly involved in a community-based project is an especially powerful approach, but the knowledge-and-skills component must be carefully structured. This knowledge will not come naturally through interactions in school and agency settings.

The Setting

The design of the setting in which service-learning occurs is a key component of the learning process as well. It is essential that service-learning experiences for novice teachers take place in settings in which strengths and resources are as evident as needs in order to avoid the reinforcement of deficit models of children and adults. Schools and agencies in which community resourcefulness is recognized and celebrated need to be located and supported. It is also important that the students have the kinds of interactions with children and adults in the community that allow a better understanding of the people's lives outside of school. Novice teachers need to understand that all of the children and adults with whom they work have experiences, traditions, and resources that can support their learning and contribute to a rich learning environment in the school. In addition, students need to be placed in settings in which they are working toward solving problems that have been defined collaboratively with community members. Involving community members in designing the service-learning experience ensures this kind of ownership and authenticity (Carver 1997). There also must be ample time in the experience for interactions and relationship building as well as action (Anderson and Erickson 1997; LeSourd 1997).

Opportunities for Reflection and Reconceptualization

Prospective teachers will need assistance in making connections between the new knowledge they have gained and the realities of the contexts in which they are working. Systemic and historic experiences that individuals have are not easily observed in many schools and agency settings and need to be made explicit for students. Resources and strengths may be subtle and easy to overlook. Questioning, discussion, and reflective writing are all effective tools for bringing beliefs and assumptions to the surface so that they can be examined and evaluated. Dialogue journals, electronic discussion groups, and case studies can also be effective instructional strategies to use in promoting reflection on experiences. Opportunities to reflect and reconceptualize need to be an integral part of the service-learning experience.

Alternative Models

This description of content, instructional strategies, and service-learning settings is far from reality in most teacher-education programs. Unfortunately, while most programs have a course or two focused on multicultural education, these courses seldom include the depth of content relating to school contexts as described above. In addition, very few school-based service-learning opportunities used in teacher-education programs meet the criteria described above. While schools and agencies may attempt to integrate some multicultural material into their curriculum, there is often little real attempt to ascertain and understand the experiences, language patterns, and traditions that the students are bringing to the learning process. Students are described in terms of needs and deficits and the activities that the college students and K-12 students engage in focus on traditional academic remediation. There is little opportunity to get to know the students' home contexts or their cultural heritage. A few program organizers may live in the community, but more often than not they are people from outside of the community. Little effort is made to include community members in identifying needs or action strategies. The novice teachers may have their beliefs challenged by the achievement of an individual child, but their beliefs about the people in the community as a whole tend to remain the same. Thus, relying on traditional teacher-education curricula and school structures is not enough. Alternative collaborative approaches need to be designed.

Recently, I have been working with colleagues and local community members to restructure our service-learning experiences for students in the teacher-education program to better meet the criteria described above. This is not an easy task. Curriculum change within a college setting is a long and arduous process. Colleges and K-12 schools are not used to collaborating closely with community members or with each other. Collaboration demands time and resources from people who have limited amounts of both. However, I think we have begun to develop some promising models that have the potential to better prepare our prospective teachers to work effectively in complex contexts.

Building on College Initiatives

It is obvious that the knowledge bases and skills described above cannot be addressed in one course or experience. Thus, one of our goals has been to integrate these perspectives into multiple courses and experiences. We also recognized that we cannot accomplish these goals solely in our education department. We discovered a valuable set of resources across the college that can support our efforts if we take the time to access them. Thus, one of our first efforts was to look for potential opportunities for collaboration and support.

Curriculum Revision

Our college recently engaged in an extensive general core-curriculum revision. This initiative gave the Education Department multiple opportunities to design and reshape classes to include the knowledge bases and skills described above. Because this initiative emphasized interdepartmental collaboration, the education and sociology departments jointly designed a general core course focusing on societal structures and schooling. This course includes much of the content relating to school contexts described earlier. It also includes a community-based action-research project so that students will be actively engaged in service and learning. The new core curriculum also includes a cross-cultural engagement requirement that is to be integrated into majors and professional programs. Resources are available from the college to assist departments in implementing this requirement. The Education Department is using these resources to help us integrate culturally responsive perspectives into educational psychology and curriculum and instruction courses. In addition, the new core curriculum requires all students to take an integrative seminar in their senior year. The Education Department integrative seminar includes a strong component focusing on school contexts and justice issues. These college-level initiatives provided the opportunity and resources for us to shape our curriculum so that we can engage students in exploring the concepts and learning the skills they need to function effectively in urban-school settings.

Community Partnerships

Our college also has the Service-Learning Center that assists departments and individual instructors in developing relationships with schools and community agencies. In addition, our administration has shown their commitment to developing community partnerships by assigning a top-level administrator to this task. We have found that there are multiple outside funding sources that are interested in supporting partnerships among schools, community agencies, and colleges. Members of the Education Department are working with the Service-Learning Center on multiple projects that involve the development of more collaborative service-learning models. Two of those projects are described here:

1. The Computer Kids Program is a collaborative effort involving the college, a local urban elementary school, and a community church. Teacher-education students and senior citizens from the church are paired with elementary students to work on computer-based reading and writing tasks. The reading and writing tasks focus on local African American history. Throughout the semester, the college student has an opportunity to interact with an adult and two children from the community in which the school is based. The senior citizen provides expertise about the history and culture of the area, the college student provides expertise in computer use and research skills, and the elementary students practice reading, writing, and research skills. The program is run by a steering committee that includes representatives from the college, a teacher from the school, and a coordinator from the church. Grant funds are used to pay the teacher and church coordinator for their work. Because the college students and community senior citizens both serve as tutors, the college students see the strengths and resources available in the community. The content of the materials help the college students better understand the background and history of the community members. A collaboratively identified need is being met. The college students, senior citizens, elementary students, and classroom teachers all report that this is a very positive experience.

2. Another program pairs teacher-education students with youth leaders and high school age students from a local church with a focus on preparing for the ACT and SAT. Teacher-education students and youth

leaders meet with young people biweekly to review math and reading content. In return, the young people prepare activities for the college students to introduce them to the community. A community scavenger hunt, visits to a church service, home visits, and talent shows are all ways in which the young people share their lives with the college students. The program is run by church youth leaders and a college student who is also a member of the local church. Again, grant funds are used to support program coordination. The college students provide subject-matter expertise, and the youth and adults provide an introduction to their community while addressing a collaboratively identified need.

The college students who serve as tutors in these programs are also involved in Introduction to Multiculturalism, a course that provides a context in which they can reflect on their experiences and gain knowledge about schools and communities. Seminars, reflective papers, and e-mail conversations assist students in analyzing and reflecting on their experiences as they work in these programs.

While these initiatives are too new to produce measurable results, they seem to offer the potential for much more effective learning experiences for prospective teachers than traditional school-based tutoring and teacher-aiding programs. The college students who have been involved in these programs so far reflect a deeper understanding of the community and children's lives than the students who are working in traditional school-based tutoring settings. They are less likely to describe their students and the community in deficit terms and more likely to discuss resources and strengths. Initial responses from church members who are involved have been positive as well.

Conclusion

Service-learning has excellent potential for providing the authentic, vivid experiences necessary for challenging assumptions and building appropriate skills for teaching in a just and equitable way. This will only happen, however, with carefully constructed experiences that include opportunities to learn about societal structures and school contexts, guided reflection, and strength-based school settings. College-wide initiatives, community partnerships, and outside funding can help provide the resources needed to design and implement these experiences. Prospective teachers can move from being bewildered observers to competent teachers who are committed to excellence and equity for all children. Our commitment to preparing this kind of teacher provides the energy that we need to undertake this challenging but essential task.

References

Anderson, J. B., and J. A. Erickson. 1997. Service learning in teacher education. In *AAHE's Series on Service-Learning in the Disciplines.* Washington, D.C.: American Association of Higher Education.

Battisoni, R. M. 1997. Service-learning and democratic citizenship. *Theory Into Practice* 36 (summer): 150-56.

Brown, J. S., A. Collins, and P. Diguid. 1989. Situated cognition and the culture of learning. *Educational Researcher* 18:33-42.

Carver, R. L. 1997. Theoretical underpinnings of service learning. *Theory Into Practice* (vol. 36 n3): 143-49.

Fitzgerald, A., and P. Lauter. 1995. Multiculturalism and core curriculum. In *Handbook of research on multicultural education,* edited by J. A. Banks and C. A. M. Banks. New York: Simon and Shuster.

LeSourd, S. L. 1997. Community service in a multicultural nation. *Theory Into Practice* 36 (summer): 157-63.

Schon, D. 1983. *The reflective practitioner.* New York: Basic Books.

Sleeter, C. 1999. Teaching whites about racism. In *Beyond heroes and holidays: A practical guide to K-12 anti-racist, multicultural education, and staff development.* Washington D.C.: Network Educators of America.

Wade, R., and J. B. Anderson. 1996. Community service learning: A strategy for preparing human service-oriented teachers. *Teacher-education Quarterly* 9 Vol. 23, n4): 59-73.

Chapter 11

SERVICE-LEARNING FOR FIRST-YEAR ENGINEERING STUDENTS

Randall Brouwer

Introduction

CALVIN COLLEGE IS A CHRISTIAN four-year liberal arts college with several professional programs, engineering being one of them. This chapter describes past and ongoing experiences the author and his colleagues have had when incorporating opportunities for service-learning into the Introduction to Engineering course. This course is required of students in the engineering program at Calvin and is typically taken during their first semester on campus. One of the primary goals of the course is to introduce students to the field of engineering. Many who come directly from high school into the college setting have been told that engineering may be the right career choice for them because they like both math and science, but relatively few have a good understanding of what the various disciplines within engineering are and what an "average" engineer may do on a day-to-day basis. Various topics are covered in the course, but one of the most important is the idea of design and how engineers go about solving a problem from the point of defining the problem to implementing the solution. In recent years, the enrollments in the course have been somewhere between 110 and 130 students.

There are numerous books and articles on service-learning in higher education that focus on the theory and management of service-learning programs (Jacoby, 1996, 5; Miller 1996) fewer that discuss applications and examples within any curriculum, and far fewer which provide examples within an engineering curriculum (Tsang and Newman 1998; Lord 1999, two good,

153

fairly recent examples). A notable example showing how service-learning can be successfully integrated into all four years of an engineering program on a large scale is EPICS (Engineering Projects in Community Service) at Purdue University (Coyle, Jamison, and Sommers, 1997). Unfortunately, the management of such a program requires a large amount of resources that is virtually unavailable in a smaller school.

Since the early 1990s, the Engineering Department at Calvin College has partnered with local agencies that assist persons with physical or mental challenges. Engineering students meet with selected clients of the organization, assess the need, develop a design to meet the need, and implement their design using basic materials. The college has embraced the idea of service-learning, and this is reflected in the expanded mission statement of the college, "Particularly important to our internal community is the way college members work together to serve communities beyond the college," (Van Harn 1996, 56). The goals of the Engineering Department include having "graduates whose Christian faith leads them to an engineering career of action and involvement, to personal piety, integrity, and social responsibility and concern." As a department, we strongly believe that Calvin engineering graduates should learn to serve the communities in which they are placed by using their talents and abilities to seek solutions to problems around them.

Robert Sigmon described a typology for learning and service (Sigmon, 1994), which outlines four approaches to service-learning. The distinctions of the typology are based on how balanced the service and learning aspects are and how intentional the link is between them. The service-learning found in these projects is close to, but not quite what he would call "SERVICE-LEARNING," wherein both service and learning are balanced. There seems to be a balance between the service and the learning aspects, and although the goals of each are not always explicit, there is an intentional link between the service and the learning. The challenge has been to help the students see that SERVICE-LEARNING is a two-way street—that there is much they can learn from the people they are working with.

The Calvin College Service-Learning Center (SLC) provides assistance as we do these projects. Staff members come to classes to explain and promote SERVICE-LEARNING both inside the course and outside the course. The SLC works with the campus transportation service to provide free transportation to nearby sites where the students will be involved in SERVICE-LEARNING, or they provide mileage reimbursement if students use their own vehicles. Also, students log their SERVICE-LEARNING hours and the SLC tabulates and provides a SERVICE-LEARNING transcript for each student.

Although there is a significant investment in time and resources to setup and manage SERVICE-LEARNING projects, the benefits to both students and the greater community are worth the effort. Some of the benefits to the students include bridging cultural differences, affirming their talents and abilities, and solving real-world engineering problems in a team setting. It is likely that the majority of engineering students (and students across the campus) have had little if any personal interaction with individuals who have significant physical or mental challenges. As students work on the projects, they will learn how to work with a wide range of persons with differing backgrounds, interests, and abilities than they typically see in their (engineering) classes. By interacting with persons from the disabled community, students will hopefully gain a greater appreciation of the challenges many people face daily. Students also gain an appreciation of how their talents can make a difference in the lives of other people. Finally, most real engineering problems are not like the canned problems found in a textbook that usually only have one solution; they are real-world problems in which tradeoffs must be made between the quality of the work, the time it takes to complete it, and the amount of resources required. Unfortunately, many of the problems students are given in class are contrived to illustrate a particular aspect under study. It is difficult to propose open-ended, real-world problems in the classroom setting. The design problems the students will face in these projects are open-ended, multifaceted, and address societal needs. From conversations with students and feedback from surveys, it is clear that students covet the chance to work on real problems.

The community also benefits from the interaction—either directly from the use of new tools or indirectly from a greater awareness by the students of the needs that are present. A number of final designs produced by teams have been delivered to the clients and, with varying levels of success, some of the clients have been able to perform tasks with greater ease. These clients have seen a small portion of the kingdom of God manifested as some of the effects of sin have been reversed. In an indirect way, the better understanding of the needs of the disabled community will be carried with the students as they graduate and continue to be involved in their communities.

Finally, the faculty benefit from their experiences with these projects. First, it is much easier and much more effective to teach students about engineering when they are able to work on real-world problems. Making a canned project effective in a class is not easy to do; the students usually realize that it is a drill exercise they must complete and that the results of their work will likely never be used. In addition, faculty benefit as they learn more about the disabled community. We often have students in our classes who have some level of disability, and through the interaction we have with the community organizations, we learn. Finally, college and/or university faculty often focus on theoretical studies. Dealing with real-world problems helps faculty to maintain a good balance.

Detailed Description of the Design Projects

The service-learning projects described in this chapter take place in the first core engineering course taken by students after they arrive on campus. The course is essentially divided into two parts, one part focuses on graphical communication, which is taught in a computer-lab setting, and the other part focuses on introducing students to the field of engineering and some design principles, which is taught in a lecture setting. The service-learning projects are part of the lecture portion of the course. Some of the topics covered include: defining *engineering*, exposing students to the variety of fields in engineering, the design process, computer tools for designing and communicating, issues of technology, ethics in engineering, and more. Although several design projects are assigned throughout the semester, the one that incorporates service-learning involves students in all aspects of the design process.

Prior to assigning the team project, the professor of the course contacts local organizations. We have worked with several organizations in the past. The most recent semester's projects were in conjunction with Goodwill Industries of Greater Grand Rapids and Hope Network. These organizations, like others we have worked with, provide supportive employment opportunities for persons with various disabilities. Some clients work in a sheltered workshop, usually assembling various articles for production. Others work in the area of sorting and hanging up donations to the organization. Still others may find employment in local businesses working on simple tasks like folding pizza boxes, office cleaning, or washing dishes at a fast-food restaurant. These clients will usually have a staff member of the organization (caseworker) who monitors and assists them in their activities. Several weeks prior to the start of the project, we contact the supervisor of these caseworkers. The supervisor will usually solicit ideas from the caseworkers, focusing especially on those persons who would be aided by having an assistive device designed and built. A list of projects and contact persons (usually the caseworkers) is then generated. The typical projects are mechanical in nature, and because most students seem to be familiar with *mechanical* engineering principles as they enter college, these projects seem to be within the scope of the students' abilities.

If we have worked with an organization for several years, then getting project ideas is usually a fairly straightforward process. However, if we are beginning to build a relationship with an organization, it is important that we consider the following:

- Are there scheduling limitations that will make it difficult to have students meet the clients?
- Are there confidentiality rules?
- Are the various projects appropriate for the students?
- Are the various projects of equal difficulty and interest?
- Will it be easy for the students to reach the contact person and do those persons expect to be contacted?
- Are there difficulties in transporting students to the site where the clients are located?

Each party in the project has much to gain, but it does take time and effort from everyone to make it work.

The projects have been assigned as follows. Three or four students are assigned to each team by the professor. While on the job in the real world, engineers seldom have the opportunity to select the persons they will work with on a project. Instead, they must learn to adapt to the dynamics of the group to which they have been assigned. Furthermore, few of the students know each other well enough to make good decisions on selecting teammates. Therefore, uniform distribution based on an alphabetical class roster has been used, which means that our students do not get to choose their teammates. This has worked well in the past. In recent years, a distribution based on class schedules and driver availability has been used. This can be very helpful if there are difficulties in scheduling meetings and site visits. The mechanisms and dynamics of teamwork are then discussed in class to help the students understand what to expect. The faculty tries to stay in touch with each team to make sure problems are averted. Peer (teammate) evaluations at the end of the projects have consistently shown that the students tend to figure out how to work together and will often create strong friendships within the group.

Each team is then assigned one of the projects from the list. The professor can assign this, or the students can request a project to work on. The students must then call their project's contact person and arrange a time at which the team can meet with both the contact person and the client. This can be difficult at times due to the complexity of merging five to six schedules together. For nearby meeting places, it is possible for students to use class time to meet the client. However, for sites further away, longer stretches of time and transportation problems would have to be worked out. Prior to meeting the client, the students are usually unsure about the whole project idea. After the meeting, however, most students get excited about tackling a real-world problem and about finding ways to help the particular person.

At this point, the students are at the beginning of the design process wherein they gather information and define the requirements of the problem. As the project proceeds, the teams will have to produce the following "deliverables:"

- Detailed problem statement
- Detailed project plan with a list of tasks that must be completed
- Sketches of preliminary ideas
- Final design sketches and drawings
- Formal design review with the professor
- Working device (prototype)
- Team-based oral presentation
- Written final report
- Regular status reports
- Peer assessment

Due to various constraints, a few years ago we did not stress the building of the design and allowed students to turn in "paper" designs. Unfortunately, most of those designs had little chance of ever working because the students did not have the opportunity to build and test their ideas. The college now has metal- and wood-shop facilities along with workbenches, small quantities of materials, and a small budget for purchasing supplies, available to the students so that they can build and test their projects. It is now a requirement of the project to build a prototype—a working device that demonstrates the design and that can be given to the client.

Following the initial meeting with the client, the students tend to work on the project with little additional interaction with that person. For the local organization and the clients, it is much easier for the clients to focus on their work when interruptions are minimized, so there are good reasons to limit the number of times the students meet with the client. Following the completion of the project (and the grading of their devices), the students are encouraged to deliver their devices in person to their clients to see how well they work and how useful they are. If they are unable to go, the professor delivers the devices. In recent years, students have done their final presentation of their project at the site where their client works, allowing the client and various staff members who work with the client to see it. Students take it very seriously when their presentations are for more than just their fellow classmates.

Project Examples

Each year we usually have a completely new set of projects for the students. Some of the projects that they have worked on in recent years include devices for

- Church bulletin folding: a device to help a person with the limited use of one hand to fold bulletins neatly.
- Spring assembly: a device to help someone with limited finger strength to insert springs into a sink sprayer assembly.
- Drinking device: a device to mount on a wheelchair so that the user can get a drink when desired instead of having to ask for a drink.
- Ring gasket assembly: a device to help in placing rubber rings on a plastic piece.
- Label peeling: a device to help workers remove sticky labels from the backing.

- Movie ticket cutter: a device to help someone tear or cut movie tickets as moviegoers enter the theater.
- Pizza box folder: a device to help someone in a wheelchair fold large pizza boxes.
- Silverware roller: a device to help someone with limited hand control stack and roll silverware inside a napkin for a restaurant.
- Portable table for a paper shredder: a strong but light-weight table that a blind person can use to hold a paper shredder.
- Jig for filling a candy dispenser: a device that helps hold a candy dispenser so a person can easily fill the dispenser and wrap it up in a package.

Not every project is equally workable. When the requirements for the project have been vague, the students have had trouble knowing where to begin and how they could help the person. Fortunately, most of the projects have been straightforward enough that the students can "run with them" with minimal direction and encouragement. It is essential to work with the organization to develop good, workable projects ahead of time.

Project Results

The students usually do a very nice job of designing a device. The limitations of time, knowledge, and budget affect the final design. In some cases, the devices look good, but do not always turn out to be useful to the clients. Furthermore, within the projects time frame, the needs of the clients can change so that the device is no longer needed by the time the project is completed. These kinds of things happen in the larger world of engineering as well, which give students an understanding of real-world constraints.

Student feedback regarding the projects was gathered in several ways: one-on-one discussions with teams or individuals, peer assessments, and an evaluation survey developed by the Calvin SLC. During the project, the instructor meets with each design team once or twice a week. During those meetings, the students provide much good feedback. Although the students were asked to leave their comfort zones and put forth an effort to understand the needs of people around them, overall, the feedback from the students has been very positive. The most common comments were that (1) they were glad to be able to work on a real-world problem and not some canned problem with a fixed solution, and (2) they thought that this project was one of the best parts of the course. Many of the students were excited about an opportunity to help someone else. It meant something to them to do a real-life design project. Students will, in general, take a project much more seriously and find it more rewarding when their work has an affect on more than just their grades. Engineers design, and if we can give students a positive design experience early on, hopefully the students will "stay the course."

Table 1: Summary of Survey Results

Question	Average Score
I understand how the ABSL in which I have been involved connects to this course.	4.3
The professor required me to reflect on my service.	4.3
My professor gave clear ABSL assignments.	4.4
I was prepared and oriented to begin my service	4.2
The supervision and guidelines provided by the site were adequate for the work I needed to do.	4.1
I made a contribution that was valuable to the organization or people I served.	4.3
This SL experience provided me with significant course-related learning opportunities.	4.4
This SL experience provided me opportunities to develop skill/gain appreciation that, although not related to the course, will help me in other ways.	4.3
I worked out reliable transportation for my service.	4.4

Unfortunately, there are often some negative experiences that occur when working in the real world. In some ways, these may have some educational benefits despite the negative character. For example, one semester the two problems that students reported most frequently were difficulties communicating with contact people at the local organization and the appropriateness of a particular project for a particular team. We found that planning and coordination with the local organization alleviated these problems. This was the first time we had partnered with Goodwill Industries, Inc. and subsequent years have been smoother for the students. There have also been cases when students have seen inappropriate and unpredictable behavior in the clients. In general, the students have shown maturity in working with the caseworkers and in dealing with the situation. Such experiences have a positive impact on students in the end.

The Calvin SLC has developed a questionnaire that students are asked to fill out after their projects have been completed. To illustrate the outcomes of these projects, the questionnaire and the results from the fall 1999 semester are shown in Table 1 (see p. 161). The students marked each with a ranking of 5 (=strongly agree) to 1 (=strongly disagree). On average, the students ranked the experience with better than a 4 (=agree), with a typical distribution reflecting those who felt the project was great and those who were discouraged by some of the difficulties mentioned earlier. These results are very encouraging and have been typical of student responses.

Conclusions

After having worked with these types of projects for several years, two ideas stand out: (1) pre-planning is very important to the success of the design project, and (2) the students learn much from the real-world experience. During their final year in the engineering program at Calvin College, the students work on team-based senior design projects (a capstone course). The students select their own projects, and in a number of cases the students have selected service-oriented projects. One example is a team that raised funding to travel to Central America to do a site survey for building a fresh-water supply system for a mountain village. After completing the design and raising additional funds for travel and supplies, the team traveled back to Central America and worked alongside the village residents build a water system that continues to be used. Another recent project was the design of an inexpensive, portable baby incubator. Although the seniors working on that project have graduated, some undergraduates have continued to work on the project on a volunteer basis.

The need around us is great, and engineering students and faculty have much to offer our communities. At Calvin College, we have found that the benefits of SERVICE-LEARNING are worth the extra effort, and the opportunities for service are excellent ways for the college community to interact with the community around us in a positive way.

References

Jacoby, B., and Associates. 1996. *Service-learning in higher education.* San Francisco: Jossey-Bass Publishers, 5.

Miller, S. 1996. *Science and society: Redefining the relationship.* Providence: Campus Compact, 1996.

Tsang, E., and J. E. Newman. 1998. Service-learning's effect on engineering students and K-12 teacher partnership in an introduction to mechanical engineering course, paper from Session S3H, Proceedings of the 1998 Frontiers in Education Conference, Tempe, Arizona.

Lord, S. 1999. Service-learning in introduction to engineering at the University of San Diego: First lessons, paper from Session 13B6, Proceedings of the 1999 Frontiers in Education Conference, San Juan, Puerto Rico.

Coyle, E., L. Jamieson, and L. Sommers. 1997. EPICS: A model for integrating Service-Learning into the Engineering Curriculum. *Michigan Journal of Community Service Learning* 4 (fall). 81-89.

Van Harn, G. 1996. *An expanded statement of the mission of Calvin College: Vision, purpose, commitment.* Grand Rapids: Calvin College.

Sigmon, Robert. 1994. *Linking service with learning in liberal arts education.* Washington D.C.: The Council of Independent Colleges.

PART III

DEVELOPING FACULTY

Chapter 12

THE DEVELOPMENT OF AN ETHIC OF SERVICE TO A PLACE

Janel M. Curry

Monroe would have dismissed such beliefs as superstition, folklore. But Ada, increasingly covetous of Ruby's learning in the ways living things inhabited this particular place, chose to view the signs as metaphoric. They were, as Ada saw them, an expression of stewardship, a means of taking care, a discipline. They provided a ritual of concern for the patterns and tendencies of the material world where it might be seen to intersect with some other world. Ultimately, she decided, the signs were a way of being alert, and under those terms she could honor them. Charles Frazier, 1997.

IN HIGHER EDUCATION WE WORK at challenging students to see issues in a framework that goes beyond the limitations of their parochial, or locally based experiences—college is meant to be a broadening experience. This is easy because, using the words of Eric Zencey (1996, 15-19), most faculty are themselves "rootless professors." Professors are supposed to belong to the world of ideas rather than places. An alternative is to see education as a deepening of local understanding. When we deepen our understanding of the places where we live, we gain a greater understanding of who we are, the intricacies of our place, and our responsibilities. Then, we may in turn have the skills to learn to appreciate and care for other places. Perhaps broadening experiences include the route of understanding the "other" via a deepening of our understanding of who and where we are. Historian Christopher Lasch (1991) claimed that allegiance to the world is ineffective because it stretches our capacity for loyalty too thin. In reality, we love particular people and places; abstract ideals need to be made concrete through loving, understanding, and caring for particular people and places.

167

The Calvin Environmental Assessment Program (CEAP) builds on this need to serve and show caretaking through the process of paying attention to that which is closest at hand. CEAP involves faculty across the college, but mainly in the sciences, who each dedicate regular lab sessions or projects to collecting data that contribute to an overall assessment of the environment of the campus and surroundings areas. Some of the initial findings show how the runoff from streets and yards of the surrounding neighborhoods impact the water quality of campus ponds. The open spaces created by the ponds are in turn used as recreational space by our neighbors. Thus, CEAP is increasing our understanding of what it means to be embedded in a natural and social system. CEAP is built on the philosophy that this knowledge must then be put to the service of the campus and the larger community, perhaps becoming the basis for a more community-based approach to campus planning. Ultimately, the hope of the Calvin Environmental Assessment Program is that students and faculty will become better caretakers and citizens on this piece of the creation and that they may in turn learn what it means to take care of the other places they encounter throughout their lifetimes.

A Reformed Christian Environmental Ethic

The overall goal of the CEAP project, to learn how to serve the creation in this place, arises from Calvin College's roots in the Reformed Christian-faith tradition. This faith perspective calls those from within this tradition to (1) understand how the creation works, (2) make creation's concerns our concerns, (3) develop ways of living that demand more sacrifice for us and less torture for everything else, and (4) work to redeem creation (Van Dyke, et al. 1996, 98-99). The CEAP program has as a goal the development of an environmental ethic built on the faith tradition of Calvin College. The Reformed Christian tradition emphasizes the continuity between this physical earth and any future eternal existence as well as the unity of mind, body, and spirit. Thus, there has never been a conflict between faith commitment and environmental concern. The universe is seen as itself a creation of God (Van Dyke, et al. 1996, 31). The redeeming work of Christ is thus not seen to apply only to individual humans. God's redemptive power can be seen in all his works, including nature (Van Dyke, et al. 1996, 34-35).

Because the earth is God's creation, its value is in glorifying God rather than just in fulfilling the use needs of humans. The creation has intrinsic value that is found outside humans and itself. God requires us to not just preserve, but to restore, bringing wholeness wherever possible (Van Dyke, et al. 1996, 48-49).

Science, Place, and Faith

CEAP is embedded in a larger discussion within the natural- and social-science academic communities over the universality versus the particularity of knowledge. Science has typically removed questions of value from the creation while valuing the development of universally applicable theories. The scientific enterprise has not been interested in complete understanding of a specifically situated phenomenon but rather emphasized partial understandings of widely dispersed but similar phenomena. This reductionism, according to its critics, has involved loss of context and applicability (Flora 1992, Kloppenburg 1991, Reisner 1992).

Local knowledge, more akin to the CEAP project, differs from scientific knowledge because it has a variety of ends rather than one, is not concerned with universal explanation, is valid only for a particular situation, and includes multiple factors rather than controlling for just one. It allows for practical experience as a valid measure of success and includes detailed knowledge of local ecological and environmental factors (Reisner 1992, 8). Local knowledge implies that understanding may be inseparable from a particular place in the sense of being embedded in the natural features of that place as well in particular labor process—environmental and social embeddedness (Kloppenburg 1991, 537). Place-based knowledge—that produced from a limited location—provides an alternative to contemporary science (Flora 1992, 93).

The Reformed Christian faith tradition has some similarities with this increased understanding of the limitations of traditional science. The Bible's presuppositions and its doctrine of creation lead in a direction different from that of traditional science and its treatment of nature. If one confesses that God has created all, then it follows that everything is dependent on God alone for its existence; thus denying that status to anything else (Clouser 1991, 173). Hence, no matter how hard scientists try to isolate aspects of reality, all of them continue to display unbreakable connections to all the others (Clouser 1991,

173, 193). Such wholeness is best understood through the emphasis on local knowledge and place.

Traditional science associates rational knowledge with certainty, truth, and justification. This rationalism in turn is founded on reductionism and the independence of individual aspects of reality. In contrast, the biblical tradition is that "knowing" is usually a function of relationships (Hart 1984, 356) for after asserting the truth of God, the Bible is mainly concerned with clarifying the ways God relates to us. God has made this the model of what it is to be rightly human (Clouser 1983, 394, 405).

Douglas Hall argues that one of the basic or foundational biblical understandings is the concept that humanity is created in the image of God. While traditional theological reflection has centered on traits possessed by humans that image God, Hall suggests that a minority tradition has identified the image of God not as a quality of being but as a quality of relationship (Hall 1988, 12-13). Hall says that this relational quality of the created order includes the natural world. This relational characteristic of our being describes our unique calling: to be in responsible relationship with God, each other, and the rest of creation (Wilkinson 1991, 285).

The Christian faith, while it has a strong element of personal commitment, demands that we soon move to the level of community, to taking care of each other. This community, especially expressed in the image of the body of Christ, is not a "building" contracted by individuals acting out of self-interest but takes on a life of its own. Suggestions of what this means are found in the New Testament. *Oikonomia* is a well-known word found in the New Testament. In its biblical context, it implies responsibility, care, and acting on another's behalf. A related term, *oikonomos*, means steward, or the steward of a household (Goudzwaard 1992, 5). Again we find these associated concepts: house(hold) and managing wisely for the good of the community (household). This is clearer in Luke 12:35-48. The wise steward is the one taking care of the household while he waits for the master. He does not settle into complacency, eating and drinking and thinking only of himself. Rather, the wise steward gives each member of the household his or her portion of food at the proper time. He is busy taking care of the household.

While the New Testament implies a certain stewardly attitude toward resources and the rest of creation, the Old Testament in particular ties body and household images, or covenantal relationships, concretely to land resources. The

Israelites were given land by God to be kept as long as they were in a covenant relationship with him. When they repeatedly mistreated the land and/or treated their fellow community members unjustly, they were banished from community and from the land. Thus, individual ownership was affirmed, but the right to the land was directly tied to one's relationship to God, the fruits of which were seen in the concern for brother or sister and for the land itself. The Law of Jubilee (Lev 25:10) guarded against speculation or the removal of land from these relationships and concerns. Again the connections are there: covenant, household, and house-building in association with wisdom and stewardship (taking care of the whole and of the land). Humans and land are part of an intertwined whole the expression of which is found at a level where covenantal relationships form.

The Reformed Christian tradition purports that the relationship between humans and the nonhuman world has implications for eternity. A Calvinistic interpretation of the future—that Christ's return will bring about a new heaven and a new earth—means that Christ will restore and redeem nature as well as humans to a wholeness not seen since the Garden of Eden. The present physical reality is connected to eternal physical realities that makes our present choices relating to the land into sacred choices. In addition, the tradition connects obedience to God's laws (most clearly expressed in the Ten Commandments) with effects on nature. Our treatment of each other and the nature of institutions are tied to the wholeness or lack of wholeness we see in nature. Perhaps the nature of the physical landscape becomes part of the ethical system of boundaries. The absence or presence of wild birds tells of obedience or disobedience. The health of a city or an institution of higher education is the measure of shalom—the coherence of people, worldview, and nature: the measure of the health of a place.

Does the commitment to a place and its intertwined relationships lend itself to alternative ways of seeing? Hassanein and Kloppenburg (1995, 727-28) contend that the development of great attentiveness to natural systems changes relationships to physical places. The process of observation and interpretation of a dynamic system leads to new ways of seeing and thinking. Those who pay attention transcend the reality of the multiple variables and acquire a wisdom that allows them to know the impact of the interrelationships of those variables. This wisdom is irreducible. Local knowledge and the practical become intertwined with the cosmological, with how one sees the world (Hassanein and

Kloppenburg 1995, 736). In this way, CEAP both reflects and enhances the tradition out of which Calvin College comes.

Wes Jackson, critic of traditional science and founder of the Land Institute, points in a similar direction. He uses Exodus 20:25 as his model. Moses has just delivered the Ten Commandments and receives instructions to build an alter of unhewn stone "for if thou lift up thy tool upon it, thou hast polluted it." Jackson interprets this to mean that we are to be more mindful of the creation, more mindful of the original materials of the universe than in our own cleverness in using them: The scientist and the artist must remain subordinate to the larger Creation (Jackson 1987, 9). The humility he requires, grounded in the origins of the Creation, asks us to approach research and teaching as though we believed that the wisdom of nature is more important, in the long run, than the cleverness of science (Jackson 1987, 10).

He states, "There is no higher standard of your performance than the land and its natural community" (Jackson 1987, 158). The land, again, perhaps tells us the story of the measure of our faith commitments.

History and Structure of CEAP

CEAP arose out of cooperation between the Natural Science Division of Calvin College and the efforts of the Academically Based Service-Learning Office. Its overall goals are:

- To engage students and faculty, particularly in the sciences, in service-learning.
- To engage students in meaningful learning in a real-life context in terms of application of course material and a group-work environment.
- To use the first two goals to provide a context in which students, faculty, and the administrative planning process on campus are meaningfully linked with the surrounding community.
- To provide data for an overall environmental assessment of Calvin College and its surrounding neighborhoods.
- To engage students at all levels and across all disciplines in quality research.
- To encourage creativity, collaboration, and curriculum change across campus.
- To develop a habit of stewardship based on attentiveness to place.

CEAP's inception came in 1997 when the science division faculty coordinator for service-learning, a geography and environmental studies professor, and the director of academically based service-learning organized a three-day summer workshop to develop the overall structure of the project. The provost's office provided the seed money for this workshop. The initial CEAP group included nine faculty from the Geography, Physics, Biology, Chemistry, Math, and Computer Science Departments. They developed a working input-output model of the campus environment, which helped to identify different areas that needed data collection and monitoring, to visualize the environment in its totality. Participants then redesigned specific lab assignments from existing courses to contribute to the data collection on various aspects of the assessment. Faculty have submitted and received equipment grants in support of the proposed research (National Science Foundation and Dreyfus Foundation). The college also received a Universities as Citizens grant on the basis of CEAP's development as a service-learning model.

The college supported a second workshop during the summer of 1998 to expand the group of participants. Faculty from the Engineering, English, Political Science, Geology, and Sociology Departments, as well as, the campus architect joined the previous participants, bringing the courses involved to twenty. In this second workshop, the overall direction of the project was designed to develop working groups of courses that addressed common problems, a strategy to increase Calvin's ties and service to the surrounding community, and an effort to integrate CEAP into the college planning process. During the summer of 1999, faculty were added from the Social Work, Economics, Religion, and Communication Departments. Throughout this process of development, the motivating force for CEAP and the philosophy of the program have been clearly grounded in the Reformed Christian tradition to which the college belongs.

The Calvin Environmental Assessment Program is unique in the country in that its structure encourages multiple goals and broad-based involvement. CEAP includes over twenty courses, and more than two hundred students in some semesters, in an ongoing environmental assessment of Calvin College and its surrounding area. At the same time, CEAP involves faculty and students in interdisciplinary engagement, undergraduate research, and academically based service-learning. CEAP is a model of a strategy to meet the national need for involvement of science faculty in service-learning while also providing a comprehensive program of undergraduate research and interdisciplinary work. CEAP's strategy of environmental assessment that, in comparison to others, is cost effective, ongoing, and well integrated into the science curriculum gives the project long-term sustainability. In addition, the structure of CEAP allows for maximum creativity among faculty and extensive impact on students while requiring a minimum time commitment by either.

These goals of sustainability, integration into the curriculum, and minimum time commitment are accomplished through involved faculty who each dedicate regular lab sessions, course projects, or focus entire courses around collecting data that contribute to an assessment of the surrounding areas. Classes sometimes form working teams and share data and specialties, modeling real-world working-group strategies. The data forms the basis for recommended changes in campus policies, for programs that target individual behavioral changes, and for identifying issues that involve and have an impact on the adjacent neighborhoods and thus form the basis for cooperation.

The major innovation of this project is its development of a model of interdisciplinary engagement for science faculty in academically based service-learning. This model directly addresses the weakness of service-learning in general as articulated by Zlotkowski (1995)—the need to ensure its full integration into American higher education through addressing the needs of individual disciplines and allying service-learning with particular academic interest groups. While ABSL has translated well into the social sciences and the humanities, ABSL organizations nationwide, such as National Campus Compact and Michigan Campus Compact, are presently targeting SEAMS (Science, Engineering, Architecture, Math, and Computer Science) faculty. Part of the difficulty of engaging SEAMS faculty in service-learning has been the time constraints that SEAMS course material places on faculty. The subject material is not easily organized around a service-learning component. In addition, labs must cover particular techniques and topics. The structure of CEAP overcomes both time and subject-matter constraints, allowing service-learning to arise naturally out of course content.

Integration among service-learning participants happens at several levels. CEAP participants are required to attend and present at end-of-the-semester poster sessions in which all data is displayed. A keynote address, focusing on environmental issues, starts off the event. These addresses have included the campus architect who talked about the state of the campus; a speaker from the

TargetEarth organization; a Christian environmental group; a local congressman, who spoke on the environmental challenges for the next millennium; and Wendell Berry, who spoke in honor of a late Calvin English professor who, like Berry, was both a writer and a strong environmentalist. The CEAP website has been developed to be used by courses as a depository of results for use by the next semester's courses. Its main purpose is to maintain continuity for all involved and to serve as a source of information for faculty, students, administrators, and people from outside the campus (www.calvin.edu/academic/geology/ceap/). Major integration of all these aspects of the campus take place during regular summer workshops that involve the academically based service-learning director, faculty, and student representatives of the campus environmental organization, as well as student's involved in summer research and service-learning and staff such as the campus architect. At that time, participants share data, set goals, identify areas of interest or need; form collaborative partnerships between faculty, between courses, and with student groups; orient new faculty into the project; and work on the next year's project proposals.

Benefits

CEAP benefits students and faculty in many ways. The CEAP program has great flexibility. Different models of learning fit different courses. One English course was entirely organized around CEAP subject matter, while most science courses include only one lab exercise. The CEAP program crosses the boundaries between academic learning and student life as well as between academic programs and campus planning. The CEAP program has increased excitement in teaching among faculty as they become connected to a larger whole. Additional faculty benefits include an increased cross-disciplinary interaction (among science faculty; between science faculty and others), less alienation from the planning process; a growing connection between word and deed; and a sense of the wholeness of research, teaching, and personal commitments. CEAP has provided a basis for getting science faculty involved in community issues based on their expertise but within the time and subject-matter constraints found within the sciences.

CEAP provides students with a greater understanding of the interdisciplinary nature of problems and the role of group work in their solutions by providing a context within which data must be shared across disciplines and through formal working groups from different courses. For example, geography students collected data on students' use of campus space to be analyzed by an advanced statistics class. This sharing of data forced the geography students to be thorough and pay closer attention to the reporting format of the data collection because others depended on their clarity and because it was going to be used for campus planning.

The CEAP project meets the need for increasing student involvement in research at all levels of their college careers. Currently, CEAP classes range from first year to senior level. Lower-level courses have tended to take on the task of environmental monitoring of elements such as water and air quality. Upper-level students have taken on more complex tasks. For example, general chemistry students identified problems of those earlier mentioned nutrient loads flowing into a set of college ponds from an adjacent neighborhood. A senior engineering design team proposed and designed a constructed wetland as a possible solution. A technical-writing class wrote a newsletter that discussed the issue in a general way for the people in the neighborhood.

Calvin College is situated in an environmental context, sharing its watershed with the surrounding community, as well as being situated in an urban context, subject to the zoning regulations of several municipalities. CEAP data provides a starting point for engagement with the surrounding community by providing natural links and service to surrounding municipalities, neighborhoods, and environmental groups. For example, analysis of the water quality of Calvin College's ponds led to engagement with the surrounding neighborhoods over chemical use on lawns and to links with local environmental groups that work to ensure the quality of the larger watershed into which Calvin's ponds drain. Concerns by neighbors over diminished property values due to proximity to Calvin's campus were addressed through an economic-geography project that found that proximity might in fact raise property values. The conservation and enhancement of open space, wetlands, and walking paths on campus are necessary for the continued enhancement of such benefits to the adjacent neighborhood.

Care of Place and Educational Philosophy

The emphases on relationship, context, and serving the place where we live are grounded in a Reformed Christian philosophy but also find support in the work of nationally known educational philosopher Nel Noddings. She starts by taking relationship as ontologically basic, meaning that we recognize human encounter and affective response as a basic fact of human existence (Noddings 1984, 4). Moral decisions are, after all, made in real situations.

The tradition of Western philosophy typically begins with a supremely free consciousness—an aloneness and emptiness at the heart of existence—and identifies anguish as the basic human effect. The view put forth in this chapter, supported earlier by theologian Douglas Hall and by Noddings is that we are rooted in relation, with the joy of relational wholeness as a basic human effect (Noddings 1984, 6).

Wholeness of relationship involves perceptive-creative modes alongside judgmental-evaluative modes. It calls forth human judgment across a wide range of fact and feeling, and it allows for situations and conditions in which judgment may properly be put aside in favor of faith and commitment. Danger occurs when a teacher is too eager to move students into abstraction and objectivity if such a move results in detachment and loss of relationship (Noddings 1984, 182). The cared for, in this case Calvin's natural setting, becomes a "problem" rather than something "cared-for" (Noddings 1984, 25). This is similar to Jackson's emphases. Our cleverness and problem solving replaces our attentiveness to the place, to nature, to the cared-for. The art of teaching is turning away at the right moment from the abstract back toward the concrete. The objective mode must continually be reframed from the base of commitment. Otherwise, science begins to serve itself, detached from nature, the object of caring (Noddings 1984, 26).

The CEAP program attempts to keep this balance. Science becomes grounded in a real place. It incorporates the range of human experiences from the aesthetics of a place to water quality—always grounded in the context of place. The attentiveness that is required leads to continual grounding that ties to basic commitments and to the development of an ethical ideal.

CEAP's goal, to develop the habit of stewardship, grows out of this attentiveness to a place. As Noddings argues, the memory of our own best moments of caring and being cared for are analogous to a transfer of learning

(Noddings 1984, 79-80). It is our best picture of ourselves caring and being cared for in an attainable way (Noddings 1984, 80). Caretaking skills are thus developed and enhanced.

Future Goals

One of the future goals of CEAP is to form interdisciplinary summer research teams built on the research done during the academic year. For example, a recent CEAP workshop identified the need for a carbon-cycle working group. This group would need the following team members:

1. A biology student would develop a measure for biomass production among different groundcovers on campus.
2. A geography student would bring computer-mapping skills needed to build a geographic information system (GIS) model to map the homes of all staff and students. The GIS model would aid in building estimates of vehicles' contribution to atmospheric CO_2. GIS skills are also needed to aid the biology student in mapping campus groundcover areas in order to compute the biomass production figures for the entire campus.
3. Economics and sociology students would bring skills in modeling different options for behavior change such as increasing mass-transit ridership and car pooling as well as aid in compiling figures on energy use and consumption over time.
4. A physics student would build on preliminary work on energy consumption by appliance type to construct a model of energy consumption on campus.

Other goals include increasing the natural vegetation plantings on campus. CEAP research has identified already existing rich native plant sites and has been involved in planting new sites with native species. At present, because of CEAP research, the college has invested in a wetland structure and berm that aids in filtering runoff as it comes off adjacent yards and flows into the college ponds. Native vegetation has been planted along the berm as well as on other places on campus. The CEAP program has the goal of increasing the visibility of these plots of native vegetation through educational materials that would encourage neighbors to come and view the wildflowers at different times of the year. Several inner-city groups have requested that CEAP aid in the development of similar projects. Those sites that already exhibit unique native biodiversity are now identified, and such identification is used to hold the planning process accountable for their conservation.

The enhancement of the physical setting of Calvin College, while crucial, does not yet address another critical issue for the Calvin Environmental Assessment Program—the reduction of the waste that is produced on campus and exported to local landfills. CEAP is beginning to address this issue as well. An archaeology class, through its CEAP garbology project, has determined baseline levels for present recycling behavior. An environmental economics course has identified the necessary institutional structures needed for effective recycling programs. The recent addition of a faculty member in business and marketing provides the missing piece that could lead to dramatic changes in waste production by the campus.

CEAP has the potential of fulfilling many of the goals that Noddings puts forth as essential for good pedagodgy. The emphasis should be on the development of skills that contribute to competence in caring, not on skills for vocational ends (Noddings 1984, 187). CEAP attempts to do this through the extension of its program beyond the scope of science majors. Noddings says that all students should be involved in caring apprenticeships, and these tasks should have equal status with the other tasks encountered in education (Noddings 1984, 188). Inherent in the CEAP program is its goal of caring for that which is close at hand which confirms Noddings who asks that professional structures that separate us into narrow areas of specialization be dismantled (Noddings 1984, 188). CEAP has been instrumental in increasing interdisciplinary interaction. Finally, Noddings says that subjects should be laid out along the entire range of human experience so that students may make multiple and potentially meaningful contact with it. This way, both personal and cultural aspects of the subject are revealed, including the meaning of the subject in individual lives (Noddings 1984, 191). CEAP crosses the range of human experience from religion to nature writing to water analysis; exploring the depth and breadth of what it means to glorify God through service to a place—a place that itself, in turn, glorifies God in its wholeness.

References

Clouser, Roy A. 1983. Religious language: A new look at an old problem. In *Rationality in the Calvinian tradition*, edited by Hendrik Hart, Johan Van Der Hoeven, and Nicholas Wolterstorff. Lanham, Md.: University Press of America.

——. 1991. *The myth of religious neutrality: An essay on the hidden role of religious belief in theories.* Notre Dame: University of Notre Dame Press.

Flora, Cornelia B. 1992. Reconstructing agriculture: The case for local knowledge. *Rural Sociology* 57 (1): 92-97.

Frazier, Charles. 1997. *Cold mountain: A novel.* New York: Vintage Books.

Goudzwaard, Robert. 1992. Creation management: The economics of earth stewardship. *Firmament* (winter): 4-5, 21-23.

Hall, Douglas J. 1988. The spirituality of the covenant: Imaging God, stewarding earth. *Perspectives* (December): 11-14.

Hart, Hendrik. 1984. *Understanding our world: An integral ontology.* Lanham, Md: University Press of America.

Hassanein, N., and J. R. Kloppenburg, Jr. 1995. Where the grass grows again: Knowledge exchange in the sustainable agriculture movement. *Rural Sociology* 60 (4): 721-40.

Jackson, Wes. 1987. *Alters of unhewn stone: Science and the earth.* New York: North Point Press.

Kloppenburg, J., Jr. 1991. Social theory and the de/reconstruction of agricultural science: Local knowledge for an alternative agriculture. *Rural Sociology* 56 (4): 519-48.

Lasch, Christopher. 1991. *The true and only heaven.* New York: W. W. Norton.

Noddings, Nel. 1984. *Caring: A feminine approach to ethics and moral education.* Berkeley: University of California Press.

Reisner, A. 1992. Tracing the linkages of world views, information handling, and communications vehicles. *Agriculture and human values* 9 (2): 4-16.

Van Dyke, Fred, David C. Mahan, Joseph K. Sheldon, and Raymond H. Brand. 1996. *Redeeming creation: The biblical basis for environmental stewardship.* Downers Grove: InterVarsity Press.

Wilkinson, Loren, ed. 1991. *Earthkeeping in the '90s: Stewardship of creation.* Rev. Ed. Grand Rapids: Eerdmans.

Zencey, Eric. 1996. The rootless professors. In *Rooted in the land: Essays on community and place,* edited by William Vitek and Wes Jackson. New Haven: Yale University Press.

Zlotkowski, Edward. 1995. Does service-learning have a future? *Michigan Journal of Community Service Learning* 2 (1):123-33.

Chapter 13

THE ASSIGNMENT OF THEIR LIVES: SERVICE LEARNING IN A COMPOSITION CLASS

Mary Ann Walters

ESPECIALLY FOR TEACHERS OF Freshman Composition, August is the cruelest month. I say *especially* because, although most teachers worth their salary feel some anxiety at the approach of a new school year, teachers of composition have a special problem. Their courses have, well, no content.

My colleagues and I agree that the course is terribly important and that in it nearly everything has to be done—students must learn to analyze, to reason, to discern, to reflect, to appreciate language, and to use it well. These goals and skills, however, do not automatically organize the course—not in any necessary, organic way. So every August, when the anxiety sets in, we teachers of composition sit in our offices and try to invent a theme for the course, one that will link what otherwise would be miscellaneous assignments and that will also, we hope, so excite our students that they will be inspired to write their very best. One colleague chooses sports, another legal cases, another environmental issues, yet another the ethics of technology. Not one of us has yet found a perfect solution to our content problem, as least not to my knowledge. Every year we reinvent the course.

Several years ago in August, Gail Heffner, one of my colleagues from the campus Service-Learning Center, popped into my office with a startling concept. "I have an idea for your course," she said. "Have your students interview elderly people in a retirement home and write about that. I will help you set it up."

I hesitated. "Give me a day to think about it."

That was a thoughtful day. Usually, I try not to think about the mission statement of the college during the angst of August, but on that day its most succinct sentence came to mind: "Calvin College seeks to engage in vigorous liberal arts education that promotes lives of Christian service." How better to prepare for a life of service than with a freshman semester of service? But would the students be inspired by the stories of elderly people to write their very best? Probably as much as they would be about legal cases or the environment. Who knows, and why not? I decided yes.

Almost immediately I had to make one other major decision—should the project be optional (surely the safer choice) or required for all? I thought of a powerful piece of advice from my favorite writing teacher, William Zinsser. "Don't be kind of bold. Be bold." Very well, then. The project would be required. Moreover, it would organize the entire course.

On the first day of class I handed out the course syllabus and read aloud its crucial paragraph:

> Early in the semester, each of you will be assigned a senior partner, a resident at the Raybrook Retirement Home. Setting up your own schedules in consultation with Mrs. Van Beek, Director of Volunteer Services at Raybrook, you will arrange to visit this person approximately one hour per week. All, or nearly all, of your papers can be about these visits. At the end of the semester you will have collected enough information to write the life story of your partner, which will be your final paper of the semester and will also be your gift to your partner and to his or her family.

No one blinked. Perhaps, I thought, I should read it again. Instead, I asked my students to think very seriously about whether the course project was right for them. I suggested they pray about it. If they came back to the second class, I said, I would assume they were committed to the time involvement and to whatever risks the project might entail. All the students were present at the second class.

On that day my "team" was also present to explain the mechanics of the project. The service-learning director told the students about the college's commitment to service-learning and about the practical help it was prepared to give them. The volunteer director of the retirement home described the place, told the students what they might expect, suggested ways they might begin their conversations, and tactfully touched on a few matters of etiquette (no baseball caps, please). My contribution to that class was to ask the students to volunteer to read from the first journal entry I had assigned—a response to this question: "What are your feelings about, or your experiences with, elderly people?" I very much wanted the three of us, my teammates and me, to hear what the students felt and thought at the beginning of our enterprise.

By the second week of class my students were off, meeting their assigned partners, forming their relationships, beginning their journeys, leaving my control.

My job, as I saw it, was to design writing assignments that could contribute in some way to the final paper. The first paper in the course, before the partner visits were firmly in place, was a personal memoir, asking the students to think about a major turning point in their lives or else to explore one of their most important relationships. I hoped that they would be better equipped to ask their partners about these matters if they had spent some time reflecting on their own lives. Later papers could contribute more directly. In response to an assignment to describe a place, for example, many students chose to describe their partner's room, the dining hall of the retirement home, or the lobby where residents socialize.

The library research paper is typically the most daunting and least successful paper in the course. I was daunted myself. I could not think of an appropriate topic. Then it occurred to me that my students would be better interviewers if they themselves had something to contribute to their conversations. So I asked each of them to find out what event, activity, or period of history their partners remembered most vividly. The students now had a reason for going to the library to read the newspapers and magazines of the 20s, 30s, and 40s. They wrote about Henry Ford, Billy Sunday, TB sanatoriums, Friesian immigration, the early life of Gerald Ford, early aviation, women's basketball in the 30s, the influenza epidemic, the Lindbergh kidnapping, and the American Red Cross. These papers were not particularly wonderful—library research papers rarely are—but at least the topics were fresh and there was even a sense of urgency about the discoveries.

One topic in particular delighted me. A male student reported that his partner told him she would have preferred a female student because her passion was knitting and she was sure her "Calvin boy" would not care about that. Determined to prove her wrong, he wrote his research paper on the history of knitting, only to discover that for many centuries and in many countries, knitting has been a manly occupation. He also learned how to knit.

We were not very far into the semester when most of my students realized that they were not particularly good at asking questions. I tried to help. I gave them a list of 150 possible questions. "When you were a child, how did your family celebrate holidays?" "How did you meet your spouse?" "What people have influenced you the most?" Questions such as that. We also practiced interviewing each other in class. Fortunately, interviewing is a skill one can only get better at. As the students learned how to ask more specific questions and how to pose follow-up questions, they noticed that their partners seemed to get better at telling their stories.

Every three weeks or so, or whenever it seemed like a good idea, I began the class with a ten-to-fifteen minute "town meeting," when the students could report on their process and talk about whatever problems or unusual situations they needed to sort out. I set up these meetings for my own benefit, actually; I wanted to know what was going on. Most of the reports were heartening, as students shared with each other the details of their growing friendships—the cookies and the birthday cards, not to mention the amazing history lessons. And when there were problems, I found the students were remarkably wise about finding solutions for each other.

"My lady doesn't think her life was very interesting," one student complained, "so she answers my questions with real short answers and I can't get her to say anything more."

"I had the same problem," offers another," but then I told him about myself and showed him some pictures of my car and my family. Now he trusts me more and tells me all sorts of stuff."

A third student had another suggestion: "I found the process actually went better when I did not ask the questions and just let her go off on her stories on her own. That is when the fun information came out."

And so it went. The simple solution given to the student whose partner did not want to talk about her marriage came from the back of the room: "So don't write about that then." When one student marveled that his partners, married for over fifty years, were still in love, there was a hush in the class until another student said, "Awesome. What I'd like to know is how you know that. Don't get me wrong. I believe you. But did they tell you that or did you, like, notice something?"

One day a student raised her hand and said, "My senior partner died last night."

Amid the quiet murmurs of sympathy and then the sounds of the members of her peer-editing group clambering over their backpacks to give her hugs, I thought about what to do. I had known from the start that the entire project was a risk and that something like this might happen. I asked her how she was dealing with this emotionally. She said she was very sad but not devastated; this was not the first death in her life. But she was worried about her final paper and what to do about the information still missing.

We had a town meeting. How much information did she think she still needed? "Did your partner have kids?" one student wanted to know. "Maybe you could call them to find out what you need."

"Do you plan to go to the funeral?" I asked. "Perhaps you could begin your paper there."

There were more suggestions, and she followed most of them. Her final paper was a tribute to her partner and, as it turned out, a cherished gift for her partner's family. At our "exam party" her senior partner's daughter and son-in-law were there to take their mother's place. They told my student that the paper about their mother's life was a healing and timely gift.

The exam party was the highlight of the semester. At the time of our officially scheduled exam we all—students, senior partners, team members— met at the hospitality room of the retirement home. I brought a large sheet cake, the retirement home furnished punch and coffee, my students brought their edited and bound final papers. This was my first chance to meet the elderly people I had read so much about, my first and only chance to actually see and hear what had happened during the semester. I saw some students carefully and skillfully push wheel chairs; saw how proud and solicitous they were of their partners; saw the hands held and patted and the shy exchange of gifts; saw how nervous my students were to give over their papers and how eagerly those papers were received; and overheard some of the little in-jokes, endearments, and concerns ("I'm famous now, aren't I, dearie." "Don't forget you're still my girlfriend.").

Gail Heffner and I took lots of photographs.

The exam party over, I still had to read the take-home exams. One of the essays asked the students to write a narrative of their journey with their senior partner—from the first visit to the last. It was only then, really, reading their narratives, that I realized the value of the experience for most of the students.

I read about the stereotypes with which some of them began the semester. One student reported on his first visit with relief: "My senior partner seemed nice, and she didn't complain about her back or any other physical ailment. She didn't flop her dentures in and out and go "Whoa!" like my grandpa does to everybody he meets." At the end of the semester this student so much admired his partner that he planned to continue his visits after the semester was over.

Other students recalled their worries about their writing competence. One wrote, "I had to make a paper good enough to give to her, an elegant and notable lady. This frightened me out of my wits. I had never been comfortable with my writing, and I certainly did not think it good enough to present to someone as a gift." Later in the essay the student's fears were allayed. "She is such a kind and giving person that I know that she will appreciate anything I give her, as long as it is my best."

Most of the exam essays described a sense of purpose. Typically, one student wrote, "When I hear other students talk about the English papers they have to write, I am grateful that my papers have a deeper meaning than simply to please a professor."

I am grateful too. I can hardly imagine going back to teaching English 101 "as usual"—whatever that was. This service-learning project has been a win-win situation. It has stretched my understanding of my role as a teacher and has given my course a fresh focus. Despite the logistical details, which can be challenging at times, this project has enlivened my teaching.

Academically, my students now write for all the right reasons. I do not have to manufacture an audience—their audience is their partners and their families. I do not have to urge them to be honest and accurate because their readers will take care of that. I do not have to worry about plagiarism. My students are not writing to please me. They worry about pleasing their partners and doing them justice.

Socially, my students also win. When I asked them what was the most important benefit from this project, many said, "friendship." One student told me he had found his soulmate. Short of that, all students learned how to ask questions, chat up a person, become curious. They were more interesting people at the end of the class than they were at the beginning.

Spiritually, too, my students benefited. They felt happy, proud even, about having made a difference in someone's life. They felt loved, and they loved in return. Many of their partners were models of faith, patience, endurance, and generosity. They taught my students what life can be like when these virtues are embodied.

They taught me something too, something I had long known but needed to be reminded of: The teacher is not necessarily the most important person in a class. In this course I was the organizer and the director but not the chief player. That role belonged to each of the senior partners. Sometimes the best teaching gets done when the teacher gets out of the way.

Chapter 14

MARKETING SERVICE

Steven Vander Veen

Introduction

I TEACH MARKETING. Service-learning is a natural component of the class because work with community groups gives students valuable experience with real products, natural audiences, and actual limitations. Students provide valuable services to companies and agencies to help them market services and products. However, while students are engaged in community work, they can also be thought of as the targets of marketing efforts. That is, their community involvement can be described as one effective way to market a product (in this case, a commitment to service) to a group (in this case, students).

Students desire a meaningful business education; small organizations desire information to make their operations more efficient and effective; Christian professors wish to instill in students the value of Christian service, defined here as obedience to Matthew 28:19-20. The Great Commission invites Christians to do at least three things: (1) go into the world, (2) tell the world about Christ; and (3) teach the world to obey the words of Christ that state that we are to love God and love our neighbor. In a marketing context, one could interpret this to mean that Christians are to meet people's true spiritual and physical needs. Calvin College's Small Business Institute program, a program housed in the Calvin Department of Business and Economics, attempts to market this calling while at the same time meeting the needs of small organizations and giving students the skills needed for these challenges.

Every marketing plan includes a careful analysis of the current situation, the articulation of marketing objectives, specific marketing strategies for matching needs with products, the implementation of plans, and the evaluation of strategies. If we think of a commitment to service as the product that we are selling to students, we can envision how all of these plan components come together in the business classroom.

Situation Analysis

A situation analysis attempts to uncover both the uncontrollable opportunities and threats that face a business and the strengths and weaknesses of that business. The goal of a situation analysis is to find where strengths can be matched to opportunities.

Opportunities

The areas of opportunity relevant to Calvin's Small Business Institute (SBI) and the concept of marketing service to our students are related to student characteristics and desires and to the educational mission of Calvin College.

What sort of experience are students seeking from higher education? From the results of student evaluations and alumni surveys, it is clear that students want to bridge the gap between business theory and practice; or, more concretely, between learning by lecture and learning by experience. On a recent survey additional departmental alumni at Calvin College indicated that the area of greatest need was in applied-business experience. Personal anecdotal evidence from the last twelve years also supports this: Exercises, case studies, and simulations are helpful, but what really makes projects meaningful is when students are empowered to make a difference. Ironically, business students are being trained to have an impact on the world, yet college provides them with few business-related experiences in which they are empowered to make a difference. This is clearly something that private Christian colleges can do to set themselves apart.

Not only do students desire meaningful educational experiences, but small organizations desire marketing expertise. Both can be provided within the context of the mission of Calvin College. Philosophically, the mission of Calvin College, to "train people by means of a liberal arts curriculum and according to the reformed faith, for a life of Christian service, means that the college sees "higher education as a God-given vocation, to be enacted on behalf of the Christian community, for the benefit of contemporary society, to the praise of God's name." Pedagogically, the college encourages "insightful and creative participation in society." Calvin also "challenges its teachers to employ pedagogical techniques that quicken the interest of students, recognize the varying learning styles and capabilities of students, and actively engage the student in learning" (Van Harn 1996, 9, 32, 33, 42). Therefore, Calvin College encourages students to participate in society as agents of renewal by using techniques that not only quicken their interests but also prepare them for this high calling.

Strengths

The mission of the college is echoed in the mission of the Department of Business and Economics, which seek to "help students make economic decisions that further God's kingdom." A significant factor in our approach to marketing, based on "Mustard Seed Marketing" (Sine 1999), as a calling is the particular business philosophy taught in marketing classes within the department and enacted through service-learning projects. Mustard Seed Marketing holds that Christians are called to meet the basic physical and spiritual needs of people—particularly the vulnerable—and advocates working in and through small non and for-profits, the primary organizations being individual churches. It holds that Christians are expected to "redeem" marketing by using it out of love. Thus, the perspective of the particular professor who teaches and directs the program is philosophically inclined toward small organizations and helping them in their strategic work in the community.

Method

The primary marketing method is student involvement in the Calvin College Small Business Institute. This institute within the Economics and Business Department exists to provide marketing opportunities for students and to match student teams with community organizations.

Typically, teams of two to four students invest between fifty and one hundred team hours into a business, usually performing some form of market research and then making recommendations regarding marketing strategy based on the research. At least half of the students' grades depend on their consulting work.

Here is a small example of how the program works. The professor agreed to work with the West Michigan Mechanical Contractors Association (WMMCA) in exchange for payment of expenses incurred in doing marketing research, the right to publicize the arrangement, and the right to use the data generated from the arrangement for conference proceedings or for other forms of scholarly work. The professor also agreed to report on the collective results of the individual projects for the Association. WMMCA agreed to work with the students and pay marketing-research expenses in exchange for marketing-related information. The students agreed to collect data, analyze data, and make recommendations for a grade. The students kept track of their hours and had them placed on their transcripts as service-learning hours. Students could have also made copies of their written reports (with the client's permission) to use in interviews with prospective employers. IN addition to WMMCA other service-learning partners include schools, social agencies, Christian-ministry organizations, neighborhood associations, development corporations, bookstores, bike shops, and golf courses.

Objectives

Objectives normally are specific, measurable, operational, and attempt to match the strengths of the internal environment to the opportunities of the external environment.

The main objective of Calvin's SBI program is to obey the words of Christ and to persuade students to do the same. The humans behind the program attempt to persuade students cognitively, experientially, and behaviorally (see Mowen and Minor 1998, for further explanation of the three perspectives of consumer behavior.) Students are challenged cognitively through lectures about marketing concepts and models, through their underlying philosophy or worldview, and through the approach of Mustard Seed Marketing. Students learn experientially by applying these concepts and models in service-learning.

We measure the success of meeting these objectives in the following ways:

1. Students are tested by way of essay exams and papers as to whether they understand marketing concepts, models, and worldviews; for example, a paper topic might be "How can we use our knowledge of consumer behavior to advance the kingdom of God?"
2. Student skills are tested by way of project presentations (oral rhetoric), project writing (written rhetoric), and research design and/or analysis of data within their project.
3. Student behavior is tested in terms of the amount of effort put forth. Effort on projects is highly correlated with project quality. Product quality is judged both by the small organization and the instructor.

Operationally, in order to break even, the program must serve at least fifty students per year and to have these fifty students engage in at least fifteen projects. Of these fifteen projects, most generate enough income through modest billing to cover the expenses of the whole project.

Segments and Targets

Marketers know that they cannot please everyone. They also know that a market is defined as those who are willing and able to pay. Furthermore, they know that they cannot enhance shareholder value unless they convince customers that they are getting what they pay for. However, small not-for-profits and small for-profits cannot afford to pay much because much of the time they are not compensated for the value they add even though it is legitimate value. For example, a neighborhood development corporation will not be compensated for attempting to rebuild a decimated community; a Christian ministry will not be paid for spreading the gospel to children. Yet, if their goal is to meet the true spiritual and/or physical needs of others, particularly of those who are not technically part of "the market" (those willing and able to pay), Calvin's SBI wants them as a service-learning partner.

On the other hand, Calvin's SBI program does not turn away other potential partner-clients: All organizations have the potential to love God and neighbor and all are part of God's providential plan for meeting the needs of people. In the same way, Calvin's SBI program does not target particular students. Everyone has the potential to serve and be served—all have a calling (cf. Martin Luther's view of work and vocation; see, for example, Hardy 1990).

Strategies: The Marketing Mix

Marketing strategies typically consist of manipulating the "4 Ps:" Product, Promotion, Place (distribution), and Price.

Product

A product is typically thought of as "whatever one offers in exchange." It consists of core benefits or attributes of the product; the tangible product, for example, the brand name; and the augmented product, for example, service, warranties, and so forth. The primary tangible product to small organizations is marketing information in the form of raw data and recommendations; to students, it is a grade and fodder for resumés. In terms of intangible product or service, Calvin's SBI program offers students the value of Christian service as calling: the idea that Christ calls us to go into the world making disciples and teaching them to love. The benefits are many. The primary benefit, however, is that business students and small organizations are preparing themselves to better live out their calling as disciples of Christ.

> I believe the purposes of God' kingdom are subversive to many of the aspirations and goals of the dominant modern commercial culture. I am convinced the purposes of God's mustard seed movement will ultimately subvert the arrogance of every Babylon that claims the authority to define what is ultimate. Therefore I believe Scripture teaches that the primary vocation of every believer is not what we do to earn a livelihood but how we devote our lives, as Christ did, to seeking to advance the subversive purposes of God's kingdom (Sine 1999, 161).

Part of the project is the Marketing logo. Because the most significant part of Calvin's SBI program is intangible, it needs concrete representation—a symbol or, in marketing language, a recognizable logo. The symbol that appears on all tangible material related to the small business institute is referred to as "The Aesthetic Triangle." The Triangle represents faculty, students, and organizational clients—each dependent on the other parts of the triangle and operating from aesthetic, not self-interested, motivation. We take the concept of aesthetic motivation from Kierkegaard's understanding of working for the betterment of society.

Promotion

Promotion is typically defined as "communicating with members of the target audience in order to persuade them to buy." It involves making the target audience aware of its needs and of the firm's product as well as persuading them to buy.

In terms of promotion to small organizations, Calvin's SBI program relies on its brand logo and brand equity, personal selling by the director and word-of-mouth communication. In terms of selling to students, Calvin's SBI program relies on word-of-mouth communication and the college catalog.

The survival of the program depends on creating "brand equity." Brand equity consists of the target audience's being aware of the brand, thinking that the brand represents a quality product, making other positive associations about the brand, and being loyal to the brand. Of course, awareness is insufficient without perceptions of quality, perceptions of quality are insufficient without other positive associations, and other positive associations are insufficient without loyalty. Loyalty in the context of Calvin's SBI program requires our building relationships with small organizations and students (who sometimes become clients). This is greatly aided by projects that last for more than one semester. Positive associations are created by way of professional behavior on the part of students and the instructor as well as from being associated with Calvin College and creating perceptions of quality requires our motivating students to do their best and teaching them the proper concepts and tools.

It is also important to build brand equity in the minds of students. Brand awareness can be built by describing the program in the college catalog and by positive word-of-mouth communication. However, if students think the courses that host Calvin's SBI program are not rigorous, the course and the program will attract academically "weak" students whose work will then reduce perceptions of quality among small organizations.

Place

Having a good product and telling others about it is important, but it is also important to have it "available in the right place at the right time in the right amount or form." In terms of distribution, Calvin's SBI program utilizes two upper-level business courses.

In Business 381: Marketing II, the goal is to utilize marketing strategies, particularly in the area of marketing communications, in Christian service. In these projects, students develop a research proposal and research method. They collect and analyze data and may make specific recommendations by way of an "integrated marketing plans book." At the end of the semester, they give both an oral and a written report.

In Business 382: Consumer Behavior, the goal is to utilize marketing research and consumer behavior from either a decision-making, experiential, or behavioral perspective in Christian service. For example, students might analyze the awareness and knowledge levels of consumers before and after promotional campaigns, they might record and analyze stream-of-consciousness, or they might manipulate a retail floor plan to see the impact on traffic patterns and "conversion rates" or sales (Underhill 1990).

Price

Price is typically defined as "what is received in exchange for the product." Calvin's SBI program charges $200 plus expenses (postage, paper, phone charges, and so forth.) to small organizations. To students we charge a significant amount of time and effort. What students receive in exchange for working on projects is a grade and resumé fodder. For instance, the project can account for 40 to 60 percent of their grade, and students can record the time they spend on their projects (e.g., 25 to 50 hours per person) as service-learning hours. Service-learning hours can then be placed on their official transcripts. The money charged to clients is used to fund projects for small organizations strapped for cash and for conference fees and membership dues.

Implementation

Business 382: Consumer Behavior is offered during the fall semester and Business 381: Marketing II is offered during the spring semester. The instructor formalizes client-student arrangements with small organizations during the summer prior to the beginning of each semester. Normally, expenses are incurred throughout the semester and submitted to clients at the end of the semester. To improve quality, the instructor contacts clients midway through the semester for feedback. During the semester, students are required within the first month to create a research-proposal document (a contract) and to have it signed by the client. Students then gather data, secondary and primary, obtaining the clients' approval before undertaking any significant activity. At the end of the semester, students present the client with an oral and written report and clients are asked to evaluate students formally at that time.

Evaluation/Control

The instructor monitors the success of Calvin's SBI program in terms of student and client feedback (including repeat and referral business) and the quality of students and clients who enter and remain in the program. Assessment data from surveys of departmental alumni suggests that participation in service-learning through the SBI helps students see business as a calling that involves service to Christ and the world.

Conclusion

Students desire a meaningful business education. Small organizations desire information to make their operations more efficient and effective. Christian professors wish to instill in students the value of Christian service. Calvin College's Small Business Institute program markets this calling of Christian service to students while at the same time meeting the information needs of small organizations. It persuades students to integrate cognitive and faith development through experiential service-learning involvement.

References

Hardy, Lee. 1990. *The fabric of this world.* Grand Rapids: Eerdmans.

Mowen, John C., and Michael Minor. 1998. *Consumer behavior.* 5th edition. Upper Saddle River, N.J.: Prentice Hall.

Sine, Tom. 1999. *Mustard seed vs. McWorld: Reinventing life and faith for the future.* Grand Rapids: Baker.

Underhill, Paco. 1999. *Why we buy: The science of shopping.* New York: Touchstone.

Van Harn, G. Calvin College. 1996. *An expanded statement of the mission of Calvin college: Vision, purpose, commitment.* Grand Rapids: Calvin College.

PART IV

BUILDING INSTITUTIONAL SUPPORT

Chapter 15

HISTORY OF THE DEVELOPMENT OF ACADEMICALLY BASED SERVICE-LEARNING AT CALVIN COLLEGE

Rhonda Berg

Introduction

THE STORY OF ACADEMICALLY BASED SERVICE-LEARNING (ABSL) at Calvin College is a story of how an idea made its way from the outer edges of the academy into the mainstream. The idea that bubbled up from within the Student Volunteer Service[1] was that educating Calvin students for the service of Christ in society could somehow be more effective if students could discuss their service with their professors in the context of their academic work. If students could integrate reading and classroom discussion with service experiences, they could perhaps become more thoughtful, humble, and helpful in their service. In the early 1990s, these thoughts began as small springs of discussion and experimentation, became a trickle, then a stream, and now a recognized tributary to education at Calvin College.

The unique aspect of this story is that the primary development of the ABSL program did not take place through political maneuvering, demonstration programs, grant funding, and the like. Rather, a small group of people, with

---

[1] The Student Volunteer Service was a small program within the Student Life Division of Calvin College. It began as a student initiative called the "KIDS" program (Kindling Intellectual Development in Students) in 1964. In the late 1980s and early 1990s 400-500 students each semester were involved in a wide array of volunteerism in educational and social service organizations in the Grand Rapids community.

sanction from the college administration, developed and shaped the concept of service-learning for Calvin College. It was a process that was communal and collegial, with the emphasis up working within the existing framework of the mission, goals, and culture of Calvin College as a Christian liberal arts institution. This chapter will trace the discussion and the issues that this group of people dealt with to provide a rationale and to build a foundation for the ABSL efforts at Calvin College.

Chronology of Academically Based Service-Learning Development

In the early 1990s, the concept of service-learning began making its way into the consciousness of Calvin College. Participants in the new organization, Campus Compact,[2] were discussing the connections between service and education, and there were some grant opportunities for developing service-learning programs. However, although the academic administration saw some potential in service-learning, it did not see any practice or models for its use that seemed to resonate within Calvin's particular mission and culture. From several discussions, questions began to emerge: Could Calvin College define and shape service-learning in a way that fit with our task of preparing students for lives of service to Christ in the world? What would happen if a group of people wrestled with this concept in light of Calvin's educational philosophy and goals?

Calvin's president and provost took up the challenge of these questions and appointed an ad-hoc committee on service-learning chaired by a tenured and respected faculty member. The committee's mandate was to define the term *service-learning* for Calvin College and to recommend its place within the curriculum. The committee did a good deal of its work at the 1992 Campus Compact Summer Institute on Integrating Service with Academic Study at Brown University. During this week-long institute, members observed and participated in what was then the foremost thinking and practice of service-learning.

By February of 1993, the committee had completed its work and presented a document to the Educational Policy Committee. The report defined "academically based service" as "service activities that are related to and

---

[2] Campus Compact is a national coalition of college and university presidents committed to the civic purpose of higher education.

integrated with the conceptual content of a college course, and which serve as a pedagogical resource to meet the academic goals of the course as well as to meet community or individual needs." The key recommendation of the report was to "encourage the faculty to incorporate academically based service, where appropriate, in courses in the Calvin College curriculum." The report also set forth criteria for academically based service and guidelines for integrating it in courses. The Calvin faculty unanimously approved the report, and the Student Volunteer Service was renamed the Service-Learning Center, signaling a shift from an emphasis on service not intentionally connected to learning (volunteerism) to service-learning in which learning is an integral component of service.

Calvin College initially supported the effort through redirecting the resources of the Student Volunteer Service toward supporting course and community-partnership development and through giving a faculty member release time to promote the program. After two years, Calvin added another staff person through the Student Life Division whose primary job responsibilities focused on developing what is now called academically based service-learning. Under a combined effort of both Academic Affairs and Student Life, participation in ABSL has grown to more than eighty faculty members, with at least forty courses each semester. With this brief chronology of the development of the academically based service-learning program, we turn now to the discussion of the issues involved in developing service-learning in a Christian liberal arts institution.

Defining Service-Learning for Calvin College

The concept of service-learning was just beginning to make its way into the broader consciousness of higher education in the United States in the 1990s. It emerged from the fringes of the academy, having been practiced in experiential educational and volunteer programs, without a clear definition of its meaning and context. Thus, "it" became something that "everyone" thought was a good idea, though for many and varied reasons. One of the Calvin participants in the Campus Compact Institute quipped, "I never met a group of people who could spend so much time talking about something without defining it." In fact, the term *service-learning* was essentially unusable in any broad discussion. Motivations for individual and institutional interest ranged widely. The concept of service-learning was bringing together people with a conservative agenda that included educating young people in traditional values as well as people who saw participation in service-learning as a way to challenge traditional cultural values and assumptions. The combination of these banners with those carrying the more pragmatic and institutional concerns of community relations, student recruitment, and retention created almost a surreal atmosphere in some of the discussions.

Earlier, in 1989, a gathering of the current leading practitioners in the field had developed "Principles of Good Practice for Combining Service and Learning" (The Wingspread Report 1989). The term *service-learning* actually comes out of a southern regional education board program in the late 1960s and was defined as the "integration of the accomplishment of a needed task with educational growth" (Sigmon 1994). The Calvin College Institute team and the ad-hoc committee stayed fairly close to the definition, defining it as "activities which are designed both to contribute to the meeting of community or individual needs, and to aid in the development of the knowledge and understanding of the service giver." They claimed service-learning first of all as a concept or strategy, not as a particular program or structure. This definition also kept service-learning broad enough to embrace its use in cocurricular programs in the institution. However, that still left the problem of talking more precisely about curricular service-learning. For this, the committee alighted upon academically based service introduced to them in a speech by Ira Harkavy of the University of Pennsylvania at the Campus Compact Institute. Academically Based Service, which was later changed to Academically Based Service-Learning, designates service-learning that is integrated with course content.

Thus, the Calvin definition is, on the one hand, a concept or strategy with potentially broad application; yet, on the other hand it remains simply a pedagogical tool. As the committee reported, "It serves curricular goals rather than shapes them." This distinguishes the Calvin definition. The National and Community Service Act of 1990, which provided the basis for K-12 service-learning, reserves the term *service-learning* only for service that is integrated into the students academic curriculum. According to this definition the words *service*, *community service*, or *volunteerism* would describe all service activities that take place outside of the curricular structure. However, at Calvin College, service-learning is not defined programmatically but as a broad spectrum of activities that meet the definition. The term *academically based service-learning* is a subset of service-learning used to describe the integration of service-learning in the curriculum.

Credit for Service vs. Credit for Learning

At Calvin College, those advocating for service-learning were not advocating its simple inclusion, but rather its integration. At that time several educational institutions were opting for the inclusion of service-learning. Those arguing for inclusion usually said something like, "If we value service as much as our mission statement says we do, then service should at least take up space in the allocation of credits." Furthermore, the argument usually continued, "If service is so important, then every student who graduates from this institution should be involved in service." These arguments for inclusion often raised the ire of people who countered with concerns about "*requiring* volunteerism" (an oxymoron), "watering down the curriculum," and the negative impact on the quality of service that would be performed by those who had been "forced" into it.

Granting credit simply for performing service was of little interest at Calvin College. Rather, the ad-hoc committee held the view that credit ought to be given for learning specific material as set forth in curricula and specific course goals. The committee members did not argue for the inclusion of service for its own sake but for the integration of service as a *means* of education. Thus, in Calvin ABSL courses, credit is not given simply for participating in a service experience. The service is viewed as an assignment or a learning task that will enable the students to understand and apply the course material. In order to receive credit for their ABSL course, students must demonstrate their understanding and competencies through "academic" work (i.e., tests, journals, papers, demonstrations). Thus, there was little interest in mandating that students fulfill service requirements outside the curriculum as a graduation requirement or for giving credit for stand-alone service experiences. Credit, per se, is given for students' documented learning, not merely for service. Weaving service-learning into the content of the course was the primary goal of academically based service-learning.

Bringing Together Ends and Means

The committee was careful in its recommendation of ABSL, defining it as a strategy rather than as a goal. It recommended that its use be voluntary, with faculty members evaluating its "potential in terms of the goals and content of their courses as well as their own ability to be effective with it." Indeed the committee was careful not to present any kind of transformational vision for education through service-learning. Perhaps it was this aspect of the report that caused one service-learning advocate from outside the institution to remark that the report was "right of center."

Rather than advocating a new vision for education, the committee pointed to the transformational vision already held by the college. This vision for education, flowing from the Reformed confessions, lays special emphasis on the sovereignty of God over every dimension of reality and on the vocation of believers, in covenant with their Redeemer, to live in gratitude as agents of renewal in the world. The report cites three major educational principles that flow from this vision:

1. Since God claims all of our communal and individual lives, both in its purpose and practice, Calvin cannot separate obedience to service from its goals or practice of education.
2. Christian education addresses the whole person—not just the mind, but the heart and the will.
3. Christian education is a communal mission directed toward a needy world, not an individualistic focus on the fulfillment of the self.

It was commitment to this vision that brought the committee to advocate for academically based service-learning as a potential strategy for Calvin. It was the result of honestly probing Calvin's effectiveness in transmitting to students the vision of education as preparation for service. Were our students catching the vision that drives the institution and its faculty? Was a Calvin education really challenging the 1990s cultural value of individual fulfillment without considering its impact on others? Had the life and educational experiences of our students prepared them adequately to understand, and then apply independently, the vision of Christian education? The honest answer was: "No, not enough."

Thus, the committee concluded that, if academically based service-learning could be integrated into courses in such a way as to engage the student more actively in the content *AND* to develop a communal vision for practical obedient service, it was a strategy that certainly ought to be promoted.

In coming to the conclusion that the end goals of a Calvin College education should have a greater influence in shaping means and methods of teaching, the committee stepped out with the thinking that philosopher Nicholas Wolterstorff expressed in a 1983 speech at Wheaton College. Wolterstorff, in his early days at Calvin College, had been one of the principal contributors to the guiding document for Calvin's core curriculum, Christian Liberal Arts Education (CLAE). In more recent years, Wolterstorff (now at Yale University) had become critical of CLAE's approach of relying on the teaching of the academic disciplines to prepare students for service to the world (Wolterstorff 1983). Central to CLAE was the concept of *disinterested study*—a study that did not seek application at every turn but sought to develop broad-based understanding and knowledge in an environment that would encourage objectivity and openness. Supposedly, from a solid basis of knowledge and understanding, students would then be equipped to apply this understanding in service to the world. However, by the early 1990s, the difficulties in this approach were becoming more evident. CLAE assumed that students would have strong motivations both for the pure study of the disciplines for their own sake and for making their own applications to service. However, as one committee member pointed out, *disinterested study* could easily become *uninterested study*. Furthermore, the notion of *disinterested study* does not take into account the student's motivation to actually apply learning in grateful service. Many a student's motivation had much more to do with applying their education in pursuit of individual achievement and wealth than in becoming more thoughtful and insightful servants.

Service-Learning as a Subset of Experiential Education

Could academically based service-learning really be an effective enhancement to the lecture-discussion method of teaching? Would not its use lead to uninformed and ill-considered activism that would replace effective education rather than enhance it? Would not its use lead to substituting important disciplinary content for touchy-feely discussions that were devoid of critical inquiry? These were among the critical questions faced by the committee. The lecture-discussion methods of teaching were familiar and comfortable for the majority of faculty members. The pedagogy of experiential education (of which service-learning is a subset) was not widely employed at Calvin College. The faculty members on the committee were "traditional academics" and enjoyed teaching through the lecture-discussion model. For the most part, they did not utilize experiential-education pedagogy in their own teaching.

In this discussion, the committee was also limited by the lack of research and evidence for the claims for service-learning as pedagogy. Although it cited David Kolb's 1984 work on experiential learning, and the 1989 Wingspread Report, it primarily relied on two more intuitive arguments: (1) respected professors at respected institutions are doing this with good results, and, (2) "Why not us?"

The Campus Compact Institute for Integrating Service and Academic Study was tremendously helpful in shoring up the first argument. The Institute, held at Brown University, had seminar leaders from Antioch, Cornell, and Stanford. The participants had in-depth discussions with several professors who were utilizing service-learning in connection with coursework, even in disciplines such as philosophy and English. Furthermore, several of the Institute participants were from Christian colleges and universities: Azusa, Baylor, Messiah, Loyola in Baltimore, and Gettysburg. Thus, participating in the Institute in the early 1990s gave Calvin the opportunity to see that becoming involved in service-learning was more than simply "jumping on a bandwagon." It was an opportunity to enter into a national discussion and to contribute to the development of a promising strategy for education.

Second, the committee took the why not us? stand for service-learning. It recognized that the lecture-discussion methods carried the weight of tradition rather than research. Thus, it sidestepped any debate between traditional academics and experiential educators. It cited the more recent emphasis within the college on pedagogical pluralism and greater recognition of the diverse levels, gifts, and styles of learning among students, and it put the decision to utilize academically based service-learning squarely in the hands of the individual professor. The closing statements of the report summarize the two arguments thus: "We do not believe that academically based service is appropriate for every course or every professor. But we are persuaded, that if done well, academically based service is a teaching strategy which is not only consistent with Calvin's educational philosophy and mission, but also promotes the college's overarching aim in new and powerful ways."

Building on Strengths

Although the movement to establish ABSL is having profound effects upon teaching and learning at Calvin College, the effort never took an oppositional or crusader-like approach. Given the lack of clarity about service-learning and its potential within the liberal arts, it would have been quite easy for the academic administration to polarize discussion rather than to seek consensus and understanding. Instead, the movement to establish ABSL built upon the strengths of the institution, one of which was a supportive academic administration, that without pushing or advocating kept the doors open for dialogue and discussion within the Calvin community. In addition, Calvin has not followed the route of other institutions to independently set up a new program or initiative that could have created resentment and resistance rather than support among faculty—ABSL comes from within the faculty.

The ABSL movement also builds upon the Calvin faculty's respect for critical inquiry and its commitment to the mission of Calvin College to prepare its students for lives of service. Among the faculty on the ad-hoc committee, there were several who did not enter the process with any expressed interest in promoting service-learning. Nonetheless they entered into an investigation and consideration of the concept with openness and careful analysis. They exemplified the ideal of being able to stand apart from a problem or issue—a necessary skill in *disinterested study*—to develop a sound foundation for a pedagogy that would promote engagement and involvement. The careful thinking and objectivity with which professors at Calvin have approached their ABSL courses has led to some very creative and thoughtful applications of the pedagogy.

Finally, rather than seek outside grant funding to begin a new initiative, the college has utilized the resources already allocated to the Service-Learning Center. academically based service-learning is built on the foundation of community relationships built over many years by the student volunteer programs that preceded the Service-Learning Center. Calvin already had good ties with area schools and nonprofit organizations. Community organizations trusted its stability and professionalism, and there were many personal relationships developed over years of working together. The community had good experience with Calvin students in their organizations; thus creating a base of organizations willing to work with faculty to provide service-learning experiences for their students. Academically based service-learning has at its disposal an entire office with a director, office coordinator and twelve to fifteen paid student coordinators, and a transportation program. Faculty members desiring to utilize ABSL do not have to worry much about the logistical factors involved for them. These resources are financed out of the general budget of the college, giving a secure base of funding.

Conclusion

No one involved in the ad-hoc committee on service-learning in the early 1990s could have predicted the growth and development of the program. Certainly our understanding and approach has matured and developed as we have gained more experience. Yet, the thoughtful approaches to service-learning and the collaboration and collegiality that still characterize the program have their roots in the way in which the program developed in those early years.

References

Kolb, David. 1984. *Experiential earning.* Englewood Cliffs, N.J.: Prentice-Hall.
Sigmon, Robert. 1994. *Linking service with learning in liberal arts education.* Washington D.C.: The Council of Independent Colleges.
The Wingspread Report. 1989. Principles of good practice for combining service and learning. Racine, Wis.: The Johnson Foundation.
Wolterstorff, N. 1983. The mission of the Christian college at the end of the twentieth century. *The Reformed Journal* 33 (6): 14-18.

About the Contributors

Rhonda Berg is the executive director of the Rehoboth-Red Mesa Foundation in New Mexico. Her field is management.

Claudia DeVries Beversluis is the dean for instruction and professor of psychology at Calvin College. Her field is clinical psychology.

Randall Brouwer is professor of engineering at Calvin College. His field is computer architecture.

Laura Hoeksema Cebulski is director of an after-school program for at-risk children in Jonesboro, Arkansas. Her field is third-world development.

Janel M. Curry is dean for research and scholarship and professor of geography and environmental studies at Calvin College.

John E. Hare is professor of philosophy at Calvin College specializing in ethics.

Susan Schneider Hasseler is the director of teacher education at Calvin College. Her field is education, with a special interest in multicultural perspectives and urban schooling.

Gail Gunst Heffner is the associate director for applied and community-based research at the Calvin Center for Social Research. Her field is resource development/urban studies.

Robert J. Hubbard is a professor of theatre and speech at Northwestern College. His field is communication and performance studies.

Michelle R. Loyd-Paige is a professor of sociology and social work at Calvin College. Her field is sociology, especially in the area of diversity and inequality.

Daniel R. Miller is a professor of history at Calvin College. His field is history, with a particular interest in Latin American history.

Steven Vander Veen is a professor of business at Calvin College. His field is consumer behavior and marketing.

Kurt Ver Beek is an associate professor of sociology at Calvin College and director of the Calvin program in Honduras. His field is development sociology.

Mary Ann Walters is professor emeritus of English at Calvin College. Her field is English, with a special interest in Great Britain.

Glenn D. Weaver is a professor of psychology at Calvin College. His field is psychology with a special interest in the relationship of psychology and spirituality.

Gail Landheer Zandee is the community partnership development coordinator for the Calvin College nursing program. Her field is nursing, especially as applied to community-based nursing.